THE REWARD SYSTEM / IN BRITISH AND AMERICAN SCIENCE

SCIENCE, CULTURE, AND SOCIETY:
A WILEY INTERSCIENCE SERIES

BERNARD BARBER, Editor

Syntony and Spark—The Origins of Radio
Hugh G. J. Aitken

Astronomy Transformed: The Emergence of Radio
Astronomy in Britain
David O. Edge and Michael J. Mulkay

The Spaceflight Revolution: A Sociological Study
William Sims Bainbridge

Toward a Metric of Science: The Advent of Science Indicators
Edited by Yehuda Elkana, Joshua Lederberg,
Robert K. Merton, Arnold Thackray, and
Harriet Zuckerman

The Reward System in British and American Science
Jerry Gaston

THE REWARD SYSTEM / IN BRITISH AND AMERICAN SCIENCE

JERRY GASTON

Associate Professor of Sociology
Southern Illinois University at Carbondale

A WILEY-INTERSCIENCE PUBLICATION

JOHN WILEY & SONS, New York • Chichester • Brisbane • Toronto

Library of Congress Cataloging in Publication Data:

Gaston, Jerry.
  The reward system in British and American science.

  (Science, culture, and society)
  "A Wiley-Interscience publication."
  Bibliography: p.
  Includes index.
  1. Research—Social aspects—United States.
2. Research—Social aspects—Great Britain.
3. Rewards (Prizes, etc.)—United States.   4.   Rewards
(Prizes, etc.)—Great Britain.   I.   Title.

Q180.U5G27   507'.2   77-17404
ISBN 0-471-29293-1

Printed in the United States of America

10 9 8 7 6 5 4 3 2 1

To Mary Frank

FOREWORD

For some time now science has been at once a great treasure and a great problem for us. It has given us all sorts of material and medical riches, but it has also produced a number of untoward environmental, economic, and social consequences. For two reasons, then—to increase the benefits of science and to reduce and cope with the harms it causes—we need to know a great deal more about how science works and how it affects society.

Happily, a whole new set of scholarly specialties has emerged since World War II to meet this need. Among them are the sociology of science, science policy studies, and the economics of science and technology. These specialties are beginning to establish a sound theoretical and empirical basis for a better understanding of science and its social consequences. Treating science largely as a set of social activities, much like other social activities, they have applied to science what is already known about human behavior in general. The stratification, communications, political, and creative processes in science have many similarities with such processes elsewhere in society. Furthermore, the new specialties studying science have successfully applied in their researches all the new knowledge from statistics, computer technique, the logic of inquiry, and research methodology that has recently been created by social scientists specializing in these areas. Finally, recognizing that controlled comparison is one social science equivalent of contrived experiment in the physical and biological sciences, the specialties studying science have more and more used comparative research designs and data, comparative both within a given society and also between them. In sum, we are well on our way to establishing a useful science of science.

This is not to say that we have achieved perfect consensus on concepts, methods, and findings in the science of science. Not so. As in the so-called mature sciences, some dissensus persists, but it is a limited dissensus, because new theoretical and research efforts are constantly devoted to resolving it. Such resolutions may create still further dissensus, but they also create greater understanding of science.

Professor Gaston's book is an especially attractive example, for the sociology of science, of all these essential characteristics and virtues of our new science of science. Focusing on the reward system in science —that system which makes science "work" as money makes a market system "work"—he carefully summarizes the present consensus of expert knowledge. Then he judiciously evaluates the points of expert dissensus, bringing out the essential elements of dispute and suggesting new theories and researches that might resolve these disputes. Throughout, he brings to bear, on matters of consensus and dissensus alike, new comparative data from his own original researches recently carried out on Britain and the United States. As a result, he has produced a model of what a social science study, in any field, should be. His colleagues in the sociology of science, those in other science of science specialties, working scientists themselves, and those who administer science in the university, in industry, and in government—all should profit from his creative, lucid, and witty book.

BERNARD BARBER

PREFACE

People often say that, from reading papers, articles, and books, one cannot tell how the scientists did the work. The process of doing research is not the way one learns "the scientific method" in textbooks. The research for this book originated from my personal interests, but it also originated from the less frequently encountered textbook method for research.

One of my personal interests for a long time has been whether people get what they deserve. I am not sure what caused me to have that interest. Maybe it was the lesson to be learned from the story of the ant and the grasshopper. Or maybe it was just a sense of fairness and equity. Whatever the origin of my personal interest, it turns out that the sociology of science involves important questions like that. Basically this book is about whether or not people get what they deserve.

The reward system in science is a very simple concept. Scientists are mostly known or unknown because of their research. As important as teaching may be to some individuals and to some institutions of higher education, unless faculty members publish textbooks that are widely used, their reputations as teachers are naturally going to be limited to the local institution. Faculty members who do publish research will have a reputation in their scientific and scholarly communities as a result. The question before us, then, is whether or not the reputations they achieve seem warranted. Of special interest is whether reputations can be explained by research productivity or by the social connections researchers may have acquired.

Research in the sociology of science over the last 20 years has raised many questions about the way social characteristics may help or hinder some scientists in achieving recognition. Some of these studies contradict each other, but the textbook scientific method requires one to synthesize the previous literature and design a research project that tries to make sense out of it. Ideally one hopes to design a project that will answer the questions once and for all, but it is rarely if ever possible to do that. This research answers some but not all our concerns, but I hope it succeeds in raising many more questions.

Although sociologists of science will be curious about this research, the book is not designed only for my colleagues in that specialty. Science policy makers and scholars of those policies will find this study pertinent to their work. Indeed those interested in the social studies of science will be able not only to understand the contents of this book but also to find topics related to their own scholarly concerns. But equally important, budding scholars and scientists in various disciplines may see their disciplines and their own actions in a way they may not have perceived before. Because they are just beginning to be part of the ongoing reward system, they should be interested now, and if not, they will certainly become interested in how this system works.

I organized this book to take the reader through the process that I actually followed in formulating the research problem and designing the study. After explaining the reasons why we see the reward system as we do and why there are many difficulties in determining whether or not people get what they deserve, I describe the information I collected and discuss the results and the implications. Then I take up the nagging problems that sociologists of science have tried to solve previously to show how my research can offer additional interpretations for what we already believe. Finally I describe some of the problems the reward system may have in the future.

This research was possible because so many people helped me. From its beginning, several students assisted, and I thank Eugene Hynes, Jen-Li Chao, Nancy Richey, Peter Wang, and especially, Frederic Wolinsky. Dr. Michael Dingerson and the Office of Research Development and Administration provided both moral and financial support. Bernard Barber provided enormous encouragement and support and arranged for publication in his series. Peter Peirce has skillfully managed the difficult (impossible?) role of editor for Wiley-Interscience. Both have my sincere appreciation. I thank Mary Frank Gaston for editorial advice and for typing the manuscript several times. My extensive quotes from Robert K. Merton's work are with permission of the author (© Robert K. Merton, *The Sociology of Science,* ed. by Norman W. Storer, Chicago: University of Chicago Press, 1973). My quotes from *The Life Sciences* (1970) were reproduced with permission of the National Academy of Sciences.

With all this assistance, I take responsibility for the errors that inevitably remain.

JERRY GASTON

Carbondale, Illinois
November 1977

CONTENTS

CHAPTER

1   The Reward System in Science as a Research Problem   1

2   The Reward System "State of the Art"   17

3   Characteristics of Disciplines and the Organization of Research   36

4   New Data on the Reward System   55

5   The Reward System in the United States and Great Britain   64

6   The Reward System in Biology, Chemistry, and Physics   86

7   The Matthew and Other Effects in the Allocation of Recognition   120

8   Cumulative Advantage, Reinforcement, and Research Productivity   133

9   Disputes and Deviant Views about the Ethos of Science   158

10   Cognitive Development, Social Organization, and the Reward System   185

Bibliography   193

Index   201

THE REWARD SYSTEM / *IN BRITISH*
                         AND AMERICAN
                         SCIENCE

Chapter 1

/ *THE REWARD SYSTEM*
IN SCIENCE AS A
RESEARCH PROBLEM

The general notion "reward system" is a relatively simple concept involving some kind of behavior and a response by others to it. Most social institutions have some type of reward system, although the expected behavior and appropriate responses differ according to the particular institution. A monetary reward system in capitalistic societies involves the amount a person is paid for working. Individual workers agree to perform work for specific wages or sums, if the wage is not set by a minimum wage or labor contracts.

At higher levels people contract for monthly, annual, or other salaries. Managers are paid in a way that reflects their effort and importance in organizing and supervising the workers in an efficient manner.

The reward system in science involves the relationship between how well scientists perform their scientific roles and what they receive for that performance. Scientists need money to live, but the reward system in science does not work as the economy does, where salary is usually the best measure of performance. The reward system of a group of scientists can, of course, be examined in terms of their salary and income levels, but that involves an entirely different type of system. Monetary rewards are not independent of the scientific reward system, because the most famous scientists are no doubt paid higher salaries than those not so well known. But scientists' salaries are not pertinent to this study. Salaries are based on many considerations, such as whether a scientist is employed in industry, government, or universities. And within these categories, salaries vary widely among different organizations. Industrial organizations are located in various parts of the country, laboratories are at different levels of government, and universities and colleges differ greatly in their prestige and salary levels.

The lack of interest in scientists' salaries results, not from this variety, but from the fact that salaries are not determined directly by other scientists as a way of acknowledging the scientific community's debt to individuals.

If money is not important for scientists in the reward system, what is? It is the recognition and honor that scientific communities allocate for contributions to scientific knowledge. Scientists are rewarded for their research performance by the community of scientists engaged in research on similar topics. The last part of that sentence is crucial. A scientist doing research in one area is often unknown to one working in a different area. Only rarely does a physicist's work, for example, have any importance for advances in chemistry or a chemist's work for advances in biology. Hence, it is incorrect to think of all practicing scientists as "the scientific community." There are really many "communities" of scientists. In many research areas these communities number as few as 10 to 20 and rarely more than 200.

Why the reward system peculiar to science operates the way it does and why it is important to scientists and science are the subjects of the remainder of the chapter.

THE CONCEPT OF REWARD SYSTEM

Robert K. Merton's research is the most important source of ideas in the sociology of science. One of his major contributions is the concept of the reward system in science. Merton did not, of course, invent it. He brought it to the attention of scholars and students and showed that it is fundamental for understanding how the social institution of science works. To place this book in an intellectual context, I review briefly the development of this concept. A recent reprinting of some of Merton's papers (Merton, 1973), edited by Norman W. Storer, makes this relatively easy. In his commentary on Merton's work as it developed through the years Storer declares that the reward system of science is the heart of Mertonian sociology of science.

Merton's concern with science as a social institution touches on many aspects of science and society, but not all those aspects are pertinent here. The focus here is on the internal operation of the reward system, which works as follows. The goal of any scientific discipline is to advance the state of knowledge in that discipline. New data are constantly collected, these data are compared to previous data, and new interpretations are advanced to explain the findings. New questions are raised in the process and then more data are collected. This is a general process, not a description of the routine of individual scientists, who usually focus only on a certain part of the process. Whether researchers concentrate on part of the cycle, rather than on the whole process, depends on the division of labor in the research area.

Scientists in different research areas do not have to decide about the goal of advancing the state of knowledge, because without question, that is the goal of all science. They decide the best approach for achieving the goal, and in doing so sometimes create differences of opinion and controversy, but the ultimate goal is not considered problematic.

Researchers are added to a specialty through training of students or by scientists, trained in related or different areas, changing into the specialty. Young scientists are socialized into the role of researcher by more senior active scientists. This process is no different from a young businessman's being socialized into the economic world. The only difference involves the values held in the highest esteem. In the business world the highest values are usually to add profits, accumulate capital, and increase the equity of the company. In the scientific world the highest value is for the research specialty or parent discipline to develop through contribution of new data and theoretical explanations to account for the data.

Science is more complicated than this simple description would make it appear. For advancing scientific knowledge as fast and accurately as possible, there are certain rules of the game. In social institutions such as the polity, the economy, and the family, most of the rules are codified into law. In education there are codified laws and also institutional regulations. In religion, rules and dogma of the church outline acceptable and expected behavior. In science, however, there are no such codified laws and no book of rules for the community. Scientists' behavior, as *scientists,* is governed by norms socialized by would-be scientists through the teachings and personal examples of mentors and teachers. The technical norms of conducting research are learned through lectures, experimentation, problem sets, and exercises. Behavioral norms are learned through admonition and personal examples. But these norms are not spelled out specifically by scientists to their students, and most scientists would not be able to discuss them directly. That this is so does not diminish the influence of these norms.

Merton (1973:267–278) suggests that four basic norms, constituting the "ethos" of science, guide the behavior of scientists: universalism, organized skepticism, communism, and disinterestedness. All scientists do not adhere all the time to all the norms, because, as is the case with all "rules," they call for ideal behavior, and it is difficult, if not impossible, for anyone to conform consistently to all the norms influencing one's behavior. Furthermore these norms are not written down for scientists to learn or presented as oaths to be taken as medical students take the Hippocratic Oath at graduation. Instead the norms of the social institution of science are essentially functional imperatives that Merton derived from analysis of the goals of science and pronouncements of scientists over a long period. In Merton's (1973:269) words, "Although the ethos of science has not been codified, it can be inferred from the moral consensus of scientists as expressed in use and wont, in countless writings on the scientific spirit and in moral indignation directed toward contraventions of the ethos."

The norms provide a basis for studying under what conditions they are more or less observed and what the negative and positive consequences are for conformity to or deviance from them. The norms thus provide a perspective for analyzing the internal operation of the social system of science. I describe these norms briefly and show the kind of behavior each norm should affect.

Universalism requires that race, sex, age, religion, ethnicity, nationality, or any ascribed characteristic should not be involved in any evaluation of any scientist's research contribution. The criteria that may be applied include only technical and scholarly considerations of the truth or importance of the new knowledge presented. Universalism is the norm most directly related to internationality in science. Although scientists as human beings may have chauvinistic tendencies, they may not let their prejudices influence an assessment of another's work. They should not dismiss something because the author is German, Spanish, or located at some lesser university or laboratory. This means also that a scientist should not attribute a positive evaluation because of social characteristics that he holds in high esteem. Contributions published by scientists at a well-known university or laboratory should not have greater influence because of the author's affiliation, in the same way that a contribution should not have lesser influence because of the social attributes of its author. Scientists should not lean over backward to avoid criticizing a contribution because it comes from an unknown author or an author at a low-prestige institution. All this is to say, of course, that a scientific contribution should be evaluated without interest in any social attribute of its presenter.

I believe that Storer's (1966:78) discussion of universalism emphasizes too much the universal nature of the content of science to the detriment of the main point about universalism when he writes that

This norm, orientational rather than directive in its intent, refers both to the assumption that physical laws are everywhere the same and to the principle that the truth and value of a scientific statement is independent of the characteristics of its author. In the words of Roger Coates, in his preface to the second edition of Newton's *Principia*, " . . . if gravity be the cause of the descent of a stone in Europe who doubts that it is also the cause of the same descent in America?"

It is this principle, too, which makes science an international community; what a Russian scientist discovers about the atom will be valid in America and his work can be appreciated by scientists everywhere. Empirical knowledge knows no national boundaries, and to reject his findings for political reasons would be totally irrational vis-à-vis scientific goals.

Whereas universalism may indeed have an orientational component, it is easy to recognize many situations where it can be applied to specific behavior.

Organized skepticism requires that all knowledge, whether originating through scientific research or any other authoritative source, such as religion or politics, be submitted to the same scrutiny before it can become a part of certified knowledge. This norm influences behavior by causing a scientist to have, in simplest terms, a questioning attitude. A scientist must realize that, although a contribution may have passed all referee and screening processes before being printed, it is still questionable. Everyone is capable of making an error. A few, a very few, are capable even of fabrication. Although it is impossible and unnecessary to replicate pertinent research to be sure it is correct, a scientist should accept the tentative nature of research and not accept, therefore, without question that others' statements are true simply because the author believes them to be true.

Communism (or communality) requires that, after a new scientific contribution has been publicized, the creator or originator has no individual claims of ownership of the new idea, information, or theory. It must be available to others to use in their work. When others use the work, they must give appropriate credit by citing the source, showing that the information was useful in arriving at their idea, in formulating a new problem, or in assisting with a technique or method. In return for this recognition scientists are not supposed to withhold crucial aspects of their research beyond a reasonable period. Publicizing the information reduces the necessity for others to solve the same problem before they can proceed to the next logical or desired step in investigating their problem.

The norm of communality is the main ingredient of Hagstrom's (1965) notions about the exchange theory of scientific research. This theory attempts to explain how social control works in science through the mechanism of scientists' publishing their work in *exchange* for scientific recognition. Because I discuss later the importance of recognition, it is appropriate to show how Hagstrom (1965:12–13) views this exchange relationship:

> Manuscripts submitted to scientific periodicals are often called "contributions," and they are, in fact, gifts. Authors do not usually receive royalties or other payments, and their institutions may even be required to aid in the financial support of the periodical. On the other hand, manuscripts for which the scientific authors do receive financial payments, such as textbooks and popularizations, are, if not despised, certainly held in much lower esteem than articles containing original research results.

Disinterestedness requires that scientists do research for the "sake of science." This may be one of the least understood and most controversial norms. It is least understood because of the conflict between "science for its own sake" and the necessity for scientists to take into account other considerations in their work.

In the first place scientists cannot drop their current work in the middle of a project and jump into another one that may hold out an opportunity for a more important discovery (modifying research is permitted and encouraged when funded by grants, but contracts are somewhat different). If that happened, the resources spent already might be wasted, especially if the new problem appeared to be more significant but only turned out to be unimportant. The funding source, whether internal or external to the university, may think that changing topics suddenly results from a fickle personality. They might not only frown upon it but also refuse to fund the new project. Moreover, graduate students working on the project may be depending on it for data for their theses.

In the second place scientists' laboratories are seldom physically equipped for other important but unrelated research. And in the third place it is one thing to believe or to know that there is a "more" important problem elsewhere, but it is quite a different thing to be able to solve it. One may not only lack the appropriate equipment or access to it but also may not be competent to work on the problem even if the equipment and funds were suddenly available. Most would argue that finding a way to cure or prevent cancer is an important scientific problem that requires *understanding* cancer (in perhaps all its forms), after which the "cure" may be obvious. Indeed the federal government allocated about $763 million in fiscal 1976 for the National Cancer Institute (not all were research funds, of course). Knowing a significant problem exists does not, however, guarantee its solution.

Doing science for its own sake means a love for truth more than doing research because it will bring fame or fortune. The positive function of disinterestedness for science is evident by the fact that, if scientists work on what is really important for the advancement of scientific knowledge, they will succeed also in obtaining fame for having solved significant problems or having made important advances. Disinterestedness then functions to influence a scientist's behavior toward concern for truth—which will ultimately produce appropriate recognition. In channeling interest toward truth scientists are channeled away from oversimplification, shoddy work, and faster results which may bring one some immediate attention. But later, when the truth finally comes out, it may lead to rejection by the scientific community because of apparent incompetence, suspected fraud, or both. The truth will come out if the problem is important enough to have merited recognition by peers in the first place.

Disinterestedness is not only misunderstood but is also controversial because it appears to be the norm least adhered to. Initial observations of many situations suggest that the scientist involved is obviously out for his own sake, not for the sake of science. Cynics can say that scientists really care only about advancing their personal careers, and there are enough instances available in the press and on television to "prove" the cynic's position. Certainly there are examples of this type of behavior just as there are bankers who embezzle, husbands who cheat on their wives, and religious people who commit sins. One or two examples described in a magazine read by millions of people still constitute only one or two examples, not millions. The thousands of scientists who work 60 to 80 hours each week and who face failure daily in their research because of problems they cannot solve at the moment would commit suicide before committing fraud. These are the modal majority whom magazine readers will never see mentioned and about whom films will not be made.

The highly publicized and isolated events describing deviance are often believed to be only the tip of the iceberg. Nevertheless science is the only social institution in which members are constantly "policing" themselves and in which colleagues caught searching for fame, at whatever cost to truth, are identified by their peers. Citizens are loath to report each other for breaches of economic laws (income tax fraud, for example); husbands are loath to blow the whistle on straying husbands; it is rumored that physicians are hesitant to bring their colleagues before medical boards for possible disciplinary action. But scientists and other scholars point out the mistakes of their colleagues in print, for all to see, and do not hesitate to deal with errant colleagues when, in the rare situation, scientists remove truth from top place in their list of values.

Universalism, organized skepticism, communality, and disinterestedness together provide a context in which maximum progress can be
made in scientific advancement. These norms function positively for
the development of science through directing behavior in the social
interaction required because, science, as much as anything, is a social
institution. All social institutions must have rules for members to live by
and patterns of behavior that others can depend on and can follow to
avoid having to decide at every turn what is the right thing to do. I
turn now to the operation of the reward system to show how these
institutional norms function in promoting scientific activity by individuals who are, of course, the actors in the social institution of science.

In developing a theory of science as a social institution, Merton
(1973:286–293) begins with a recurrent observation about the history
of science. Looking through those pages of history, one finds frequent
descriptions of scientists involved in disputes over priority of discovery.
"During the last three centuries in which modern science developed,
numerous scientists, both great and small have engaged in such ac-
rimonious controversy" (Merton, 1973:287).* He recounts how Galileo
fought for priority in his invention of the "geometric and military
compass," how one Father Horatio Grassi tried to diminish his contribution to the invention of the telescope, how Scheiner claimed priority on observation on sun spots, how another tried to rob Galileo of
glory through pretending not to have seen his previous writings on the
discoveries, and how Simon Mayr (Marius) claimed priority in first observing the Medicean planets by using a deviant method of dating the
publication that announced his discovery. His using the Julian calendar
rather than the Gregorian resulted in an earlier date.

Merton describes how Newton fought battles with Hooke about
priority in optics and celestial mechanics and with Leibniz about invention of the calculus. Hooke fought with Newton and also fought with
Huygens over the invention of the spiral-spring balance to regulate
watches.

These were seventeenth-century disputes, but the eighteenth and
nineteenth centuries did not escape their share. Merton (1973:288)
writes:

Perhaps the most tedious and sectarian of these was the great "Water
Controversy" in which that shy, rich, and noble genius of science, Henry
Cavendish, was pushed into a three-way tug-of-war with Watt and

*With permission of the author, © by Robert K. Merton, *The Sociology of Sci-
ence,* ed. by Norman W. Storer (Chicago: University of Chicago Press, 1973).

Lavoisier over the question of which one had first demonstrated the compound nature of water, and thereby removed it from its millennia-long position as one of the elements. Earthy battles raged also over claims to the first discovery of heavenly bodies, as in the case of the most dramatic astronomical discovery of the century in which the Englishman John Couch Adams and the Frenchman Urban Jean LeVerrier inferred the existence and predicted the position of the planet now known as Neptune, which was found where their independent computations showed it would be. Medicine had its share of conflicts over priority; for example, Jenner believed himself first to demonstrate that vaccination afforded security against smallpox, but the advocates of Pearson and Rabaut believed otherwise.

Throughout the nineteenth century and down to the present, disputes over priority continued to be frequent and intense. Lister knew he had first introduced antisepsis, but others insisted that Lemaire had done so before. The sensitive and modest Faraday was wounded by the claims of others to several of his major discoveries in physics: one among these, the discovery of electro-magnetic rotation, was said to have been made before by Wollaston; Faraday's onetime mentor Sir Humphrey Davy (who had himself been involved in similar disputes) actually opposed Faraday's election to the Royal Society on the ground that his was not the original discovery. Laplace, several of the Bernoullis, Legendre, Gauss, Cauchy were only a few of the giants among mathematicians embroiled in quarrels over priority.*

Merton considers various hypotheses to account for these observations. Priority disputes could result from human nature. Egotism being part of that nature, scientists would exhibit egotistical behavior by making claims about the priority of their discoveries. That explanation does not, however, stand up, because there has been little success in explaining specific conduct by attributing it to human nature. A second hypothesis is that, whereas egotism is part of human nature, it is not evenly distributed among all human beings, and persons who select themselves to be scientists have an unusual quantity of egotism. But that explanation does not stand up to the fact that scientists who have pressed claims have often been extraordinarily quiet men and in many instances the claims have been pressed by friends and colleagues. The "respect by association" that might accrue to such friends and colleagues does not account for their dedication to duty that is involved. Merton (1973:292–293) explains why this hypothesis does not hold and what the best explanation is for priority disputes:

*With permission of the author, © by Robert K. Merton, *The Sociology of Science,* ed. by Norman W. Storer (Chicago: University of Chicago Press, 1973).

Now these argumentative associates and bystanders stand to gain little or nothing from successfully prosecuting the claims of their candidate, except in the pickwickian sense of having identified themselves with him or with the nation of which they are all a part. Their behavior can scarcely be explained by egotism. They do not suffer from rival claims to precedence. Their personal status is not being threatened. And yet, over and again, they take up the cudgels in the status–battle and, uninhibited by any semblance of indulging in self-praise, express their great moral indignation over the outrage being perpetrated upon their candidate.

This is, I believe, a particularly significant fact. For, as we know from the sociological theory of institutions, the expression of disinterested moral indignation is a signpost announcing the violation of a social norm. Although the indignant bystanders are themselves not injured by what they take to be the misbehavior of the culprit, they respond with hostility. They want to see "fair play," to see that behavior conforms to the rules of the game. The very fact of their entering the fray goes to show that science is a social institution with a distinctive body of norms exerting moral authority and that these norms are involved particularly when it is felt that they are being violated. In this sense, fights over priority, with all their typical vehemence and passionate feelings, are not merely expressions of hot tempers, although these may of course raise the temperature of controversy; basically, they constitute responses to what are taken to be violations of the institutional norms of intellectual property.*

Scientists do not own the results of their research. The only intellectual property scientists have is the recognition as the one who contributed that knowledge to the advancement of science. This recognition, the response to a contribution to knowledge, constitutes the second half of the reward system. The first half is the contribution—the second half is the appreciation shown by other scientists in using and acknowledging that contribution. The norms of science provide the structure that causes this to happen. Disinterestedness requires that scientists do research that is best for science, not for themselves; organized skepticism requires that scientists' work be scrutinized; universalism requires that the scrutiny occur without consideration of the contributor's social attributes; and communality requires that scientists publicize their findings and that others who use it appropriately acknowledge its usefulness either by the usual citation, or in more unusual circumstances, by a special note of acknowledgment.

The most important goal of science is to extend knowledge, and unless a scientific publication is original in some way, it is not useful to the

*With permission of the author, © by Robert K. Merton, *The Sociology of Science,* ed. by Norman W. Storer (Chicago: University of Chicago Press, 1973).

scientific community. Originality has both a substantive dimension and a time dimension. A contribution that replicates or explicates earlier work may be original, but it probably is not so important for science as the first work reported. Thus originality is a variable that is not dichotomous, original or unoriginal, but is bound by some continuum from truly original to original only in some small way. The time dimension becomes evident when the first person to make an announcement of discovery is more likely to be recognized for it because it is the most valuable to science. Independent simultaneous discoveries may be good for science because two discoveries increase the probability that they are correct. But if the process leading to the first announced discovery or creation is correct, it needed only to have been done once. This is not to suggest that redundancy is to be avoided, because redundancy and duplication have some important functions. What it shows, however, is that the time of making or announcing a discovery is important. A later, second announcement by an independent discoverer does not add *new* knowledge; it only increases the confidence in the validity of the previously announced discovery. The independent discoverer may have used as much creativity and hard work as the first scientist, but even if the second announcement comes only shortly after the first, it is still announcing something already known.

Merton (1973:293) describes this process by saying:

> The ways in which the norms of science help produce this result seem clear enough. On every side the scientist is reminded that it is his role to advance knowledge, and his happiest fulfillment of that role, to advance knowledge greatly. This is only to say, of course, that in the institution of science originality is at a premium. For it is through originality, in greater or smaller increments, that knowledge advances. When the institution of science works efficiently—and like other social institutions, it does not always do so—recognition and esteem accrue to those who have best fulfilled their roles, to those who have made genuinely original contributions to the common stock of knowledge. Then are found those happy circumstances in which self-interest and moral obligation coincide and fuse.*

The best evidence against this picture of the scientific community would be to prove that scientists do not care about recognition. If they avoided or rejected recognition due them, one would have to question the assertion that they want recognition or that they understand the process of exchanging their scientific discoveries and creations for rec-

*With permission of the author, © by Robert K. Merton, *The Sociology of Science*, ed. by Norman W. Storer (Chicago: University of Chicago Press, 1973).

ognition from their peers. To say that scientists want or expect recognition is in no way to accuse them of impure or pathological motives. When people who contract to perform a service complete their job, they want and expect their pay, but that is not considered impure or pathological. Even people who actually do not need the money want it just the same.

There is a story about a famous professor who signs over his check to his university. Upon being told he would not get a raise, because he would, in any case, return it to the university, he replied that it was his prerogative to make a decision to return the salary and that had nothing to do with the raise. The university official was ignorant of the nature of the exchange between professional services and salary level and of the fact that salary was an important measure of the worth of the professor, regardless of how he used it. Was this impure or pathological? Of course not. It was entirely appropriate according to the institutional norms of the economy.

Scientists have told me that sociologists put too much emphasis on their concern for recognition. But that is not true. Sociologists do not emphasize the desire for recognition, the institution of science does, and the evidence is scientists' behavior. Merton (1973) reports examples recorded over three centuries. But unless one thinks this evidence is relegated to the pages of history, all one has to do is examine Hagstrom's (1965) rich source of quotations from contemporary scientists from various disciplines, read my own (Gaston, 1973) interviews with high-energy physicists, listen closely at any party where scientists are in attendance, or scan publications such as *Science* or *Nature* in which the letters to the editors frequently involve misplaced priority or unacknowledged contributions.

Merton (1973:293) writes that "As Darwin once phrased it, 'My love of natural science . . . has been much aided by the ambition to be esteemed by my fellow naturalists.' " And with much insight Hans Selye said (Merton, 1973:341):

> Why is everybody so anxious to deny that he works for recognition? . . .
> All the scientists I know sufficiently well to judge (and I included myself in this group) are extremely anxious to have their work recognized and approved by others. Is it not below the dignity of an objective scientific mind to permit such a distortion of his true motives? Besides, what is there to be ashamed of?*

*With permission of the author, © by Robert K. Merton, *The Sociology of Science*, ed. by Norman W. Storer (Chicago: University of Chicago Press, 1973).

Hagstrom (1965:14) writes about a theoretical physicist who, when told that another scientist was unconcerned about an instance of being anticipated and unable to publish his work, said:

> I think I would admit to not having such pure interests. I must admit to a desire for recognition. I suppose it doesn't make much difference whether one wants to glorify himself or have others glorify him.

A mathematician told Hagstrom (1965:14) that

> A field in mathematics may become popular if the more popular mathematicians, the big shots, become interested in it. Then it grows rapidly. Junior mathematicians want recognition from the big shots, and consequently work in areas prized by them.

One of the best situations to derive information about scientists' concern for recognition is the case where other scientists do not refer to a scientist's prior publications. Hagstrom (1967:127) reports that, for a large sample (1235) of American scientists, from 46 to 60 percent, depending on discipline, believe that others have failed to refer to their work. From 16 to 36 percent, depending on discipline, believe that others probably knew of their work but failed to refer to it anyway. Among British high-energy physicists, 50 percent believed that others had failed to refer to their work when they should have; 20 percent knew the scientists involved who they thought intentionally did not refer properly to previous work (Gaston, 1973:110).

The failure to refer to prior published work may result from several causes, but even if the cause is an "innocent" one, it does not eliminate the hurt feelings of the slighted scientist. One scientist told me (Gaston, 1973:111) that "it very often happens that people who haven't published much will not refer to your work because the only way they can get their paper into print is by not referring to the preceding paper that has done the same thing." A theorist said:

> Possibly a reference to my work would distract from the importance of their work, because what I've done so far in my field has always been new. The approach has always been better than what was done before and what has happened since. There's been very little improvement.

In Mitchell Wilson's (1949:103) novel *Live with Lightning,* Erik Gorin, a fictitious Columbia University physicist talking to his wife Savina, says:

I *am* ambitious, Savina. I've got it so bad I'm afraid if I once let it get started, it'll run away with me. A long time ago, I told you that I ache with wanting success. . . . It's not that I want to be famous or rich. What I want, what I burn for, what I'd give damn near anything in my life for, is to be good enough to deserve being famous, as a scientist.

Finally, a contemporary scientist, in reviewing a book that he thought overemphasized scientists' concern for recognition, could contain himself no longer. "Yes, Virginia," he said, "scientists do love recognition, but only since Pythagoras" (Lederman, 1969:169). These statements show that, like others throughout history, scientists still want recognition for discoveries or creations.

THE FUNCTION OF THE REWARD SYSTEM

Some people may wonder what all the concern is about the reward system in science. The answer is simple. The reward system operates to promote the advancement of knowledge, and a major concern of any social study of science is to discover how the social components of science affect the production of new knowledge. If scientists are strongly motivated to continue the hard work and frustration that accompanies most, if not all, worthwhile research, then their behavior must be reinforced by positive responses by their peers in the scientific community. This does not mean that scientists are abnormally anxious to have their work recognized, but recognition for scientific research is an important reinforcement of the value of their activities. It helps to assure the scientific community that scientists responsible for important research in the past will continue to do research. Failure to obtain appropriate recognition (I point out later in the book that "appropriate" does not mean all scientists expect or have to receive the Nobel Prize) would encourage highly competent and productive scientists to engage in activities that would lead to some other kind of rewards, perhaps monetary. Although scientists are generally paid at a level to provide comfortable livings, anyone who believes that they, or most other scholars, could not earn much higher salaries by engaging in quite different occupations is simply mistaken. Scientists cannot be totally motivated to conduct research by the level of monetary rewards. Because of this there has to be some other explanation for their putting themselves and their families through the ambiguities and frustrations about which nearly all scientists will testify. To some the activity itself has its rewards; to most the recognition by peers that the work is worthwhile has to be the major reward. Any other currently possible explanation will not withstand a comparison with the facts.

Turn again to Merton's (1973:293) statement: "When the institution of science works efficiently—and like other social institutions, it does not always do so—recognition and esteem accrue to those who have best fulfilled their roles. . . ." At this point in the history of the development of Merton's notions about the reward system (originally published in 1957) there were no specific hypotheses suggesting the conditions under which the social institution of science would operate either efficiently or inefficiently, or in a universalistic or particularistic manner. Of course, the severe effects of particularism as observed under Nazi rule in Germany were well known. But since 1957 some research in the sociology of science has involved problems that provide the bases for suspecting that certain variables affect the operation of the reward system.

The main question I address in the remainder of this book is this: Are there differences in the reward systems of various scientific communities based on the effect of cognitive differences in disciplines or on the structural differences created by the social organization of science in a nation?

This question deals both with aspects of the cognitive elements, or content of science, and the social structural aspects of science. It assumes that the social system of science is influenced by internal or intellectual characteristics and also by external characteristics. The latter are beyond the control of science or scientists and are imposed by historical processes that are largely political. To be more specific, contemporary scientists have had little influence on the organization of science in their particular countries. Any nation's organization of science is a development over time that ultimately, no matter how much "advice" scientists give, results from political compromise. Taking advice from experts, whether from practicing scientists or scholars of science, specifically science policy specialists, would not necessarily have produced a "better" organization of science. In the first place scientists have specific preferences, but their ideas are often based on nothing but bias. In the second place science policy experts do not have a knowledge base sufficient to prescribe an organization that would be the most "efficient." This is not to suggest that science policy experts are ignorant. It is to suggest only that efficiency in most cases is not well defined and that governmental science policy is, in reality, a political policy. As a political policy it may not be the most advantageous to the goal of advancing certified knowledge. Governmental science policy, after all, is no different from any other government policy. It indicates how government views science in concert with all other positions governments have to take.

This book is not an attempt to show how nations go wrong in organizing their scientific activities. It is a study of how the internal operation of the reward system is affected by the nature of the organization of scientific activities and by the content of science. Chapter 2 describes the published studies dealing with the reward system and shows how these raise important questions about cognitive and structural elements and their potential influence on its internal operation.

Chapter 2 / THE REWARD SYSTEM
"STATE OF THE ART"

All observers of the social dimension of science agree on one fact: There is enormous variation in the number of papers scientists produce. Some scientists complete their PhD degrees and publish nothing from that research. Others publish something from their theses and are never heard of again. Others continue to publish at a very slow rate. Others publish at a steady rate over a period of years and then fade away. And others publish at an enormous rate even before they receive their PhD degrees and continue to publish for as long as they live.

The possible range of publications generally expected in any sample of scientists extends from zero to more than 100. Price (1963:41) reports a study by Wayne Dennis of men listed in the *Biographical Memoirs* of the National Academy of Sciences for 1943–1952. Of the 41 who died after age 70, the highest producer had 768 publications; the lowest had 27. The average number was more than 200, and only 15 had fewer than 100 publications. These figures represent data from the highest echelons of the scientific community, and 100 publications is a rare achievement obtained by only a small percentage of all practicing scientists.

Observers of science also agree that the reputations of scientists vary enormously. Scientists who have never received any acknowledgment are on the low end of the scale. They are followed by those with some visibility who are known in very limited circles. Much higher up on the prestige scale are those for whom processes, measurements, or "effects" are named; members of honorary elected academies of science; and winners of prizes and medals. Of course, the ultimate prestige is being awarded a Nobel Prize. It is clear to most observers that the most pro-

17

ductive and prolific scientists are also the ones with the most prestige. As Price (1963:41) says, " . . . although there is no guarantee that the small producer is a nonentity and the big producer a distinguished scientist, or even that the order of merit follows the order of productivity, there is a strong correlation. . . ."

Such variation in both productivity and recognition seems to beg for explanation. Some research has examined personal and contextual variables involved in differential productivity, but these studies have been less than satisfactory (see Berelson, 1960; Halsey and Trow, 1971; Lazarsfeld and Thielans, 1958; Manis, 1951; Meltzer, 1956). A study using psychological variables such as motivation, intelligence, work habits, and other individual data is not likely to be able to explain adequately the variation in scientific output. Moreover, a study using sociological variables exclusively is not likely to be able to explain variation sufficiently to be comprehensive. I am not aware of any study that has explained most of the variation in scientific productivity, although it is easy enough to find rather large correlations between productivity and other variables. It is not that we know nothing about scientific productivity, only that the enormous variation has not been explained completely.

In contrast to the many studies dealing with correlates of scientific productivity, few studies have attempted to explain the prestige of scientists, because it is common knowledge that this is derived mostly from scientific contributions (see Caplow and McGee, 1965; Orlans, 1962; Sturgis and Clemente, 1973; Wilson, 1958). Of course some cynics would argue that a scientist's prestige is, to a large extent, a matter of successful political activity, grantsmanship, organizational and entrepreneurial skills. (For a forceful argument negating this, see Cole and Cole, 1973:247–252). In some ways these characteristics may help determine a scientist's prestige. Indeed, in some instances, these characteristics may be a necessary condition for research accomplishment and may be important at some types of universities. But these are not sufficient to explain the status of scientists at the higher levels of prestige.

Studies of either scientists' productivity or their prestige constitute only one component of the reward system and are not sufficient to deal with questions about its operations. Five systematic studies on the reward system, influenced by the Mertonian model of science, have been published since 1965. I now consider in detail each of these studies.

FIVE STUDIES ON THE REWARD SYSTEM

The most important empirical research on the reward system, exclusive of Merton's research, are the studies by Crane (1965), Cole and Cole (1967), Hargens and Hagstrom (1967), Gaston (1970), and Blume and Sinclair (1973). Unless these papers are quoted directly or different work by these authors is referred to, I do not repeat the reference each time and thus I avoid cluttering the page with parentheses. The samples used in these studies included British and American scientists and representatives of biologists, psychologists, political scientists, "physical" and "biological" scientists, eminent physicists, high-energy physicists, and chemists.

Crane's American Biologists, Psychologists, and Political Scientists

The purpose of Crane's (1965:700) study was to analyze "information about the distribution of scientific productivity and recognition, in an attempt to assess the importance of talent and achievement relative to that of academic environment." Whereas her original intention was to test their effect as affected by academic environment, there was no explicit measure of talent except the inference that scientists attending a prestigious graduate school probably had more ability in general than those attending a less prestigious one ("departments" are the pertinent units in later studies because of Cartter's [1966] study of departmental quality). Judged from the use of Crane's study, most scholars are not alluding to her data on the advantages of research environments at major universities; rather they refer to her conclusions about the lack of congruence between scientific productivity and recognition.

Crane personally interviewed 150 scientists at three universities of varying prestige: one with a long and prestigious research history, another with a tradition of research in some departments with some national visibility, and one that, like so many other state universities in America, began active (and often uneven) research efforts only since World War II. The three universities provided comparisons between the research atmosphere and the effect of that climate on the scientist's productivity.

Her study shows that scientists trained at a university among the top 12 in Berelson's (1960) scheme were more likely to be productive than those trained in other universities. Productivity took into account the time since the scientist had taken the PhD and the nature of scientific publications. Books counted as a major publication, and a series of articles on the same problem was counted as a major publication. Scientists currently at the major university were more likely to be productive (41 percent were highly productive) than those trained at an unprestigious university (36 percent were highly productive) but now at the major university in her sample.

An evaluation of the reward system should consider the same variables for recognition as are considered for productivity. Recognition was measured by the number of honors the scientists had won, divided into high and low categories that took professional age into account, requiring more awards if the scientist had been active over a longer period. The more prestigious category involved presidencies of national professional associations or some special-purpose association; membership in the National Academy of Sciences, the American Academy of Arts and Sciences, and the American Philosophical Society; an honorary doctorate from an institution other than the current or degree-granting institution; and the Nobel Prize. The secondary honors included prestigious fellowships, such as Guggenheim, Rockefeller, National Research Council, National Science Foundation Fellowship, National Institutes of Health career development awards, and service of various types on governmental or professional advisory boards. No scientist with less than five years since the doctorate had received any such honors, and these were omitted from her analysis of recognition. (It is significant that these young scientists had not received "recognition" as measured by Crane, and this kind of problem will appear later in the chapter.)

Similarly to the pattern for productivity, more scientists currently at the major university had high recognition (58 percent) than those at the next prestige level (35 percent), where, in turn, more scientists had high recognition than those at the state university (17 percent). The connection between a scientist's recognition and the prestige of the university where the PhD was obtained was different from the pattern for productivity. Whether or not scientists were trained at the top 12 or other universities, more scientists currently at the major university had high recognition. Scientists trained at lesser institutions and later appointed to the major university had achieved more recognition than those trained at a "top 12" university but later appointed to the two institutions in the study with lesser prestige.

The important question about the reward system is whether or not scientists receive rewards commensurate with their scientific productivity, and if they do not, one must ask what decreases the universalistic allocation of recognition. Crane found that recognition and productivity are positively correlated, but the correlation is less than perfect, and it is different for scientists affiliated with universities of different prestige. Crane (1965:710) writes:

> Although the very productive were most likely to have won the highest honors, highly productive scientists at the major university were more likely to have won recognition than highly productive scientists at a lesser

school. The latter were, in fact, no more likely to win recognition than unproductive men at the major school. Evidently, productivity did not make the scientist as visible to his colleagues in his discipline as did a position at a major university.

There are two types of reasons why a scientist at a higher prestige university may receive more recognition, for apparently equivalent work, than one at a lower prestige university. A universalistic reason for differential recognition is that some scientists' work is more important than others'. Important work, even if not in large quantity, deserves recognition more than a larger amount of less important work. Particularistic reasons for differential recognition include the "halo" effect of being located at a highly respected university where it is simply assumed that "better" scientists are located. A scientist at a prestigious university may also be more visible to other scientists, especially if there are eminent colleagues who can sponsor one's work and help to make contacts with other respected scientists in the discipline. Crane could not test these possible reasons for differential recognition, but she leaned toward explanations that involved particularistic reasons.

*Hargens and Hagstrom's American Physical
and Biological Scientists*

Berelson's (1960) data obtained from a questionnaire survey of 4440 faculty members of American graduate institutions were the basis for Hargens and Hagstrom's study of the reward system in American science. They used only a subsample of the larger sample of graduate faculty, the physical and biological scientists, a total of 576. Their study originated from concerns, expressed by several writers, that the career of a scholar is heavily influenced by attending a prestigious graduate school. They cite Caplow and McGee (1965:193), who believed that "the initial choice of a graduate school sets an indelible mark on the student's career. In many disciplines, men trained at minor universities have virtually no chance of attaining eminence."

Hargens and Hagstrom say that, after writers make these assertions and give some evidence that people trained at the top end up there, while people trained at the bottom stay there, the writers usually do not invesitgate the effect that scholarly merit (scientific productivity) has on that process.

The purpose of Hargens and Hagstrom's study was to determine the relative influences of graduate school and of research productivity on a scientist's location in the academic stratification system. If attending a prestigious graduate school is more important than performance for scientists, then it is clear that the reward system is not operating to recognize performance but rather operating to reward particularistic, ascribed criteria.

They examined the data in several ways to assess the relative influence of scholarly productivity and prestige of graduate school. Of the scientists with high productivity (upper half of the distribution for unweighted totals of all papers and books for the previous five years), 51 percent of those taking PhDs in high-prestige institutions, contrasted to 24 percent of those in other institutions, were currently appointed at a university in the highest prestige category. Of the scientists with low productivity (lower half of the productivity distribution) 22 percent with PhDs from high-prestige institutions were at a university in the top prestige category, but only 10 percent with PhDs from low-prestige institutions were now at a top ranking university. This result parallels Crane's finding. Productivity is rewarded by appointments at top institutions, but, to some extent, so is low productivity if one chose the right institution for a PhD. Hargens and Hagstrom (1967:32–33) conclude:

> ... being from a high prestige doctoral institution may help a scientist to obtain a position in the upper ranges of the stratification system, but will not save a scientist from placement in the bottom level of the system. On the other hand, being highly productive can help scientists to stay out of the bottom level just as much as it can help them to obtain positions in the top level.

They divided the sample into two groups: scientists currently affiliated with an institution in Berelson's two top prestige categories and those in the bottom two prestige categories. They compared the differences between levels of productivity and placement in the upper part of the high and low categories. Hargens and Hagstrom (1967:33–34) concluded that

> ... in the higher ranges of the academic stratification system, the prestige of a scientist's doctoral institution is as important as his productivity for high placement ... [and for those] .. in the lower ranges of the academic stratification system, productivity is more important for high placement than the prestige of one's doctoral institution.

Finally they divided the sample into two groups, those receiving their PhDs before and those after 1950. They decided that, whereas identification of a scientist with his doctoral institution seems to affect his location in the prestige hierarchy, the effect becomes less important as time passes. In the early postdoctorate years, with little time to demonstrate research abilities, having studied at a high-ranking institution is important. In later years one can be held accountable for scholarly productivity or the lack thereof, and regardless of academic origins, one can end up in a relatively unknown university. Their abstract summarizes the nature of the reward system in their study: " . . . the prestige of an institution where a scientist received his doctorate is related to the prestige of his present affiliation even when the effects of his productivity are controlled" (Hargens and Hagstrom, 1967:24).

Cole and Cole's American Physicists

Cole and Cole selected their sample of 120 physicists by stratifying the population of university physicists along four dimensions: age, rank of department (Cartter's 1966 report), productivity, and number of honorific awards. Later Cole and Cole (1973:264–265) describe the sampling in more detail, adding that 86 departments were involved, selected on the basis of having granted at least one PhD annually during the period 1952–1962. The stratified sample had 128 sampling cells (although they state it is a $4 \times 3 \times 2 \times 4$, which results in only 96). The sample made no claims to represent all American physicists, and they deliberately chose it to overrepresent eminent scientists. Solid-state physics (a less spectacular specialty than many others, probably claimed by scientists at less prestigious departments) was the only specialty whose representation did not conform closely to its relative size in physics.

Cole and Cole's purpose was to see whether the reward system operates to recognize excellence, regardless of where it is found. If the reward system operates to give recognition to scientists who produce long lists of trivial papers, then the negative implications of the publish-or-perish doctrine are evident. If, however, it operates to recognize excellence, then it operates in a universalistic fashion.

They examined data on the number of publications, quality of publications (number of citations), number and prestige of honorific awards, prestige ranking of departments, and percent of the physics community familiar with the prior research of the physicists in the sample. Cole and Cole (1967:385) concluded that "It is the quality of research rather than its sheer amount that is most often recognized through honorific awards." The general conclusion from their study is that science, at least physics, operates in a universalistic fashion.

Although they describe the reward system in science as operating in a universalistic fashion, Cole and Cole (1967:390) note that

... some preliminary evidence suggests rank-of-department differentials in the working of the reward system. When we take honorific awards as the dependent variable and introduce quality of research (weighted citations) into the regression equation, we account for 44 percent of the variance. When we introduce rank of department into the equation, we increase the percent of variance explained to 53. This indicates that high quality research by men in the highest ranked departments is more often recognized in the form of awards than comparable work in the lower ranked departments.

In spite of the general universalistic operation of the reward system, rank of department accounts for some of the scientists' recognition. Departmental prestige is an ascribed, particularistic characteristic, and it represents, of course, the same kind of interference with the reward system suggested both by Crane and by Hargens and Hagstrom.

Gaston's British High-Energy Physicists

My data were obtained by personal interviews with 203 British high-energy physicists at 20 universities (the four colleges in London University totaled individually) and three research laboratories. This specialty was selected because it is highly competitive and is "frontier" physics. Studying one specialty reduced the variation many different specialties create and also included scientists at a sufficiently large number of universities so that any effect of the prestige of universities could be considered. In the analysis of effect of university prestige, scientists at laboratories were omitted.

My purpose was to assess the operation of the reward system in British science. The concern with British science originated from the popular, if not prevalent, notion that the Oxford–Cambridge axis controls the academic, and to a degree, the intellectual life in Britain (Halsey and Trow, 1971:213–225). This has caused a suspicion that scientists at Oxbridge are superior to those at other universities in Britain. Part of this suspicion stems form the traditional presumption of superiority of Oxbridge undergraduate education. Whether there is justification for generalizing that to the research level is questionable.

Information on scientific productivity, recognition, social origins, and academic affiliations produced no pattern showing that recognition accrues for any reason other than research productivity. One method of demonstrating this is to regress an indicator of recognition on number of publications. This indicates the extent of "over" or "under" recognition based on the assumption of a linear relationship between recognition and productivity. In the results a minus number equals less recognition than expected, a plus number equals more recognition than expected, and a zero denotes equity. The figures for the regression residuals show the following: Oxbridge, −.33; London, .09; Redbrick universities, .06; Scottish universities, −.16; and the laboratories, .12. The differences between these figures are neither statistically nor substantively significant. If the reward system does not operate in a universalistic fashion, one would expect a high positive score for Oxbridge scientists and a high negative score for scientists at other universities. What did show important differences was comparing experimental with theoretical scientists. The mean residuals for experimentalists at all institutions were negative; those for theorists were all positive. But theorists are not uniformly "over" recognized. Two types of theorists, phenomenologists and intermediate, have positive mean residuals, while abstract theorists have negative ones. The conclusion is that, while there are differences in the pattern of the relationships between productivity and recognition, these are based on scientific considerations and not on any social attributes of the scientists. In short, as research activity, theoretical work is more prestigious than experimental work, and this prestige comes from the value that theoretical work has in advancing scientific knowledge. (It is not accidental that more Nobel Prizes are awarded for theoretical studies than for experimental accomplishments.) Theoretical work, regardless of where it is done, is highly recognized; experimental work is not "over" recognized, whether done at the famous or other universities. If scientific criteria are used to allocate recognition for outstanding work, one must conclude that, to the extent that British high-energy physics reflects British science in general, which cannot be argued logically, then one must conclude that the reward system in British science operates in a universalistic fashion.

Blume and Sinclair's British Chemists

Blume and Sinclair surveyed the 1537 faculty members in the 58 chemistry departments in the United Kingdom. They achieved a response rate of 55 percent, which represented very closely the actual distribution of the academic ranks among chemists. Blume and Sinclair's (1973:127) purpose was to describe the reward system of science in chemistry in the United Kingdom.

Scientists reported the number of papers they published in the previous five years and the types of honors they had received over their careers. The chemists provided peer evaluations, which Blume and Sinclair used as a measure of quality of chemical research, as responses to questions about which researchers the chemists feel are "pacemakers" in Britain and in the world. Quality scores were computed for each scientist by assigning 1 point for being mentioned as a pacemaker in the UK and 3 points for being mentioned as a pacemaker in the world. Only 25 percent of the scientists responding to the survey received any mention. Thus 75 percent were coded "zero" quality, 15 percent were coded "low" quality (1 to 3 points), and 10 percent were coded "high" quality (4 or more points). Blume and Sinclair (1973:129) note that the distribution resulted from the obtrusiveness of the question. About half the scientists did not complete the question, and many of them stated they objected to it. Scientists might have been nervous about helping to establish reputations of other scientists through this method because the survey was sponsored by the Department of Education and Science, on the advice of the Council for Scientific Policy. Both agencies at the time had responsibility for recommending the future of chemical research. Specifically the idea that initiated the study, that some of the groups might be too small to be effective in research, created possible resistance to the inquiry, if chemists were indeed aware of the motivation.

Blume and Sinclair found that scientific productivity and quality scores in chemistry were positively related (gamma = .63) and that productivity and recognition were positively related (gamma = .66). Quality scores and recognition scores were also positively related (gamma = .75). When they considered the relationship between quality and quantity of research and recognition earned, they found that only 8 percent with low productivity and zero quality had received high recognition, but 87 percent with high productivity and high quality had received high recognition. This shows convincingly that the reward system operates to recognize both quality and quantity of research.

Blume and Sinclair (1973:134–135) established a context for examining the ascriptive factors in the reward system, comparing the results of my study with Halsey and Trow's findings in *The British Academics*. They state that Halsey and Trow conclude that much prestige is attached to Oxford and Cambridge because these institutions have not only provided the models for many newer universities but they also remain attractive to British academics. Furthermore Oxbridge faculties are distinguished from others because they come from high social classes and hold the lion's share of memberships in the Royal Society (33 percent) and the British Academy (63 percent). Thus Halsey and Trow's conclusions are in conflict with any generalization of mine, that current affiliation does not affect the allocation of rewards. They wanted to see if rewards are inequitably allocated to chemists affiliated with the Oxbridge universities.

The statements on the characteristic of Oxbridge are correct, but it does not follow that affiliation has any effect on the allocation of rewards, in the sense meant by Blume and Sinclair. Even if all memberships in the Royal Society were held by Oxbridge scientists, it would not prove that particularism exists. The reward system should allocate recognition where it is due on the basis of merit. If Oxbridge scientists merit more recognition than others, they should receive it. They would not be receiving it because they are Oxbridge scientists; they simply happen to be affiliated with Oxbridge. That is not deriving unmerited recognition from affiliation. Halsey and Trow did not consider the reward system specifically in their work. They discussed only variables usually considered when a reward system is examined. They did not look at the relationship between productivity and recognition while holding constant affiliation or other ascribed characteristics.

When Blume and Sinclair described aspects of the reward system and how ascriptive factors such as university affiliation affect it, they chose to consider quality, recognition scores, and affiliation. They did not include scientific productivity, although quantity appeared to be more important than quality of research in obtaining recognition, according to their tables 2, 3, and 4 (apparently they do not accept this, judged from their own comparisons of the gammas involved).

They conclude that there are ascriptive factors involved because of these results. Of the chemists with "zero" quality scores, 54 percent at Oxbridge, 17 percent at London, 12 percent at Scottish/ Welsh/ Northern Ireland, and 12 percent at all the other universities have achieved high recognition. Of the chemists with "low" quality scores, 85, 83, 89, and 67 percent respectively have achieved high recognition. Of the chemists with "high" quality scores, 72, 69, 48, and 47 respectively have achieved high recognition. The only potential variance with the equitable operation of the reward system is the larger percentage of Oxbridge chemists with high recognition in the zero-quality category. In the low-quality category, only 3 percent more Oxbridge scientists than London University scientists have high recognition; in the high-quality category, Oxbridge is not the university category with the largest percentage of scientists with high recognition. Only at the zero-quality level do Oxbridge scientists appear to achieve more recognition than they deserve. This is explained later. Blume and Sinclair (1973:136–137) conclude that, as other studies had shown in the United States, the most productive chemists were also those who had produced the highest quality research, based on peer evaluation. They further conclude that both quantity and quality of research are highly correlated with recognition. Although they say that quality of research is the more important, my interpretation of their data is that quantity is the more important. Whereas awards are strongly related to quantity and quality of research, they believe that this relationship is affected by institutional affiliation and that receipt of rewards depends on a scientist's affiliation. Scientists at Oxbridge, they say, have an advantage. Blume and Sinclair (1973:137) conclude:

> Our findings thus diverge from those of Gaston, who found no evidence for ascriptive allocation of rewards in high energy physics in Britain. They are, however, consistent with Crane's account of the institutional advantages to be had in the U.S.A., and with Halsey and Trow's discussion of the peculiar prestige attaching to Oxford and Cambridge within the British university system. They may to some extent account for the high concentration of Fellows of the Royal Society in those institutions.

PROBLEMS WITH STUDIES OF THE REWARD SYSTEM

A brief review of the five studies reveals many methodological problems. Crane concludes that her data on American science show considerable deviance from the norm of universalism in science. Hargens and Hagstrom's conclusions are indeterminate, but they conclude that the system is universalistic, at least if given enough time for careers to develop. Cole and Cole conclude that the reward system operates in a universalistic fashion, some deviation resulting from prestige of department. I concluded that my data show a universalistic operation of the reward system of science in Britain. Blume and Sinclair conclude that university affiliation (prestige) is a strong factor in British chemistry and therefore cast considerable doubt on the generalizability to the whole of British science on the basis of my conclusions. All these studies used different methods of statistical analysis and involved different levels of measurement. The studies are not directly comparable, but by making careful assumptions, is there some way that the results can be reconciled?

If Crane's data had included a measure of quality, the study might have resulted in different conclusions. For example, a scientist who achieved recognition that appeared to be unmerited may have been what Cole and Cole refer to as a *perfectionist,* one who publishes few but high-quality papers. Similarly the few scientists who appear to have merited recognition on the basis of the number of their publications but who had not achieved the proper recognition might simply have been undeserving, or, to use Cole and Cole's label, they may be *mass producers.* These are scientists who publish a large number of inconsequential papers. If only 10 or so scientists had been categorized differently, the resulting percentages would not have been large enough to produce the statistically significant differences obtained.

Consider now the possible differences that Hargens and Hagstrom might have obtained. Their study is the least comparable to the other studies because they measure recognition by "current affiliation" at a prestigious institution. Few doubt that appointments at prestigious institutions are indications of scientific recognition. Few doubt either that there are scientists in lesser known institutions who are highly recognized if different criteria are invoked. If Hargens and Hagstrom could have known the names of the scientists used in the secondary analysis, they could have obtained a measure of recognition different from "current institutional affiliation." Then they might have found that the scientists who obtained PhDs at a prestigious institution and who had not published much in the *most recent five years* had nevertheless deserved their position because of work prior to that time. If career productivity had been available instead of only the most recent five years, the highly productive scientists might not have deserved much recognition, because they had produced little until recently. This possibility is not highly plausible, because scientists' publications do not go on and off like a water faucet. These questions are hypothetical, and even if true, most scientists probably would not have had their categorization changed. It would not, however, take many changes to produce weaker trends that would have to be interpreted that the reward system operates much more in a universalistic than in a particularistic fashion.

The one additional item in Cole and Cole's study that might have reduced any hint of particularism, and there was not much to begin with, is consideration of the effects of the division of labor in science. Their work was originally published in 1967, and so it is not clear whether they were aware of Hagstrom's ideas on the subject published in 1965. Their research may have been begun long before Hagstrom's work was published. The effect of division of labor may have been tested and found unimportant, but they do not discuss this subject. Hagstrom's (1967) study of nearly 2000 scientists and my (1970) study both showed important differences between experimentalists and theorists. It would not be unreasonable to suggest that, if "type of scientist" were introduced into their analysis, any evidence of particularism might be eliminated entirely. To put this differently, is it possible that the residual particularism was in fact due to the difference between the scientific community's evaluation of the importance of theoretical work over experimental work?

It is probably clear by now that I have been attempting to show that the studies other than my own, which showed no evidence of particularism, might also have shown no such evidence if only slightly different or additional data had been used. My purpose is not to criticize the other studies unduly but rather possibly to explain why they concluded what they did. To be accurate, I admit that, with a small assumption about my data on British scientists, the results could have changed. Specifically, if I had measured quality of research, it could have turned out that scientists at any prestige category of universities actually had produced demonstrably higher quality research. If, as a consequence, they had failed to receive high recognition, I would have concluded that some degree of particularism was operating.

Blume and Sinclair's study would require only a very minor assumption to change the conclusion that the chemistry community's reward system operates to reward Oxbridge scientists more than they deserve. Recall that the only apparent problem with the reward system was in the zero-quality category. These scientists were not named as currently being a pacemaker in chemical research in either the United Kingdom or the world. More scientists in this category at Oxbridge than at other universities had received "high" recognition. If only 11 scientists who caused Oxbridge to have the highest percentage were to be categorized differently, Oxbridge would not have this distinction. The best explanation for this apparent particularism is not that the chemistry community makes invidious distinctions between scientists affiliated with different universities; it is best explained by the particular and strange methodology used. I shall be more specific.

The variable "quality of research" is based on who is reported *currently* to be doing the most important research. The recognition variable is an index based on number of expense-paid invitations abroad within the past five years, number of senior visitors from abroad received in the scientist's own laboratory, *current* service on a Research Council or other grant-awarding committee, membership of the council or editorial advisory board of a learned society, number of medals received, and Fellowship in the Royal Society. The recognition index is entirely appropriate, but the problem arises in correlating these honors with peer assessment of *current research*. Neither the age of scientists nor the prior research record produced over entire careers is taken into account. On the one hand it is impossible for a young scientist, who may be known for good *current research*, to achieve these kinds of honors as quickly as he can become "known" as a competent researcher through giving a lecture or publishing a paper or series of papers. On the other hand, and more importantly, a scientist who is not doing current research of great significance could still merit these honors for previous research. I do not know whether Oxbridge scientists are older, on the average, than those at other institutions. The rapid growth of university faculty since 1960 in the new universities, compared to less rapid growth at Oxbridge, suggests this is the case (Halsey and Trow, 1971:144). Whether it is the case for chemistry is an empirical question. Blume informed me that data on scientists' ages were not available.

If Oxbridge scientists are older, then they are not obtaining recognition for being at Oxbridge to the disadvantage of scientists elsewhere. They are obtaining it for their past research record. If the variable *research productivity* had been the number of papers published over the scientist's career rather than the number published only in the past five years, the results easily could have been different. Or if the data on age of scientists at the various universities had been taken into account, the explanation proposed here might have become obvious.

SOCIAL ORGANIZATION, CODIFICATION OF KNOWLEDGE, AND THE REWARD SYSTEM

With only a few minor assumptions the five studies could be reconciled to show that the reward system of science in Britain and the United States operates in a universalistic fashion. Another appropriate strategy is to assume that the data in the studies show exactly what the authors claim. If that is true, then the reward system of science operates differently in various scientific communities within the same country. In the United States the physics community is more universalistic than the natural and biological sciences when aggregated into one group. These communities are more universalistic, in turn, than an aggregation of biological, psychological, and political scientists. In Britain the high-energy physics community is more universalistic than the chemistry community. If these relationships are correct, then it becomes necessary to try to determine why scientific communities have reward systems that apparently differ in the extent to which they operate universalistically. Two possible influences on the operation of the reward system are worth consideration. Either of these influences has potential for significant impact on this operation. The first involves the level of codification of knowledge and the second involves the social organization of scientific research in a particular country.

Codification, or development, is a continuum. It ranges at the low end from a complete lack of agreement on the boundaries of a discipline or specialty to the high end, where there is strong consensus about what the important research questions are, which of them ought to be taken up next, and how the results should be evaluated.

Zuckerman and Merton (1973a:507) explain that "Codification refers to the consolidation of empirical knowledge into succinct and interdependent theoretical formulations." Disciplines and their specialties differ in their degrees of codification. Apparently physics and chemistry are different from botany and zoology in the extent to which research findings are integrated by general ideas. The mode of gaining competence in a field is influenced by how codified it is. In the less codified fields, experience is probably more important than in more codified areas. In the former, scientists have to learn an array of descriptive facts and low-level theories, whose implications are not clear. Zuckerman and Merton (1973a:507) state that "The comprehensive and more precise theoretical structures of the more codified fields not only allow empirical particulars to be derived from them but also provide more clearly defined criteria for assessing the importance of new problems, new data and newly proposed solutions." If this is true, there should be greater consensus among scientists in highly codified fields about the significance of new knowledge and the continuing importance of the old.

In a scientific field where a large percentage of the papers submitted for publication are accepted, there is a high level of codification, although rejection rates are certainly not the only measure of codification. This is another way of saying that scientists can, and do, agree on what the important questions and appropriate methods are. Physics exemplifies this level of codification. Conversely, in a discipline where a large percentage of the papers submitted for possible publication are initially rejected, there is a low level of codification because scientists and gatekeepers cannot and do not agree on what the important questions and appropriate methods are for dealing with the problem. Sociology presumably exemplifies this level of codification.

Consider how codification of knowledge, a cognitive or intellectual component of research, varies with the different social activities that are also components of research. Studies show some important differences between scientific disciplines that may affect the way the social system of science works. This is not simply an assertion that the content of disciplines differs, because that is obvious.

The observable differences between the social activities of disciplines are numerous. Scientific disciplines differ in the amount of anticipation of discovery that scientists experience, in the consequences (ability to publish anyway) after work is anticipated, and in the amount of concern scientists express about being anticipated in their current research (Hagstrom: 1974:3–4). Disciplines differ in the age of the literature referred to by scientific papers (Price, 1970). Scientific disciplines differ in the average number of papers scientists produce annually and the relationship between time spent on research and productivity (Hagstrom, 1967:53, 63). Disciplines differ about the extent to which there is disagreement among scientists over the validity of published answers to research questions (Hargens, 1971:35) and the average number of reprints sent by scientists to others outside their own institution (Hagstrom, 1967:115). Disciplines differ in the use of textbooks compared to original research papers (Kuhn, 1970) and in the extent that mathematics is used in research (Storer, 1967). And if these are not enough, Hargens (1971:95–132) shows disciplinary differences in the extent to which scientists got "hung up" in working on research problems, or were able to plan a day's work in detail. Co-authorship patterns differ as do opinions that less productive periods result from lack of research assistants and ability required to solve research problems; and the number of different research problems being worked on simultaneously differs.

Finally, Hagstrom (1967:33, 44) found differences between disciplines in their reliance on assistants to make all or most of the observations and measurements and in the fact that scientists collaborated in their research because of the necessity for the division of labor where various collaborators supplied special skills. In view of all the things that produce differences among the social activities of scientific disciplines, it is surprising that greater differences were not found in the studies of the reward system, because of the mixture of scientific disciplines involved.

Codification of knowledge, or the level of scientific development of a discipline, specialty, or problem area, is only the first of two influences to be considered. The second potential influence is the nature of the social organization of science in a country. As part of a nation's culture, the scientific enterprise is related to other social values. Becoming a scientist, working as a research scientist, the scientific career, and the context in which these processes happen are organized differently in every country. These differences are not always as great as those between daylight and dark; some are only subtle. But others are more explicit.

National differences in research activities are not the invention of sociologists. Watson (1969:19), after spending time in the United States, Britain, and the continent, observed the differences in the social aspects of research between countries, and aptly wrote:

> . . . the English sense of fair play would not allow Francis [Crick] to move in on Maurice's [Wilkins] problem. In France, where fair play obviously did not exist, these problems would not have arisen. The States also would not expect someone at Berkeley to ignore a first-rate problem

merely because someone at Cal Tech had started first. In England, however, it simply would not look right.

Whether a country organizes its scientific research policy and funding in a *centralized* or *decentralized* method is the interesting dimension of the social organization of science. That is, are policies made and research funds allocated by a centralized authority or by dispersed authorities? To describe any country as either centralized or decentralized overlooks the obvious state of affairs in which some scientific fields are more centralized than others in the same country. This results from the nature of research, where in certain fields little research assistance, other than one's own time, is needed, as in mathematics. At the same time large, centralized laboratories are the only organization currently possible for research in experimental elementary particle physics, regardless of the country.

The way social organization can affect the operation of the reward system is this. In a decentralized system unequal competitive opportunities can easily affect the allocation of rewards because there is less social control possible than in a situation where policy and funding are centralized. If that is correct, then we should find that the centralized social organization in Britain results in a more universalistic operation of the reward system. Suppose my study of British high-energy physics is correct in finding no evidence of particularism. Suppose further that Blume and Sinclair's study of British chemists was incorrect in finding evidence of particularism when in fact the results arose from the method used to assess the effect of institutional affiliation. If both conditions are met, then the conclusion must be that the reward system in Britain appears more universalistic than it does in the United States. This comparison fits the differences between the organization of research in Britain and America and gives support to the idea that social organization affects the reward system.

The degree of codification of knowledge may be just as strong an effect on the reward system. Both studies reviewed involving physics showed the operation of the reward system to be highly universalistic. The next most universalistic communities were probably the British chemists and the American natural and biological scientists. Crane's sample of biologists, psychologists, and political scientists was the least universalistic. This ranking of disciplines fits neatly the hypothesis that codification of knowledge and the objective evaluation possible in highly codified fields affect the operation of the reward system.

Which is more important, codification of knowledge or the social organization of science? It is not possible with the current studies to determine which is or what the relative effects of both are. Chapter 3 describes in detail the characteristics of the disciplines and the social organization of science in the countries pertinent to this book. I describe how disciplines rank on the codification of knowledge continuum and how the organization of scientific research differs in Britain and the United States.

Chapter 3 / CHARACTERISTICS OF
DISCIPLINES AND
THE ORGANIZATION
OF RESEARCH

One purpose of this book is to explore the effect of the level of development or codification of knowledge on the internal operation of the reward system in science. Previous studies suggest that the cognitive nature of scientific research provides evaluative criteria that vary, depending on the development of the research area. Another purpose is to explore the effect of a nation's organization of scientific research on the internal operation of the reward system. Previous studies suggest also that organization of research provides an atmosphere in which the reward system can operate more or less universalistically.

It is important, no matter how sophisticated about science and scientific research a reader is, to have an idea of how disciplines and countries are compared on these dimensions of cognitive development and social organization. This chapter describes, in an elementary fashion, the three scientific disciplines in this study and the organization of research in the two countries. The purpose is not to prove that these disciplines are developed at different levels, because there is certain to be disagreement among scientists and philosophers of science about this. The purpose is to present opinions that rank the disciplines, in progressive levels of development, from biology, to chemistry, to physics.

For the dimension of social organization there is no doubt that, historically and currently, the United States is the most decentralized of any country and Great Britain is more centralized, though there are other countries where science is more centralized than in Great Britain.

CODIFICATION IN THREE DISCIPLINES

Traditionally, biology, chemistry, and physics are considered to follow that rank order of development of codification. There are both cognitive and social reasons to believe this order is correct. Scientists tend to see these disciplines ranked in that order, but that in itself would not constitute valid evidence that the order is correct. Social indicators that coincide with this ordering add further evidence to its validity. I consider first the writings of scientists who suggest the order of cognitive development is biology, chemistry, and physics.

Biology

Dillon (1964:6) writes that "*Biology* may be defined as that natural science which is concerned with the study of life and of things that possess life, including their relationships to one another and to their environment." This definition covers enormous material that must be learned before biology can know its subject matter as chemistry or physics know and understands theirs. No doubt biology can tell us more about diseased organisms than social scientist can tell us about "diseased" personalities or societies. That is only another way of saying that biology is more developed than the social sciences, and in general, few would argue with that proposition.

Carlson (1967:1) believes that "Biology is primarily a descriptive science. To understand life we must observe life. . . . In the twentieth century the descriptive preoccupation of biologists gave way to experimental approaches. This trend to experimentation has never ceased." Biology has developed rapidly over the last 75 years, but chemistry and physics were well on their way to understanding their subject matter while biology was still very young. Hellman (1971:9–10) gives a personal view of biology and its relationship to other disciplines:

> Biology is usually defined as the science or the study of life. The simplicity of the definition stands in strong contrast, however, to the complexities of the subject. For one thing, there are a number of levels at which the biologist can perform his studies. The atom is the building block of all matter. In trying to understand life, the biologist might study the connection between the structure and function of an atom and the life processes. . . .
>
> It turns out that atoms and their parts (protons, neutrons, and electrons) have traditionally been considered the province of physicists. But the biologist often uses information provided by the physicist.

At the next level, we find ourselves in the world of molecules, which are groups of atoms. Now we have invaded the traditional realm of chemists, and indeed are coming close to the level of life. For the next step up is the cell, which is generally conceded to be the building block of life, and cells are made up of molecules. . . .

Since World War II science has been given strong social and financial support by governments. Budgets have increased dramatically over prewar support. Since its foundation in 1950 the National Science Foundation (NSF) has seen its budgets rise from about $225,000 to more than $500 million (Schaffter, 1969:45). This is, of course, only a small part of total research funds in the United States.

During the 1960s the future prospects for research became problematic for the scientific community. This was partly based on perceptions that funding was inadequate and partly on the reality that future financial support could not continue increasing at the rapid rate it had in recent history. The rate clearly had to slow, as Zuckerman and Merton (1973a:505) point out, "Otherwise, as Derek Price is fond of writing, and as many others are fond of quoting, 'We should have two scientists for every man, woman, child and dog in the population, and we should spend twice as much money as we had.' "

The inevitability of the reduction in the growth of resources did not eliminate scientists' anxieties about it. The National Academy of Sciences Committee on Science and Public Policy anticipated this problem and in the early 1960s appointed several committees to examine the status and future prospects of research in various disciplines. The reports for biology, physics, and chemistry give some insight into the nature and problems of these disciplines. I should caution, however, that these reports had two perhaps conflicting purposes. On the one hand they gave the respective scientific communities an opportunity to lay claim to important accomplishments and thus justify past expenditures. On the other hand they were expected to be used as a basis for claims to higher levels of support. This produced a natural tendency to downgrade the current state of knowledge in order to assert the connection between additional funds in the future and the imminent breakthroughs if only more resources were available. I am not competent to judge whether these reports gave a balanced view, although they are straightforward and appear to be well balanced.

The report on biology was issued later than others. The Committee on Research in the Life Sciences (CRLS) (1970:vii) explained:

For several years an equivalent study of the biological sciences was deferred. Whereas the physical sciences are usefully divided along conventional lines, no equivalently justifiable division of the life sciences seemed rational, and the entirety of the life sciences appeared to be so broad as to escape the grasp of any survey committee.*

This statement recognizes the importance of the biological sciences, but it also recognizes the difficulty in considering them as a coherent discipline. This problem is exemplified by the committee's surveys of academic departments and practicing scientists. They had 1256 responses to a mailed questionnaire to academic departments showing 195 distinct departmental titles; the responses from individuals produced 300 additional distinct departmental titles (CRLS, 1970:282). The committee acknowledged that classical disciplinary labels have lost their meaning; more than 100 subdisciplines are included under the label biological or life sciences (CRLS, 1970:276).

Biologists' research questions are extremely varied and include the following (CRLS, 1970:33):

> Of what chemical compounds are living things composed? By what means are the materials of the environment converted into the compounds characteristic of life? What techniques have been employed to reveal the structures of the huge macromolecules of living cells? How are living cells organized to accomplish their diverse tasks? What is a gene and what does it do? What are the mechanisms that make possible cellular duplication? How does a single fertilized egg utilize its genetic information in the wondrous process by which it develops into a highly differentiated multicellular creature of many widely differing cell types? How do differentiated cell types, combined to form organs and tissues, cooperate to make their distinct contributions to the welfare of the organism? What is understood of the structure and function of the nervous system? What is a species? How does speciation occur? What factors give direction to evolution? Is evolution still occurring? Is man evolving still, and if so, can he control his own evolution? What relations obtain among the species in a given habitat? What governs the numbers of any one species in that habitat? Are there defined physiological bases for behavior? What is known of the bases for perception, emotions, cognition, learning, or memory, for hunger or satiety? For few of these questions, today, are there exact answers; yet the extent to which these are approximated, even now, constitutes a satisfying and exciting tale.*

It is not unreasonable to expect that research into various areas of biological science has produced uneven results. In the chapter "Fron-

---

*Reproduced with permission of the National Academy of Sciences.

tiers of Biology" the committee discussed 10 different major areas, each having subareas. Some areas appear close to understanding major questions, but others have instructive statements at the end. About "cell division" the committee (CRLS, 1970:71) remarks that "Cell–cell interactions are of immense significance in cell life, but the molecular bases for such events remain totally obscure."* About "development of an organism," the committee (CRLS, 1970:74) states: "Thus description of the early stages of mammalian life has become much more detailed, but understanding of the process is surprisingly meager."* And, to give a final example about development of the nervous system, the committee (CRLS, 1970:75) concludes that "The capacity of developing cells generally to form intercomplementary groupings lies at the basis of essentially all embryonic events at cellular and higher levels, but the origin of these abilities and their nature are largely unknown."*

Unanswered questions do not "prove" a lack of codification in a discipline, but they suggest a ranking or a position on a continuum below other disciplines on which they depend for help in reaching ultimately both the questions and answers. The committee writes:

> Until the laws of physics and chemistry had been elucidated, it was not possible even to formulate most of the important, penetrating questions concerning the nature of life. For centuries, students of biology, in considering the diversity of life, its seeming distinction from inanimate phenomena, and its general inexplicability found it necessary, in their imaginations, to invest all living objects with a mysterious life force, "vitalism" (CRLS, 1970:32).

> Biology has become a mature science as it has become precise and quantifiable. The biologist is no less dependent upon his apparatus than the physicist. Yet the biologist does not use distinctively biological tools; he is an opportunist who employs a nuclear magnetic resonance spectrometer, a telemetry assembly, or an airplane equipped with infrared photography, depending upon the biological problem he is attacking. In any case, he is always grateful to the physicists, chemists, and engineers who have provided the tools he has adapted to his trade (CRLS, 1970:34–35).*

Chemistry

The Committee for the Survey of Chemistry (CSC) (1965:vii) defined chemistry as " . . . the science dealing with the composition of substances, and the transformations that they undergo. As such, it attempts to account for the properties and behavior of every material

*Reproduced with permission of the National Academy of Sciences.

thing in the universe." Basic research in chemistry, the committee says (CSC, 1965:2–3) "is both an experimental and a theoretical science. It begins with observations of materials as they occur in nature. It goes on to devise conditions under which ideas about nature can be tested and new materials not found in nature can be invented."

Chemistry has been around for a long time, but there is much more to it than filling in the periodic chart of the elements. There are fundamental problems still to be resolved. The committee (CSC, 1965:5) admits that

> Despite the great advances being made in chemistry, our ignorance is profound. We cannot yet predict from fundamental principles the boiling point of a liquid or the melting point of a solid; we cannot predict (except approximately, with semi-empirical rules) the spectroscopic properties of the millions of known compounds; we have only an incomplete working theory for collisions in the gas phase, and no satisfactory quantitative predictive theory for chemical or photochemical reactions. Synthesis has accomplished practical miracles, but the reactions of chemistry are almost ridiculously non-specific when compared to those of enzymes—and we do not yet understand enzymes.

One would not imagine that chemistry is without important questions in spite of its inability, at the time of the report, to provide answers to very perplexing problems. The committee argues that original developments and novel ideas will probably arise both from within chemistry and other sciences to create as many new opportunities for the future as there have been in the past. "Especially because chemistry is so flexible and so varied, because it is practiced effectively in so many laboratories, and is not tied to a relatively few expensive installations [as is some physics], we can look forward to a continuation of unpredicted innovations from creative scientists throughout the world" (CSC, 1965:5).

Consider now the relationships between chemistry and biology on the lower side of development, and chemistry and physics on the higher side. The committee (CSC, 1965:2) acknowledges these relationships by saying that

> With the discoveries of the electron, atomic nuclei and the principles of quantum mechanics, physicists during the first quarter of the twentieth century provided all of science with fundamental ideas that chemists promptly applied to the understanding of molecular phenomena. . . .
>
> At present, the principles of molecular structure and reactivity serve as the fundamentals of chemistry, as an essential guide to the interpretation of biology, and as a challenge to chemical physicists.

The relationship between chemistry, physics, and biology is discussed also by a separate report issued by the Panel on Theoretical Chemistry (PTC), organized by the Committee for Chemistry. This panel (1966:1) differentiates physics and chemistry by noting that physicists try to describe properties of matter not sensitive to the particular system, but chemists try to deal with the system-sensitive aspects of matter. The basic goals of chemistry are to understand and be able to control the particular reactions and properties of particular substances.

Chemistry owes a large debt to physics. The theoretical panel (PTC, 1966:22), as well as the committee previously quoted, acknowledged the debt by showing how the development of chemistry depended on the *prior* development of physics.

> The credit for many of the theoretical developments and the experiments which led to our present extensive knowledge about nuclei and nuclear reactions belongs to physicists. But if the physicist gave us the fundamental understanding, the chemist has contributed and continues to contribute much to make this knowledge useful for mankind.

The second sentence shows that chemists would like to have their appropriate credit for *application* of the physical and chemical processes. If chemistry owes part of its intellectual progress to physics, mankind in turn owes a lot to chemists and chemistry. This is not the place to discuss why chemists feel compelled to state this claim, but it is only further evidence that chemistry sees itself lower than physics on the level of scientific development and acknowledges the position of physics.

As a summary of the relationship between biology, chemistry, and physics, at the theoretical level, at least, the PTC (1966:24) had this to say:

> Chemistry underlies all the sciences, for the substance of almost all experiments is finally some chemical entity. Theoretical chemistry is, in principle, indistinguishable from theoretical physics or theoretical biology. In all three disciplines, the goal of the theoretician is to provide incisive analysis that connects the generally accepted laws of microscopic motion with macroscopic observation. In practice, however, there are appreciable differences between theoretical physics, theoretical chemistry, and theoretical biology—differences which are engendered by the complexity of the systems being studied. Theoretical physics is usually (although not always) concerned with the analysis of systems containing but few particles (solid-state physics is an exception and here the methodology and philosophy of physics and chemistry almost converge). On the other hand, systems of interest to chemists almost always involve many parti-

cles, directional forces, and other factors, while biological systems are still more complex by several orders of magnitude. Consequently, the standards of explanation alter from field to field. Whereas a satisfactory explanation of a phenomenon by a physicist may require the introduction of no concepts other than those inherent in fundamental quantum theory, some of the principles of chemistry are essentially representative of approximate solutions of the complex many-body problem (for example, the octet rule in valence theory). Of course, description of biological systems is still more primitive, and at present is either phenomenological or uses general theory to provide a structure from which unknown parameters may be determined.

Physics

"The science through which we seek to understand matter, radiation, and energy-transforming processes at the most fundamental and general level is the science of physics" (Physics Survey Committee [PSC], 1966:1). Many areas in physics are involved in this general definition, but there are not as many specialties as in chemistry and biology. The PSC divided physics into six subject areas: (1) astrophysics, space physics, cosmic rays, and gravitation physics; (2) atomic and molecular physics and quantum electronics; (3) elementary-particle physics; (4) nuclear physics; (5) plasma physics; and (6) solid-state (and condensed-matter) physics.

The beauty, elegance, and sophistication of physics result from the discipline's attempts to deal with the simplest and most fundamental components of matter. Atomic physics deals with the "behavior" of atoms and with simple molecules with five atoms or less. Contrast that complexity with chemical processes in which there may be hundreds of molecules involved. It is hardly questionable that the subject matter claimed by physics is one important reason why it has become the most developed of the physical sciences. If the subject matter and problems of physics and chemistry were reversed, then, of course, chemistry would be the more advanced. In other words it is the fact that physics deals with the most fundamental systems that enables it to be highly developed. This is not to say that everything knowable is known. It is only to say that the focus of inquiry is clear and well defined.

The boundaries of physics are prescribed and accepted. The committee had no problem in acknowledging the unity and coherence of physics. Consider the idea about the relationship between experiment and theory (PSC, 1966:75).

Physics is an *experimental* science, which means that the principles and relationships developed by the theorists must stand the test of experiment. The theoretical physicist is thus distinguished from the mathematician, who invents and manipulates mathematical formalism for its own sake without constraint imposed by the realities of nature.

When one considers its breadth as a science and the extent of its applications, physics is remarkable for its high degree of unity. Concern for the simplest and most fundamental laws of nature inherently lends unity, because the generality of these laws provides a common foundation for all of physics.

Responsibility for maintaining this unity falls increasingly to the theoretical physicist, as rapid growth and extension of physics activity holds the possibility of its degeneration into a conglomeration of apparently uncorrelated professions. . . .

The unity of physics is appealing to the keenest minds and therefore important in attracting them to physics. . . .

Because of the functions of the committees whose reports I am describing, it is only to be expected that the practitioners in each discipline wish to show that the discipline not only is worthwhile on its own right but also is valuable, if not indispensable, for progress in other scientific disciplines. Physics is no exception to this pattern. "Physics interacts with other scientific fields, stimulates them into new areas of exploration, and often provides illumination of the concepts and laws originating in those fields," the committee believes (PSC, 1966:4). The basic sciences are called "basic" because they are able to provide illumination for other fields. And it is clear with this criterion that physics is the most fundamental of the basic sciences. The history of modern science has seen other disciplines trying to develop connections with physics, and a principal aim of those connections is to enable those disciplines, such as biology and chemistry, to explain their principles in terms of the laws of physics (PSC, 1966:4).

The descriptions of biology, chemistry, and physics place them in that order on the level of scientific development or the degree of codification found in the discipline. This book deals both with British and American scientists, but I have relied on American sources to describe the differences in and the relationships among fields applicable to all countries. The discussion of the ordering of biology, chemistry, and physics has been completed from the perspective of practicing and prestigious scientists. I turn now to other aspects of these disciplines to see how the ranking follows from the cognitive characteristics of disciplines.

SOCIAL MEASURES OF CODIFICATION

One of the possible measures of codification is the use of mathematics in a discipline. High-level theory and mathematics are a sign of degree of codification, and high-level theory is not possible without mathematics. There is clearly more mathematics involved in physics than in chemistry and more in chemistry than in biology. It is only recently that mathematics, at what could be considered a sophisticated level, became important for the biological sciences.

There is a perfect rank order correlation between codification of biology, chemistry, and physics and measured intelligence in a scientific field. Price (1963:52) quotes Lindsey Harmon's study of PhDs graduated in 1958 showing that the mean AGCT scores were, for physics, 140.3; for chemistry 131.5; and for biology 126.1. This does not prove biologists are incapable of using mathematics. Indeed, some biologists are no doubt as bright as some physicists, and certainly if measured intelligence at a certain level were necessary for using mathematics, then anyone with that level of intelligence could use it. All I mean to suggest is that the rank order of codification follows the order of mathematical usage in the discipline and that it is common knowledge that many biological students detest mathematics. Some of my physical science colleagues tell me that many students go into biology because they cannot hack mathematics. If measured intelligence means follow the rank order, it is at least interesting, even if there is no causal connection. The PhDs in mathematics were second ranked with a mean measured intelligence score of 138.2, just under the first-ranked physicists.

Another indicator of the degree of codification in a field is the consensus about the important problems, the appropriate methods to answer the research questions, and the appropriate criteria to evaluate the results. These indicators are crystallized in various ways, but one way to make the concept of consensus operate is to examine rejection rates of journals. In highly codified fields rejection rates should be lower than those in less codified fields. Zuckerman and Merton (1973b:471) examined the rejection rates of 83 journals in various areas of scholarship ranging from history to physics. Their results did not confirm a perfect relationship between rejection rates and how one might intuitively rank disciplines, but the pattern obtained tended very much toward that kind of ranking. For example, history had the highest rejection rate and physics the third lowest. That physics was not the lowest probably arose from Zuckerman and Merton's methodology. The sample of journals did not represent the intradisciplinary ranges. Geology, with the second lowest rejection rate, was represented by only two journals. And linguistics, with the lowest rejection rate, was represented by only one.

If more journals in these disciplines had been studied, physics probably would have shown the lowest rejection rate. Eleven of the 12 physics journals had rejection rates between 17 and 25 percent, but the 12th journal, *American Journal of Physics* (a journal about physics, rather than of physics) had a rate of 40 percent. The 12th raised the average rate.

The average rate for the 12 physics journals was 24 percent; for biological science, 29 percent (based also on 12 journals); and for chemistry, 31 percent (based on 5 journals). There is no reason to believe the five chemistry journals reflect an accurate rejection rate for all of chemistry, but if they do, then there is an anomalous ranking of biology over chemistry. An argument could be made that perhaps the low rejection rate in the biological sciences reflects lower standards of research and more publishing opportunities (journals and pages) than in chemistry, but I do not have data to deal with that hypothesis. This ranking of codification, then, puts biology over chemistry. It is probably safe to assume there is some plausible explanation for that ranking other than to assume that biology is more codified than chemistry.

For a final consideration of the indicators of codification Lodahl and Gordon's (1972) survey of 80 university graduate departments involving four disciplines is pertinent. Their study tried to determine the correlates of "paradigm development," which is synonymous with my use of the concept "codification." Physics and chemistry represented disciplines with highly developed paradigms while sociology and political science represented the opposite extreme. Before they examined these correlates they tested the assumption that these disciplines indeed had the characteristics attributed to them. Scientists in the four disciplines were asked this question (Lodahl and Gordon, 1972:59):

> Scientific fields are often said to vary in their degree of development or maturity. Whether or not you agree with all of the implications of this statement, it is probably true that in some scientific fields scientists are more uniform in their scientific practice than in others. This is because their field has a larger body of generally accepted theory and agreed-upon methodologies—paradigms upon which to base their present investigations. Please rank the following fields on the degree to which you feel there is consensus over paradigms (law, theory, methodology) within the field (1 = most consensus).

They asked scientists to rank biology, chemistry, economics, physics, political science, psychology, and sociology. Scientists in all four disciplines (biological scientists were not among the respondents), on the average, ranked the seven disciplines the same. Physicists and chemists ranked political science sixth and sociology seventh in development, while both political scientists and sociologists reversed that ranking. Political scientists agreed with sociologists that sociology has a more developed paradigm than political science, even if only slightly more developed.

Physics ranked first in development, chemistry second, and biology third (Lodahl and Gordon, 1972:60). Because of the amount of evidence presented on codification, I shall assume that this order is plausible. If other disciplines were involved, biology would not, of course, necessarily be considered the least developed.

ORGANIZATION OF SCIENCE IN TWO COUNTRIES

The perspective I want to follow in looking at the reward system of science is to consider both the level of development of a discipline, which is a cognitive influence, and the extent to which the social organization of science in a country is centralized or decentralized, which is a social influence. Because there are so few previous studies on the reward system, it is not possible to suggest precisely how this matrix of cognitive structure and social structure should affect the reward system. These studies suggest, however, that this matrix does affect it.

I discussed the cognitive component of the matrix in the previous section. I turn now to the social structural component. I shall outline the organization of research in Great Britain and the United States. The task is not to explain how the particular social organization came to exist, which is an entirely different problem. I focus on how science is organized and how that type or organization can be called centralized or decentralized.

Any current description may, and probably will be, different by the time this book is read. Indeed a current description does not take into account the changes that have occurred over the lifetime of the scientists included in this study. Britain and the United States have not written their science policy in stone. They seem to change it, in some minor way, with every session of Congress or Parliament, but throughout the period covered by the careers of the scientists in this study, the two countries have not changed their relative position to each other. Britain has always been more centralized than the United States. Whether it will continue so is a different question and one that no one can answer now.

Organization of Scientific Research in the United States

Most basic research in the United States, but not most research, is done in universities. In 1972 approximately $29 billion was spent for Research and Development (R & D) from all sources (National Science Board [NSB], 1973:109). Of that total, only about $4.1 billion was spent on basic research; of that, $2.335 billion (57 percent) was spent by universities and colleges (NSB, 1973:114). The university scientists doing basic research and their social system of science are the focus in this book.

These basic researchers are affiliated with university departments that, in most instances, have graduate programs to train the next generation of research scientists. Because scientists are generally involved both in teaching and research, the educational system in the United States (as in Britain) must be included in any discussion of the context of the social organization of research. The intersection between the educational system and the national scientific enterprise is the place to examine the nature and consequences of a decentralized social organization.

The situation found in the United States is this. Most primary and secondary education is planned and performed by local school districts. States exert some pressure on school districts, but there is considerable freedom in many areas for local initiative. Most states require attendance at school until age 16 or older. After graduation from high schools students go to college or do something else, but an increasing number of students in this century, beginning with only a very small percentage and increasing to around 50 percent during the 1960s, have entered higher education.

The choice of a college or university is a big decision because there are now more than 2600 institutions of higher education although many do not award baccalaureate degrees. Some universities are public, others private, and among the private are sectarian and nonsectarian institutions. Most of the "better" colleges compete for the best students among the graduating classes in any year.

As is the case with secondary schools, public colleges and universities are administered "locally" on a statewide basis. They are responsible to 1 of the 50 states for their programs and dependent on the states for most of their operating budgets. Thus 50 different state "systems" of public higher education exist in the United States. The reputation and actual quality of the systems, and the institutions within a system, vary. With so many different systems and so many students from secondary schools of uneven quality, there has to be great diversity. The quality of students ranges from below average to the level of genius because about 50 percent of the high school seniors go to college. Because some students have previously dropped out of school, some with more than average intelligence, those who enter college are not precisely drawn from the top half of the intelligence distribution. In student populations there are many with less than average intelligence, a distribution that obviously increases the range of student abilities.

After college graduation potential scientists can apply to dozens of universities for advanced training. Even if the variation in the abilities of college graduates has been reduced, compared to the variation of students entering college, there is still great diversity. Graduate departments seek to recruit the best students for admission into their advanced degree programs. Departments with highly visible faculty and successful graduates are at a competitive advantage for recruiting the best students, who will become the next generation of scientists. Once a prospective scientist has received the PhD, there is competition from the numerous colleges and universities to recruit the best recent graduates for their faculty. That may sound strange after the situation of the last few years, when the number of positions has not seemed to equal the number of scientists looking for positions. In spite of the current tight job market the description is generally true. There is always some competition for the best people, and the rate of unemployment for scientists never reached the level of the total work force (engineers and applied scientists may have suffered differentially).

The substance of this description is that the United States has a highly decentralized and competitive academic system. At any point of entry and exit there are many alternatives, and this situation produces competition for the best talent available. At any point also, there is opportunity for the social stratification of institutions—the various degrees of prestige ascribed to their graduates—to influence the movement of a scientist up, down, or laterally. The potential for benefits or disadvantage resulting from the social stratification of institutions suggests that in a decentralized and competitive situation there is more opportunity for particularistic criteria to enter the evaluation of a scientist's work.

Suppose our scientist reaches the PhD stage of a scientific career and has a position, what next? Depending on the type of scientist, one of the first tasks may be to search out sources of funds for setting up a research program. At this stage one begins to see very clearly the difference a highly decentralized social organization of science makes.

Depending on the scientist's specialty, there are many sources to look to for funds. The first and most obvious is one's university, which, if a public institution, very likely receives part of its operating budget for research. Certainly, if it has a research orientation, it will provide less than 100 percent teaching responsibilities so that some time is available for research. But time is not enough in most experimental scientific disciplines. A scientist also needs equipment, supplies, research assistance, publication costs, and funds for travel to professional meetings.

In addition to the local source of university funds, where can the scientist look for possible financial assistance? If one is a physicist, chemist, or biologist, there are numerous places in the federal government where one may apply for funding. There are in addition, of course, private foundations and industrial sources. A 1956 publication of the NSF listed eight different sources for research funds for any of these disciplines. Since then, there has been some centralization of these sources through transfer of function, but many of the American scientists in this study were operating research programs at that time, and so the data are still pertinent.

All three disciplines could apply for funds at the Departments of Agriculture; Defense (with separate funds from Army, Navy, Air Force); Health, Education and Welfare; and Interior. Moreover, the Atomic Energy Commission, the Smithsonian Institution, the National Academy of Science, and the NSF had funds for the three disciplines. Physics could look also to the National Advisory Committee for Aeronautics; chemistry and biology, to the Tennessee Valley Authority; chemistry, to the Treasury Department; and biology, to the State Department. Within the various government departments more than one division often has research funds. It is a conservative statement to say that any of these scientists could apply for funds from at least 5 sources and probably 10.

The situation in the United States, then, is one in which there is, as I have heard Derek Price say, a "pathological" decentralization of science policy. Each source of funds has to justify its mission to the President and to the Congress at budget time. One of the basic philosophical principles has been that, in a competitive process, the best researchers will get funds, they will do the best research, and science and the country will benefit in the long run from this competition. If that philosophy sounds similar to the ideas behind the operation of a free-market, capitalistic economy, it is no accident. If research ideas are tested in the atmosphere of a free market place, presumably the best will win out, and the fastest progress in science will result.

Organization of Scientific Research in Great Britain

Most basic research in Britain, but not most of all research, is performed in universities, as is the situation in the United States. The current level (1975–1976) of government spending on R&D includes about 116 million pounds for educational institutions; 246 million pounds for trade, industry and employment; and about 550 million pounds for defense (Sherwell, 1976:275). The portion going to university and other higher educational institutions is from 12 to 13 percent. The universities include some applied research in their programs, but this is negligible compared to their basic research function.

The British educational system and the organization of science are considerably more centralized than the educational system in the United States. At the elementary school levels not only is British education controlled by Local Education Authorities (somewhat comparable to our school districts), but also there is a strong influence from the central government. Some regional schools, often named direct-grant grammar schools, are more directly influenced by the central government. These schools serve "catchment" areas larger than the area served by local grammar schools.

After students complete a grammar school, a public school (not financed by the government), or a sectarian school, they must take advanced work preparatory to going to a university. Students are previously tested for their aptitude to do further work at the preparatory levels that lead to university admission. Successful students are then encouraged to do the preparatory work. Other students are encouraged to study for more practical futures. The school-leaving age is around 14 years. In effect the British elementary system forces students to make decisions about their futures at an earlier age than that at which their American cousins must decide.

Students have to apply to a university, and admission is competitive, but most students who qualify are able to attend a university. If they need financial assistance to do so, it is available. The number of universities is small, around 44, and they are all national universities, regardless of their original foundation. There is 1 national system, unlike the 50 state systems in the United States, and there is no private or sectarian system. The private system in the United States, in spite of the large sums private universities receive from the federal government, promotes diversity and competition for excellence. There is no British equivalent to Harvard, Columbia, Yale, Princeton, Cornell, Chicago, Vanderbilt, MIT, California Institute of Technology, and Stanford.

Before arriving at a university, a student, by virtue of preparation for university, is already part of a small elite. There is only a small percentage of the population in the age grouping, by American standards, enrolled in any university. The percentage increased from less than 1 percent in 1900 (Halsey and Trow, 1971:246) to about 7 percent in 1961. At that time the Labour government initiated a strong push to expand the number of student places in universities. They founded several new universities and promoted some of the colleges of advanced technology to universities. By 1971 the percentage of the relevant age group in universities increased to 17 percent and is expected to rise to 22 percent in 1981 (*Nature,* 1972:373).

When a student enters a university, the choice of subject to be studied has already been made. Application for admission is for a place in a specific subject. Currently the distribution of places between subjects is about 45 percent in the "arts" and 55 percent in the "sciences" (*Nature,* 1972:372).

After the usual three years of undergraduate studies the student receives the BA degree, and if the student plans a career in basic research outside industry (where there is some but not much basic research) but especially in an academic or research laboratory environment, then the usual pattern is for the student to remain at the same university for research training and the PhD. And it is not infrequently the case that the student remains at the same university for a postdoctoral, if not a permanent, position after the research training. At this point, then, a student has been brought through the stages of a career, having been carefully screened at each entry point, and has become part of an extremely small elite that gets through the educational system.

Science in Britain is organized around a dual system of funding but it is still highly centralized. The universities receive operating funds and capital grants from the University Grants Committee (UGC). The UGC, comprised of academics or former academics, advises the Department of Education and Science on the allocation of funds. The level of funds, especially those affecting research activities, is closely coordinated with the advice of committees designed to allocate these funds among the various scientific disciplines and the different universities. These funds also originate with the Department of Education and Science; before 1965 they were in a Department of Scientific and Industrial Research.

The advisory mechanisms have changed recently, but the overall pattern of centralized funding and decision making has not been affected to any large degree. Until recently the Council for Scientific Policy (CSP), appointed by the education and science minister, advised the ministry on the division of funds among the research councils that in turn distribute funds for scientific research projects. The CSP was comprised of scientists and science statesmen, who acted as "representatives" of the scientific community. And so, although the policy decisions were centralized, they were at least informed by the opinions of practicing scientists. The CSP has been eliminated and replaced with the Advisory Board for the Research Councils, with representation from the various research councils plus certain government departments. The representatives from government are there to influence allocation of funds so that the research councils will not ignore the stake that the government and the taxpayers have in a research policy that, to some extent, promotes research leading to practical application. Because of this concern the recent reorganization has shifted some funds from the Agriculture Research Council and Medical Research Council to the government departments responsible for application in these areas. The government departments are to contract with the research councils, in turn, to produce research according to the consumer's (government's) perceived needs.

The research councils distribute virtually all the basic research funds in the country. They are the Agricultural Research Council, Medical Research Council, Natural Environment Research Council, Science Reseach Council, and Social Science Research Council. Whereas biological scientists may conceivably receive funds from the first three councils, chemistry and physics are supported predominantly from the Science Research Council, the largest council, which spends more than 50 percent of the funds.

In spite of the appearance of multiple sources from which scientists could receive research support, multiple funding is not likely to happen, because of the communication among the research councils, the UGC, and the Department of Education and Science. Representatives from the various organizations sit on each other's committees as assessors. This is designed to monitor the procedures and decisions. Thus if a scientist wants funds for a certain project, it is not likely that multiple submissions for funding portions of the projects would be encouraged. That contrasts considerably with the situation in the United States, where multiple submissions are often encouraged and where sometimes agencies literally compete with each other to fund scientists with reputations for doing outstanding research.

Every effort is made to support the research of university faculty, and this is accomplished through a particular strategy. Suppose a department wishes to initiate research in a special problem area. The UGC gets a request for a faculty position and the Science Research Council gets a request for support costs. Each will not act on this kind of request without assurance that the other will support it. In this way the expansion is planned, orderly, and very much under control.

Unlike the British situation, if a department in the United States has the backing of the university administration to initiate research into a particular subject, the department is authorized to hire faculty. In the process they may agree to support the research from local funds until funds can be obtained from outside. Most likely the procedure would involve "buying" scientists already funded away from their current institution. The scientists would get their grants or contracts transferred to the new institution. This kind of wheeling and dealing would not happen in Britain. For one thing it is too "crass." For another thing the system would simply not encourage it, even if it were permitted.

Education and science in Britain are controlled to a large degree from offices in London. Education and science in the United States are hardly controlled at all, compared to the planning that occurs in Britain. In Britain, education, they argue, is very democratic. Everyone capable of doing well at university level studies is supported by government funds, if necessary, to study at that level. In the United States, education, we argue, is very democratic. Everyone who wants to try can try. The provision of resources is a different question. While the British system keeps out the stupid, the American system keeps out the poor.

The British system is tight but supportive; the American system is loose but competitive. If it appears that the two systems mirror the basic philosophy of the economic systems of the two countries, it is no accident. They exemplify cultural consistency.

Having described the ranking of disciplines on cognitive development, and the comparative social organization of science, I describe in Chapter 4 the data and research strategy for studying the effects of these cognitive and social influences on the reward system. Chapter 4 also describes the rationale for measuring variables and strategies for testing their effects.

/ NEW DATA ON THE
REWARD SYSTEM

Science is an international activity, but its reward system is organized around national scientific communities. Foreign memberships in honorific national academies and the Nobel Prize are the major international awards formally bestowed on scientists. Important, but not institutionalized, recognition is allocated in a simple way by having one's work cited by scientists in various countries. But scientists look to their countrymen, by and large, for recognition of their work. Scientists enjoy international recognition if they have it, but the importance of the reward system for reinforcing continued high-quality work in science is not based on receiving recognition from scientists in other countries. It is sufficient that a scientist has recognition from peers in his own nation.

Because all previous studies of the reward system have compromised with various design problems, no study is adequate for science as a whole. Crane's (1965) purposive sample did not have any population to which the results could be generalized. Cole and Cole's (1967) sample represented eminent physicists, but it is clearly not generalizable to all physicists. Hargens and Hagstrom's (1967) sample probably represented all scientists in the specific disciplines who were affiliated with American graduate institutions. But that excludes large numbers of PhD scientists. In any case Hargens and Hagstrom did not present their data by disciplines, and so interdisciplinary comparisons are not possible. My study (Gaston, 1970) of British high-energy physicists represents neither all British physicists nor all British scientists. Blume and Sinclair's (1973) sample adequately represented British chemists but certainly not all of British science.

Showing that all previous studies compromised with design problems does not prove that they are not a reasonable description of an entire scientific community in a discipline or a country. The problem is that it is not possible to know to what extent one of the previous samples represents any scientific community. Moreover, saying that previous studies compromised with design problems does not mean it is easy to design a study that will not have to make some compromises. I designed this study to reduce compromises to a minimum.

Because of the research questions posed for this study I needed scientists from different disciplines and different countries. I selected biologists, chemists, and physicists because of the evidence that these disciplines are developed to various degrees. I chose Great Britain and the United States because they are similar in an important way; for example, basic research in both countries is conducted primarily in universities. They are also different in a crucial way because the countries have different degrees of centralization in the organization of science.

The most elegant research design would be a random sample of all scientists in each country, but it is not possible to obtain a list of all scientists in a country. I compromised by using the 11th edition of *American Men of Science* (1965–1967) for the American scientists, and *Who's Who in British Science 1971/72* (1971) for the British scientists. Neither of these reference sources represents the entire number of scientists with PhD level training in science, but they are not lists of elites.

The editors of the *American Men of Science* (1965:v–vi) listed these criteria for inclusion:

1. Achievement, by reason of experience and training, of a stature in scientific work at least equivalent to that associated with the doctorate degree, coupled with presently continued activity in such work; or

2. Research activity of high quality in science as evidenced by publication in reputable scientific journals; or, for those whose work cannot be published because of governmental or commercial or industrial security, research activity of high quality in science as evidenced by the judgment of the individual's peers among his immediate co-workers; or

3. Attainment of a position of substantial responsibility requiring scientific training and experience of approximately the extent described for (1) and (2).

For *Who's Who in British Science* the criteria are less specific. The publication grew out of a general directory of British scientists starting in 1961, which was finally discontinued because of the costs involved. The reference contains 10,000 names, and although that must favor somewhat the more accomplished scientists, it does include scientists from all academic ranks and is not merely a list of eminent ones. John Grant (1971:v–vi), the editor, sets out the criteria for inclusion this way. Only scientists invited may be included and no fees are involved directly or indirectly. The editor must determine if a scientist has achieved distinction in some branch of the biological or physical sciences, in academic life, industry, or a profession. Medicine and veterinary science are not included, because they are adequately listed elsewhere. Anonymous referees are used, and so no pressure for inclusion may be placed on anyone. Of course it is possible for individuals to withhold their names if they desire. Consequently *Who's Who* is a listing subject to some possible human and other errors, but 10,000 individuals nevertheless constitute a large population from which to draw a sample of British scientists.

The most appropriate type of sample, a simple random sample, would require listing all eligible scientists and selecting randomly from that list. That procedure would have required reading each entry and then deciding if it was appropriate for inclusion in the list. That procedure requires more time and trouble than necessary. The procedure I used to select the names approximates a random sample closely enough to use statistical procedures that would be appropriate for a simple random sample. For each country 300 random numbers were selected. The first 100 numbers constituted one discipline, the next 100 numbers a second discipline, and so forth. If the scientist chosen by the random number was appropriate for the discipline, the name was included in the list. If the scientist was a different type, the next appropriate scientist on that page or succeeding pages was selected.

After the 600 scientists were selected and the biographical information recorded, each scientist's publication record was obtained from *Science Abstracts* (Physics), *Chemical Abstracts,* or *Biological Abstracts.* The publications for each scientist were recorded beginning two years *before* the PhD or terminal degree and ending in 1972 inclusive. Determining publication information this way was preferable to sending questionnaires because of the problems of response rates and the lack of confidence in self-reported information on publications. There are errors no doubt in the various abstracts, but the errors should not be systematically biased for this sample. Moreover, by use of the abstracts, data could be obtained for every scientist, a "response" rate that could never be reached through a survey questionnaire.

In the abstracts it is possible to determine the senior author of co-authored papers. This enabled us to get a more precise count of citations to the papers a scientist has published. For example, when looking for citations to work by Jones and Smith, if Smith is the scientist being studied, one must look up the name of Jones to determine whether or not that particular paper has been cited. After all the data for the scientists were collected, it was possible to measure several variables that would provide a test of the effects of discipline and country on the operation of the reward system.

PERTINENT VARIABLES

A description at this point of the variables and how they were measured will eliminate the need to discuss them in detail in later chapters. In addition to information on country and discipline, I collected information on sex, birthday, year when the BA degree was obtained, year when the PhD was obtained, and prestige of both the BA and PhD institution (in Britain) or department (in the United States). I recorded the number of different universities attended and taught at, whether or not a university post was the only type of position held, and, if not, what other types of positions the scientist held. When the scientist had achieved a professorship, an important accomplishment, I computed the speed of this achievement.

I determined the prestige of scientists' current affiliations and the awards they have received from the scientific community. From the publication data it was possible to code for each scientist the number of publications for the period before taking the PhD (or terminal degree) and for each five-year period afterward. Of course the career total of all publications was available. The use of citation data is described in a later section.

Most of these variables are commonly used and require little explanation, but because the specific treatment here varies somewhat from previous usage, a brief description is desirable. There are no prestige rankings of undergraduate programs in the United States for the span of time covered in this study. My measure of prestige of BA university followed the Cartter (1966) rating of graduate programs with slight additions. If an American scientist graduated at any time from one of the departments listed in Cartter's top four categories, the scientist was assigned that category for prestige of BA degree institution. Because Cartter dealt only with graduate institutions, I adapted a procedure to assign prestige to institutions not in his top four categories. Adding three points to his top four categories and creating three lesser categories gave a range of 7 to 0. Category 3 included liberal arts colleges; category 2, state universities; category 1, private universities not in his list; and category 0, all other institutions. This is my way of making prestige operational, and it should not be confused with "selectivity" as Astin (1965) defines it. I suspect that his selectivity and my prestige rankings are highly correlated. The 0 through 7 scores are used in statistical procedures that assume an interval level of measurement. The categories are not interval levels of measurement, of course, but it is not inappropriate or misleading to assume interval levels and then compute the appropriate statistics.

For prestige of PhD departments in the United States physics and chemistry presented few problems, but biological science departments have several different names. I took all the Cartter rankings for biological sciences and assigned a department in a particular university to the category with the highest rank achieved by any biological science department in that university. That procedure overestimates the prestige of the degrees of some biologists, but it should not create gross distortions.

There are no prestige rankings for British universities comparable to the American Council on Education studies, but the general categories of universities in Britain tend to serve as an implicit prestige ranking (see Halsey and Trow, 1971). For example, Oxbridge universities (Oxford and Cambridge) are ranked at the top (category 4); next follow the various constituent colleges of London University (category 3); next are the older Redbrick and Scottish universities (category 2); next are the newer universities (category 1); and at the bottom are all other institutions (category 0). The 0 through 4 scores are used in statistical procedures that involve interval levels of measurements. The categories are not interval levels as mentioned before, but it is not inappropriate or misleading to assume interval levels.

CITATIONS TO SCIENTISTS' PUBLICATIONS

Questions about the reward system in science invariably deal with the number of publications scientists produce. Productivity indicates the extent to which a scientist contributes to the community's goal of extending certified knowledge. Merely summing the number of papers a scientist has published creates problems, however, because there is a consensus that all papers are not equally important. Evidence on how crucial some papers are proves that not all papers are equal. If this is so, and the numbers cannot simply be totaled, an additional measure of a scientist's contribution is desirable.

Concern about citations to previously published research is prevalent in the scientific community. If any scientist doubts this, just remember what a colleague has to say the next time he sees a paper that should have cited some of his publications. This failure is a frequent occurrence and is often seen as an intentional act by certain individuals who do not want to give credit where it is due (Hagstrom, 1967).

Concern about citations is not limited to responses of personal disappointment at not seeing one's publications cited. The Committee for the Survey of Chemistry (CSC) (1965:30–32) used counts of papers and citations to evaluate the status of chemistry in the United States. Counts of papers showed the United States the leader in research output as late as 1960, but the CSC (1965:30–31) adds that "A better gauge of basic research, because it measures significance as well as quantity, can be obtained from the count of the references in articles in foreign journals." The committee noted that scientists tend to refer to research performed in their own country more often than to the research of foreign scientists. These "domestic" references totaled between 30 and 45 percent of all the citations. Excluding references scientists make to their countrymen shows that references to the papers of American scientists comprise nearly half of all the nondomestic references for a selected sample of countries. "Since the United States contributes only about a quarter of the total chemical literature, these data show that our research is preferentially read and cited" (CSC, 1965:32).

To reduce suspicion that concern about citations is a peculiar trait of chemists, I point out that the National Science Board (NSB) (1973), representing the total scientific community in the United States, also uses citations to evaluate the status of American science. Computing a ratio of citations to publications, where 1.000 denotes equivalency, more than 1 equals overrepresentation, and less than 1 equals underrepresentation, the NSB (1973:105) shows that the ratio is higher for the United States than for the United Kingdom, Germany, France, the USSR, and Japan in the fields of physics and geophysics, chemistry, metallurgy, molecular biology, engineering, and psychology. Unfortunately the United Kingdom's ratio is higher than that of the United States for systematic biology and mathematics, although mathematics has a ratio of 1.10 and systematic biology approaches equality (at .97). If the governing board of the National Science Foundation (NSF) uses citation analysis to measure significance or quality, then sociologists should not be too severely criticized for doing the same thing.

The introduction of the *Science Citation Index* (*SCI*) in the 1960s opened up an enormous data source for scholars interested in questions of quality and quantity. The *SCI* was designed originally to permit scientists to discover and trace important work in a research area, but it has turned out to be one of the most useful sources of information yet "invented" for scholars of science.

One of the earliest systematic uses of the *SCI* in sociological research was Cole and Cole's (1967) research showing that, for a scientist to achieve eminence, quality of research, measured by citations to a scientist's work, is more important than mere quantity of publications. Later, after careful examination of citation patterns, Cole and Cole (1972) suggested that, because the publications of great numbers of scientists are apparently inconsequential, the number of scientists in the community could be reduced—but not funding support—without harming the progress of science, provided the right scientists were encouraged to enter science as a career.

This conclusion created controversy among some scientists. In the exchange that followed, Goudsmit (1974) pointed out that scientists often do not refer to papers originally detailing a technique, and so counting citations would underestimate the true importance of their research. McGervey (1974) claimed that popularity of scientific fields affected the number of citations a scientist would receive. Yaes (1974) suggested that negative citations would be counted as a positive indication of a contribution to science. Cole and Cole (1974) effectively demolished these arguments by invoking the fact that, contrary to Goudsmit's concern, such important scientists do receive large numbers of citations, even if they are not always referred to when they might be. For McGervey's point they noted that popularity of a field, another way of saying number of researchers involved, does not influence citation counts, because there are more papers available to which scientists can refer. In response to Yaes's comment they reminded him that citations accumulate to any degree only if the original idea or piece of research, however wrong it may have been, was an important topic to the scientific community.

Cole and Cole (1973:27–36) discuss problems that have been raised about the use of citation counts for measures of individual scientist's status: size of scientific field and number of scientists in a discipline or specialty, contemporaneity of scientific research, important papers no longer cited because of integration of the discovery as common knowledge, and stability of citations through time. They show evidence and argue that none of these problems creates measurement errors that reduce the utility of citation analysis.

There are, of course, technical problems with the *SCI*. There are errors in the *SCI* because it uses what authors list in their published papers as references, and these are sometimes inaccurate. The human process of transferring the information from journals to a machine-readable format adds more errors. Because these errors are probably not systematic, they are not likely to bias the results of any particular study.

None of these problems constitutes the most serious argument against using citation analysis. Most criticism stems from the different functions of references in papers and the failure to take these differences into account and weight them in some way. Suppose scientist A has two papers, cited a total of 10 and 5 times respectively in a given year. Suppose scientist B has two papers, cited a total of 5 times each. Of scientist A's total of 15 citations the 10 citations are to a paper that is pointed out by the citers to be erroneous. The remaining 5 acknowledge an intellectual debt to the other paper. In the case of scientist B with only 10 citations, all acknowledge an intellectual debt, that scientist B's papers had important implications that assisted the citers in formulating new research. Which of the two scientists, A with 15 citations or B with 10 citations, has the highest quality research?

One could argue that scientist B with only 10 citations, all acknowledging an intellectual debt, has far higher quality research than scientist A with 15 citations, 10 of which point out errors. One could argue, however, that scientist A's research was more important. After all, if the paper had not attacked a problem that was judged by referees and editors to be important when it was accepted for publication, it would not have been printed. If the erroneous paper had dealt with an unimportant problem, no one would have taken the time and trouble to correct it. Even if one cannot prove that A's or B's work is of higher quality, one would have to agree that the research of both scientists is more important than that of scientists who receive only a few or no citations. And it is the ability to differentiate quality rather than to measure it absolutely that is important.

Recently scholars have attempted to analyze the content of citations to determine the context in which they are used (Chubin and Moitra, 1975; Moravcsik and Murugesan, 1975). This line of inquiry is important and eventually may produce typologies useful in citation analysis, though it has not yet produced a comprehensive typology. Because the present study was initiated well before these typologies were measured and published, I do not attempt to use any in this study. If later research should show that some general constant seems to hold so that X percent of all citations, on average, are to former teachers, Y percent to the top "names" in the field, and Z percent to important prior work, these constants could be applied to the data in this study. I would rather risk criticism about the ambiguities of citation counts and keep the data simple than appear to have sophisticated, precise techniques, only to find in the near future that the typologies have limited scope and are valid only in the research areas where they were initially tested.

In addition to information on yearly publication, beginning two years before the scientists received their PhD or terminal degrees through 1972, I collected information from *SCI* about which papers were cited in 1972, excluding, of course, citations to one's own work. A problem with this procedure is that scientific papers produced more recently are more likely to be cited than those published at the beginning of scientists' careers. There is evidence (Cole and Cole, 1973:29, 30) that recent publications are more heavily cited, but because that is the case for everyone in the sample, bias would result only if there are differentials in this pattern among the disciplinary subfields or specialties. If one of the disciplines has specialties that show patterns different from this statistical norm and the other disciplines do not have such deviations, then the bias would be serious only when disciplines are compared. Since the sample selected for this study is not likely to contain many scientists in any one specialty, that problem should be negligible. The fact that recent publications, more than older publications, are likely to be cited remains a problem if one is comparing younger with older scientists. An older scientist with twice the number of publications of a younger scientist may receive citations only to papers printed within the past 10 years. A younger scientist's total publications may have been printed in the same period of time. The relationship between number of publications and number of citations to a scientist's life's work would be reduced because of the larger number of the older scientist's uncited papers. It is possible to handle this problem by controlling for the professional age of scientists. Professional age is defined as the number of years since scientists received their PhD or terminal degrees. This eliminates the effect caused by the number of years a scientist could publish papers that potentially could be cited.

The advantage of the data in this study over previous data is that these were collected over the period of a scientist's career. For questions relating to the reward system this advantage can be significant. I turn now to discuss this question: How does the reward system operate in Britain and the United States?

Chapter 5 / *THE REWARD SYSTEM
IN THE UNITED STATES
AND GREAT BRITAIN*

If the way a society organizes the funding and decision making for its scientific research has any effect on the reward system, it should be possible to discover the impact by comparing this system in two countries such as Great Britain and the United States. The basic thesis is that, in a highly decentralized country such as the United States, the reward system cannot operate as efficiently and smoothly as in a centralized country such as Great Britain. In the United States there is more opportunity for competition, and where there is competition, usually not everyone competes with the same degree of advantage or disadvantage. In a decentralized and competitive situation the scientific community is less easily monitored by its members.

Size of a country could be the crucial variable rather than the extent of centralization. Britain is smaller geographically and has fewer universities and scientists, who are located relatively close to each other. It is not easy to dismiss the possible effect of size, although there are theoretical reasons for the predicted relationship between social and cognitive factors and the reward system. It is impossible to design a study that controls for the size of scientific and educational communities, because the United States, in both size and extent of decentralization, is in a category by itself. That no comparable country exists does not mean I think size is unimportant, but I am forced to put aside that hypothesis for lack of data.

The strategy I follow is first to describe the operation of the reward system without reference to a specific country. This uses combined data on all 600 scientists. Then I separate the British and American scientists so that I can compare the two countries. Chapter 6 regroups the data into biologists, chemists, and physicists to assess the importance of the cognitive development of disciplines on the operation of the reward system.

THE REWARD SYSTEM FOR BOTH COUNTRIES

A scientist's purpose is to contribute new knowledge through research and publication of the results. The cynical view of publishing, often expressed through the pejorative phrase "publish or perish," seems to be held mostly by people who themselves either cannot, or do not, produce much noteworthy research. The major part of the activity of a scientist devoted to science, rather than to the "teaching" of science, is normally directed toward research results that are ultimately publishable. So it is to publications, as measurements of research productivity, that one looks for important information about the way the reward system operates.

The sample of 600 scientists in this study, selected by precise random procedures, is representative of virtually the total population of biologists, chemists, and physicists in the United States and Great Britain. These 600 scientists published an average of 27.9 papers over an average professional career, after their terminal degrees, of 18.4 years, making a yearly rate of 1.5 papers. The standard deviation for career publications is 27.1 papers. The range of publications is from zero (28 scientists) to 98 or more (again, 28 scientists). I did not expect more than 98 publications. Not giving "credit" for more than 98 will affect the results only in a conservative fashion; it will not change the directions of any results. The publication quartiles are 7, 18, 39 and, of course, 98 papers. From these figures it is easy to see, as other studies show, that the distribution of publications is skewed; most scientists produce fewer than average for the sample.

Only 22 of the 600 scientists (3.7 percent) are female. That percentage is lower than that of all PhDs in science who are female. As a dummy variable, sex status (in all tables, males are coded 0, females 1) was correlated with all other variables, except total papers produced, at less than .10. Females are not excluded from the analysis because sex status in this sample shows a negligible impact.

Some scholars (Allison and Stewart, 1974; Hagstrom, 1967; 1971; 1974) use number of citations to indicate number of publications, and there is a high positive relationship between the two measures. I use citation counts in various ways, depending on the context and what

seems the most logical. The correlations between selected variables and
(1) total career publications and (2) total citations in 1972 to career
publications give first approximations to the nature of the reward system (see Table 1).

The correlations suggest that prestige of current affiliation is related
to scientists' productivity. It is not, however, possible to determine the
sequence, whether productivity preceded or followed appointment to a
prestigious department or university. The information about career
movements between universities for British scientists was inadequate
for coding the information. Whether or not scientists are more productive at some institutions than at others is not a major consideration in
questions about the reward system. Although knowing that a certain
type of institution or a certain type of atmosphere promotes scientific
productivity is important, scholars have not been successful in explaining much of the variability in productivity by social or contextual variables (Clemente, 1973).

Notably absent from the selected variables correlated with publications and citations are social–psychological variables such as degree of
commitment to science as an activity or profession, activities as a child

TABLE 1   *ZERO-ORDER CORRELATIONS BETWEEN
SELECTED VARIABLES AND PUBLICATIONS, CITATIONS*

Selected Variables	Publications	Citations
Sex status[a]	−.11	−.09
Age at PhD	−.28	−.28
Prestige of PhD department or university	.17	.18
Chronological age	.22	.02
Professional age	.31	.12
Number of universities awarding scientist a degree	−.07	−.06
Number of universities at which scientist has held position	.06	.02
Number of visiting positions scientist has held	.06	.06
University position only type of position[b]	.01	.00
Number of books published	.38	.32
Number of years after PhD full professorship attained	.16	.04
Prestige of current university affiliation	.36	.39
Awards	.51	.41
Number of publications	−	.82

[a]Male = 0; female = 1.
[b]Yes = 0; no = 1.

dealing with "scientific" ideas and problems, ability to solve problems in general, a burning desire to be famous as a scientist, and many other attributes that presumably affect the ability and motivation of a scientist to conduct research and publish the results successfully. These types of variables might produce high positive correlations with scientific productivity, but the reward system, not the level of scientific productivity, is the primary focus here.

I thought that professional age would be highly correlated with scientific productivity because, among British high-energy physicists, the zero-order correlation coefficient was .65 for professional age and publications and .56 for chronological age and publications (Gaston, 1970:721). The higher correlation in the high-energy physics specialty demonstrates how confining attention to a single specialty reduces variation between specialties, a variation exemplified in this sample of 600 that includes many specialties. Among high-energy physicists the pattern of research is reasonably standardized, so that the longer a scientist has to do research and publish the results, the more publications he accumulates. Scientists in the same specialty are more homogeneous, in attributes that may be related to productivity, than a sample consisting of many different specialties.

Any reward system is characterized by the relationship between performance and rewards. In the reward system of science the relationship between productivity and recognition received from the scientific community constitutes the system. I have discussed the distribution of publications among the sample of 600 scientists. The measures of recognition are the number of awards and the number of citations, both of which measure the extent to which a scientist's publications have been recognized. The honorific awards a scientist receives are without question part of the reward system, but using citations as a measure of recognition requires some explanation.

Cole and Cole (1973:34) suggest that using citations as a form of recognition is legitimate. The question is how citations are a form of recognition. The answer involves consideration of honorific awards, the need to have measures of recognition in addition to institutionalized awards, and the logical use of citations as measures of recognition. Honorific awards are scarce, by definition, for if they were abundant, they would bestow no distinction or prestige on the persons receiving them. Because they are scarce and few people achieve these institutionalized, recognized awards, and because in this study I did not survey scientists either personally or by questionnaire to discover other important but less obvious forms of recognition, the number of awards obtained in the sample of 600 scientists is, as expected, quite scarce.

The range of awards is from zero through nine or more, and only one person exceeded nine (a Nobel laureate). The distribution is as follows: 491 scientists (82 percent) have no awards; 63 (11 percent) have one; 22 (4 percent) have two; 12 (2 percent) have three; 6 (1 percent) have four; 2 (0.3 percent) have five; 3 (0.5 percent) have six; and 1 (0.16 percent) has nine (compare Cole and Cole, 1973:48).

It is not certain, of course, that awards were reported to the editors of the biographical references, but the usual problem is that people tend to report more in such instances than actually justify reporting. It is possible that a reticent scientist might not report all accumulated awards. Probably much more frequent are instances where scientists report they have been "advisors" or "consultants" to an agency or organization when in reality they were only asked to evaluate a proposal for possible funding or referee a paper for possible publication. I do not question scientists' integrity; I only point out human tendencies.

It is not just the scarcity of awards in this sample that causes me to use citations as a measure of recognition. The scarcity of awards for the deserving scientists is aptly described by Merton (1973:439–443), who writes of the problems of scientists who occupy the 41st chair. These scientists are equal in all respects to the scientists holding, in this story, the 40 chairs of the French Academy, but because of limitations on numbers, only 40 may be members at a time.

The 41st-chair syndrome is found throughout the social world. A person may have two equally desirable mates. Law requires, and conformity wins out, and so only one eligible person becomes the legal mate. Search committees may determine that any one of several people are qualified to become dean, vice president, or president, but, because there is only one position, only one is chosen. Departments may narrow a selection process to five applicants, but only one can be offered the position. The cliché that many are called but few are chosen has more than a grain of truth.

Even if awards are scarce in this sample, and even if social restrictions consistently produce the phenomenon of the 41st chair, the use of citations to measure recognition would not be acceptable unless there is a logical reason to use them. The best evidence that scientists view citations to their work as a form of recognition is seen through their responses of satisfaction when their work is cited. When it is not cited, in situations where scientists perceive their work should have been, they can become angry, to put it mildly. (My personal experience plus reports by others lead to no other conclusion: Seeing one's work cited is an important indication of the scientific community's appreciation of that work.)

When interviewing British high-energy physicists, I asked them if people had failed to refer to their work when it should have been cited (Gaston, 1973:110). One who said yes, added, "Some of them were my friends and I told them off." Another told about his experience with an eminent scientist, Dr. *Y.*, which is illustrative:

> I remember giving a review talk at the ___ Laboratory. *X* and *Y* were buddies at one time. Well, I mentioned in this talk that work was done by *X* et al. I didn't include *Y*. *Y* was there, and when it was over he took me aside and told me I should refer to him also. I kind of laughed, but he was quite serious and took it to heart.

Finally citations are not so severely affected by the syndrome of the 41st chair. Except on the rare occasion of being asked to reduce references because of space, authors are usually able to refer to all the previous work they think appropriate. As a consequence all can be cited, if their work is significant, even if they cannot be elected to 1 of the 40 chairs. Information on the norms governing whom to cite, of all possible relevant scientists, is only now being studied.

The distribution of citations shows far more dispersion, as expected, than the distribution of awards. The range of citations is from zero to 98 (as with publications, 98 was the maximum allowed). The mean citations in 1972 to career publications is 27.8; the standard deviation is 32.2. The citation quartiles are as follows: 2, 14, 39, and, of course, 98 citations.

The correlation coefficients in Table 1 show that publications and correlations are highly related. Publications, more than citations, are correlated to awards. In contrast, as an indication of recognition, citations, slightly more than publications, are correlated to current affiliation. The question that raises most problems about the extent to which the reward system operates universalistically is this: Are there any controlling variables, that is, social categories, that lessen or strengthen the relationship between productivity and recognition?

The critical feature of all studies on the reward system is whether being at a prestigious university or department provides an unfair advantage to a scientist for obtaining recognition from the scientific community. If scientists at these universities have more recognition than others, there is nothing wrong with that, as long as the recognition is based on superior scientific performance. Differential recognition cannot be attributed to the "halo" effect or to presumed unfair competitive advantages when recognition is compared to performance. This is where Halsey and Trow (1971:216–218) err in concluding that

Oxbridge professors seem to have unusual advantages based on over-representation among memberships in the various honorific societies. Their conclusion may be correct, but they failed to produce evidence that the recognition of Oxbridge professors does not follow from their performance as scholars.

I shall look at the problem by using various techniques. One way to examine the influence of a scientist's university or department prestige on recognition is to see what the relationship is between publications and recognition, when prestige of current affiliation is controlled for (see Table 2). This answers the question, Is recognition allocated to scientists according to levels of performance, regardless of their affiliations? The data show only a slight tendency for scientists at the highest prestige levels to obtain more recognition for their publications. The table collapses all publications beyond 50 into one category, and so that can influence the appearance of more recognition at the highest levels. Tabular presentations are important because the reader can visualize the relationships, but a more sophisticated and powerful presentation of these data is possible through product-moment correlations.

The zero-order correlations for the three variables in Table 2 are these: Prestige of current affiliation with number of publications equals .36; prestige of current affiliation with awards equals .25; number of publications with awards equals .51.

Publications have more impact on awards than prestige of current affiliation, but that does not eliminate all the effect of the prestige of the scientist's current affiliations. To test for that requires partial correlations, somewhat equivalent to the data in Table 2. The correlation between number of publications and awards, when prestige of current affiliation is controlled for, is .46. That means that, after the effect of prestige of current affiliation is taken into account, the correlation between publications and awards is still .46, reduced only from the original .51. A question could also be asked about the relationship between prestige of current affiliation and awards when the number of publications is controlled for. This question asks, If one takes into account the number of publications, is there any relationship remaining between prestige of current affiliation and awards? The correlation is only .08, showing only a small effect of prestige of current affiliation on receiving awards. Prestige of current affiliation explains only 0.64 percent of the variance in awards, a minuscule amount. Thus controlling for publications eliminates most of the effect but does not eliminate completely the impact of prestige of current affiliation on receiving awards.

Recall that the distribution of rewards is heavily skewed toward no awards but that citations are also an important indication of recogni-

TABLE 2   *PUBLICATIONS BY AWARDS, WHEN PRESTIGE OF*
CURRENT AFFILIATION IS CONTROLLED FOR, FOR TOTAL SAMPLE

Current Affiliation Category	Awards	Publications					
		0-9	*10-19*	*20-29*	*30-39*	*40-49*	*50+*
0 (low)	0	99	91	83	100	67	55
	1	1	9	17	—	17	36
	2	—	—	—	—	8	—
	3+	—	—	—	—	8	9
		100	100	100	100	100	100
	N:	97	34	29	7	12	11
	Gamma:	.75					
1	0	93	100	100	80	88	82
	1	7	—	—	13	—	18
	2	—	—	—	7	12	—
	3+	—	—	—	—	—	—
		100	100	100	100	100	100
	N:	28	24	17	15	8	11
	Gamma:	.39					
2	0	97	89	82	90	60	38
	1	—	11	11	—	20	24
	2	—	—	7	10	20	21
	3+	3	—	—	—	—	17
		100	100	100	100	100	100
	N:	32	36	27	10	10	29
	Gamma:	.69					
3	0	94	90	68	50	80	39
	1	6	5	26	25	—	39
	2	—	5	—	—	20	3
	3+	—	—	5	25	—	18
		100	100	99	100	100	99
	N:	18	20	19	4	10	33
	Gamma:	.61					
4 (high)	0	100	100	80	75	33	41
	1	—	—	20	25	33	14
	2	—	—	—	—	33	14
	3+	—	—	—	—	—	32
		100	100	100	100	99	101
	N:	3	11	5	8	9	16
	Gamma:	.78					

tion. Consider recognition again, but use citations instead of awards to measure recognition. That correlation matrix is as follows: Prestige of current affiliation correlates with publications, .36; prestige of current affiliation correlates with citations, .39; publications correlates with citations, .82.

Publications, more than prestige of current affiliation, has a strong effect on citations, indicating that scientific performance in one's career is more important for receiving citations at the time of this study than where a scientist is located. When prestige of current affiliation is controlled for, the partial correlation between publications and citations equals .79, hardly reduced from the original correlation of .82. Controlling for number of publications does not eliminate completely the relationship between prestige of current affiliation and the receipt of citations. That correlation is .18, which means that, after publications is controlled for, prestige of current affiliation still explains a little more than 3 percent of the variance in number of citations.

The first strategy to test the importance of ascribed characteristics on the reward system in Table 2 used a technique that physically controls for prestige of current affiliation and examines relationships within categories of prestige. The second strategy (not presented in a table) used zero-order and partial correlations to control statistically, rather than physically, the effect of prestige of current affiliation on recognition. This becomes confusing when more than three variables are involved. The third strategy is to use regression techniques that control simultaneously all but one of the independent variables and compute its effect on the dependent variable. This is a superior strategy and is especially helpful for seeing what is affecting the allocation of recognition. The second strategy showed that, after publications was controlled for, there was still a small effect of prestige. Consider now what the effect is when additional variables are controlled for at the same time (see Table 3).

The variables in Table 3 were entered in the regression analysis in the order listed. This ordering represents, as much as is possible to determine, the chronological ordering of the variables. The impact of each independent variable is what is possible at that particular point. In a stepwise regression, for example, variables are taken in the order of decreasing impact, and in such an analysis, this same list of variables has a different order.

The most important question is what variables have an independent effect on awards and citations, the two indicators of recognition achieved by these scientists. In the case of awards professional age explains 13 percent of the variation when it is entered before publications,

TABLE 3 REGRESSION ANALYSIS ON CITATIONS AND AWARDS FOR 600 SCIENTISTS

Independent Variables	Awards		Citations	
	Regression Coefficient	R^2 change	Regression Coefficient	R^2 change
Sex status[a]	.26	.00	.06	.01
Prestige of BA institution	-.00	.01	-0.29	.01
Predoctoral publications	.05	.01	-0.86	.04
Predoctoral citations	-.01	.00	1.82[b]	.01
Prestige PhD department/institution	-.01	.01	1.12	.02
Prestige of current affiliation	.06[b]	.05	2.16[b]	.12
Professional age	.02[b]	.13	-0.51[b]	.02
Publications	.01[b]	.11	.98[b]	.50
Citations	.00	.00	—	—
Awards	—	—	.65	.00
Total R/R^2	.56/.31		.85/.72	
F	27.58		154.46	
Significance	.001		.001	

[a] Male = 0; female = 1.
[b] Regression coefficient is more than twice its standard error.

73

but publications still explains 11 percent after professional age and the other variables have explained all they can. Because professional age and publications are related at the zero order ($r = .33$), professional age entered before publications, as in Table 3, explains some of the same variation that publications explains when entered before professional age. Professional age seems to be more important than publications, but when publications is entered before professional age, publications by itself explains 26 out of 31 percent of the total explained variation.

Even after publications explained all it can, there is a lingering effect of professional age (and of course chronological age). This happens simply because it is not possible to allocate recognition, in the form of honorific awards, immediately after research is completed and published. There is a demonstrable time lag between earning recognition and actually receiving it. These kinds of results caused me to criticize Blume and Sinclair (1973) in Chapter 2 because they did not consider the possibility that age was responsible for the differential rewards of Oxbridge scientists, who presumably are older, on the average, than scientists at other institutions. While professional age, like chronological age, is an ascribed characteristic, it is not so negative a factor in the reward system as is sex status or prestige of a university where a scientist is located. The problem of professional age and recognition is discussed in more detail in Chapter 7.

Prestige of current affiliation explains 5 percent of the variation in awards when entered before professional age and publications, but when it is entered after, it explains only 0.65 percent, a level of influence that can be ignored safely when the reward system for all 600 scientists is considered.

Number of publications is the most important independent variable for explaining variation in citations. In Table 3 the effect is to explain 50 percent after everything else has been considered; in a stepwise analysis it enters first, explaining 67 percent out of the total of 72 percent explained. Professional age, entered *before* publications, explains only 2 percent, and entered *after* publications, still explains 2 percent. In contrast, however, prestige of current affiliation among the 600 scientists explains 12 percent of the variation in citations when entered before publications and professional age; when entered after, prestige of current affiliation explains only 0.87 percent. So, with citations, as with awards, prestige of current affiliation has a surprisingly small independent effect when compared to the conclusions of previous studies. The question now is whether that influence is stronger in the

United States or Britain, such that, when considered in the aggregate, the effect is eliminated. Originally, on the basis of the effect of differential social organization, I predicted the greatest deviation from universalism would occur in the United States. I turn now to the reward system in each country, to see if the pattern found in the sample of 600 is different in some important way from the sample of 300 scientists in each country.

THE REWARD SYSTEM IN EACH COUNTRY

This section separates British and American scientists to see whether country has a demonstrable effect on the way the reward system operates. I present the same type of data as I did for discussion of the reward system in both countries. I attempt to follow the previous format as much as possible to permit the reader to make comparisons as conveniently as possible.

Most of the zero-order correlations for each country are only slightly different from the sample of 600, but some of the correlations show slight differences (see Table 4). The correlation between prestige of PhD-granting department or institution and publications and citations is stronger in the United States than in Britain. Similarly the relationship between prestige of current affiliation and publications and citations is stronger in the United States than in Britain.

The same explanation holds for both those relationships. In the United States the quality of potential scientists and their training are more variable than is the case in Britain. The differences between the Oxbridge universities at the top of the prestige ladder and those on the lowest rung of the ladder are much less in actual quality than the similar categories in the United States. The faculty in Britain have been trained at far fewer institutions, and their training and experience vary less than those of graduate faculties in the United States. American scientists have been exposed to extremely diverse faculties, both the faculties at enormously different undergraduate institutions and the less varied, but still uneven, faculties at graduate departments. Some data on publications support this view, which I have also expounded elsewhere (Gaston, 1970:729–731). The average number of publications for British scientists is 32.01 during an average professional age of 16.34, producing a mean rate of 1.96 papers per professional year; for Americans the comparable figures are 23.74 papers during 20.38 years for a mean of 1.16. The British standard deviation for papers is

TABLE 4 *ZERO-ORDER CORRELATIONS BETWEEN SELECTED VARIABLES AND PUBLICATIONS, CITATIONS*

Selected Variables	British		American	
	Publications	*Citations*	*Publications*	*Citations*
Sex status[a]	-.11	-.11	-.11	-.07
Age at PhD	-.24	-.23	-.27	-.26
Prestige of PhD department or university	.10	.14	.26	.25
Chronological age	.37	.17	.17	-.03
Professional age	.43	.26	.29	.09
Number of universities awarding scientist a degree	.11	.13	-.09	-.05
Number of universities at which scientist has held position	.20	.13	.01	.02
Number of visiting positions scientist has held	.11	.14	.03	.00
University position only type of position[b]	-.07	.00	.16	.06
Number of books published	.43	.37	.25	.18
Number of years after PhD full professorship attained	-.02	-.16	.22	.09
Prestige of current affiliation	.23	.30	.45	.42
Awards	.51	.40	.52	.42
Number of publications	—	.84	—	.78

[a]Male = 0; female = 1.
[b]Yes = 0; no = 1.

28.81, less than the mean; the American standard deviation for papers is 24.60, more than the mean. British scientists are more homogeneous than American scientists.

The correlation patterns between publications, citations, and awards are remarkably similar for British and American scientists. Because these patterns may hide subtle differences, the next step is to examine the tabular material that presents the distribution of awards and publications among the various prestige categories of current affiliation (see Table 5). For British scientists, only one gamma coefficient is reduced below the similar statistics for the sample of 600. One might have expected the smallest gamma to be in the highest prestige category, where scientists might receive awards by virtue of their position and regardless of their publication performance, but that is not the case. For some reason, not readily apparent, scientists in the next to lowest category are most subject to having awards without large numbers of publications. There are so few cases in many categories that percentages must be read with extreme caution. This was not the situation with the total sample, but this table has 120 cells, and only 300 potential scientists to distribute in them, and so many cells are blank.

For American scientists two gamma coefficients are lower than the similar statistics for the sample of 600. The divergence is in the two categories adjoining the top category, but the correlations are nevertheless still rather high as such correlations go for sociology. The only possible explanation for this is that an insufficient number of variables is being considered and that important variables are not considered in this table.

At this point, while there is a small hint that the American reward system is slightly less universalistic than the British, the evidence is far from precise. Consider now the product-moment correlations for each sample. For the British scientists (and Americans in parentheses) the correlation between prestige of current affiliation and publications is .23 (.45); for prestige of current affiliation and awards it is .19 (.31); and for publications and awards it is .51 (.52). The correlation between publications and awards is stronger than the other coefficients, which suggests that performance generally has more impact on awards than the prestige of the university where a scientist is located does. The relationship between publications and citations, when prestige of current affiliation is controlled for, is .49 for British scientists and .45 for Americans. Both correlations are reduced only slightly and are strong indications that, regardless of the prestige of a scientist's location, publications are strongly related to receiving rewards.

A different question is: What is the relationship between prestige of

TABLE 5   PUBLICATIONS BY AWARDS, WHEN PRESTIGE OF
CURRENT AFFILIATION IS CONTROLLED FOR, FOR
BRITISH AND AMERICAN SCIENTISTS

Current Affiliation Category	Awards	Publications					
		0-9	10-19	20-29	30-39	40-49	50+
British							
0 (low)	0	100	83	100	100	75	—
	1	—	17	—	—	25	—
	2	—	—	—	—	—	—
	3+	—	—	—	—	—	100
		100	100	100	100	100	100
	N:	12	6	5	2	4	2
	Gamma:	.80					
1	0	89	100	100	70	100	80
	1	11	—	—	20	—	20
	2	—	—	—	10	—	—
	3+	—	—	—	—	—	—
		100	100	100	100	100	100
	N:	18	19	11	10	5	10
	Gamma:	.29					
2	0	95	90	86	100	57	32
	1	—	10	5	—	29	24
	2	—	—	9	—	14	24
	3+	5	—	—	—	—	20
		100	100	100	100	100	100
	N:	21	29	22	8	7	25
	Gamma:	.71					
3	0	92	83	79	100	100	31
	1	8	8	14	—	—	39
	2	—	8	—	—	—	—
	3+	—	—	7	—	—	31
		100	99	100	100	100	101
	N:	13	12	14	1	4	13
	Gamma:	.80					
4 (high)	0	—	100	100	80	—	62
	1	—	—	—	20	—	—
	2	—	—	—	—	—	15
	3+	—	—	—	—	—	23
		—	100	100	100	—	100
	N:	—	5	3	5	—	13
	Gamma:	.80					

TABLE 5   PUBLICATIONS BY AWARDS, WHEN PRESTIGE OF
CURRENT AFFILIATION IS CONTROLLED FOR, FOR
BRITISH AND AMERICAN SCIENTISTS (continued)

Current Affiliation Category	Publications					
	Awards	0-9	10-19	20-29	30-39	40-49	50+
American							
0 (low)	0	99	93	79	100	63	67
	1	1	7	21	—	13	22
	2	—	—	—	—	12	—
	3+	—	—	—	—	12	11
		100	100	100	100	100	100
	N:	85	28	24	5	8	9
	Gamma:	.75					
1	0	100	100	100	100	67	100
	1	—	—	—	—	—	—
	2	—	—	—	—	33	—
	3+	—	—	—	—	—	—
		100	100	100	100	100	100
	N:	10	5	6	5	3	1
	Gamma:	.93					
2	0	100	86	60	50	67	75
	1	—	14	40	—	—	25
	2	—	—	—	50	33	—
	3+	—	—	—	—	—	—
		100	100	100	100	100	100
	N:	11	7	5	2	3	4
	Gamma:	.58					
3	0	100	100	40	33	67	45
	1	—	—	60	33	—	40
	2	—	—	—	—	33	5
	3+	—	—	—	33	—	10
		100	100	100	99	100	100
	N:	5	8	5	3	6	20
	Gamma:	.51					
4 (high)	0	100	100	50	67	33	11
	1	—	—	50	33	33	33
	2	—	—	—	—	33	11
	3+	—	—	—	—	—	44
		100	100	100	100	99	100
	N:	3	6	2	3	3	9
	Gamma:	.88					

current affiliation and awards, when number of publications is controlled for? For British scientists it is .09; for American scientists it is .10. These partial correlations, as they did with the total sample, show there is a small but persistent effect of prestige in spite of the fact that scientists are generally rewarded for their publications regardless of their location.

Awards are only one indication of recognition, and the same strategy now should be used to gauge the impact of prestige on scientists' having their life's work cited. The zero-order correlation between prestige of current affiliation and citations for British scientists is .84; for American scientists it is .78. The correlation is higher for British scientists than for the total of 600 (which is .82), while for American scientists it is somewhat lower. The relationship between publications and citations, when prestige of current affiliation is controlled for, is .82 for British scientists and .73 for American scientists. Scientists' publications were cited, in large part, as a function of the amount of research they had published.

If the number of citations is largely accounted for by the fact that highly prolific scientists achieve large numbers of citations, is there still something operating that causes scientists at prestigious institutions to receive more citations than are justified on the basis of their publications? The answer requires looking at the partial correlation between prestige of current affiliation and citations and controlling for number of publications. The pertinent correlation for British scientists is .20; for American scientists it is .12. This is the only indication so far suggesting that prestige in Britain, more than the United States, may have an impact on the reward system.

Recall that citations are highly correlated not only with publications but also with awards. Citations and awards are both correlated with prestige of current affiliation. In the case of these scientists, awards preceded citations to their work in 1972, because the measure of awards is based on the number received throughout a scientist's career. The zero-order correlation between awards and citations for British scientists is .40; for Americans it is .42. What happens to the relationship between awards and citations when prestige of current affiliation is controlled? For British scientists the relationship dips only to .37, and for Americans it dips only to .34. If papers are cited because the authors have received awards and gained visibility, then the work is cited regardless of scientist's location. Any halo effect that might attract attention receives that attention, whether scientists are at a more or less prestigious institution.

Consider now the regression analysis for awards to determine what the important variables are that determine awards while several other variables are controlled for at once (see Table 6). For British scientists professional age is the most important determinant of awards; but for Americans publications is most important for awards. Publications, if entered prior to professional age, explains 27 percent of the variation among American and 26 percent among British scientists. In both instances professional age is the second most important variable, explaining 2 percent among American but 9 percent among British scientists. This adds more credence to my hypothesis about the effect of professional age, which Blume and Sinclair ignored when considering institutionalized awards. One variable that is particularistic and that has an impact on awards is prestige of BA institution. Among British scientists this factor, explaining 3 percent of the variation in awards, is more important than prestige of current affiliation, which explains none. To the extent that these 300 scientists represent British science the main intrusion into the reward system involving honorific awards is through the effect of undergraduate institution. One could speculate that capability, measured by quality of undergraduate experiences, is the dimension actually being measured rather than the effect of some ascribed status.

In Britain prestige of BA institution plus prestige of current affiliation explain a total of 5 percent of the variation in awards. In the United States prestige of PhD department plus prestige of current affiliation explain a total of 10 percent of the variation in awards. If these variables are entered after publications, the total for British scientists is 1 percent, and for American scientists, slightly less than 1 percent. The effect shown in Table 6, then, is largely a consequence of the ordering, not the impact, of particularistic influences.

Consider now the determinants of 1972 citations to career publications (see Table 7). For British scientists a large amount of variation in citations is explained by publications. Indeed publications explains nine times more of the variation than the next most important variable in the list. If publications is entered prior to professional age and prestige of current affiliation, the former explains 71 percent rather than 54 while the latter explain a total of 3 percent rather than 12. Prestige of BA institution changes to 0.10 percent. Awards does not explain any variation in citations in either case.

For citations in the United States number of publications is the most important variable. Particularistic variables such as prestige of undergraduate institution, PhD department, and current affiliation explain 18 percent of the variation. Awards in American science, as in British science, explains none of the variation in citations.

TABLE 6 REGRESSION ANALYSIS ON AWARDS FOR BRITISH AND AMERICAN SCIENTISTS

Independent Variables	British		American	
	Regression Coefficient	R^2 Change	Regression Coefficient	R^2 Change
Sex status	.27	.00	.26	.00
Prestige of BA institution	.08	.03	−.04	.00
Predoctoral publications	.04	.02	.03	.00
Predoctoral citations	.00	.00	−.02	.00
Prestige PhD department/institution	−.04	.00	−.02	.02
Prestige of current affiliation	.02	.02	.08[a]	.08
Professional age	.04[a]	.22	.02[a]	.07
Publications	.01	.06	.02[a]	.14
Citations	.00	.00	.00	.00
Total R/R^2	.60/.36		.56/.31	
F	16.22		14.03	
Significance	.001		.001	

[a] Regression coefficient is more than twice its standard error.

TABLE 7 REGRESSION ANALYSIS ON CITATIONS FOR BRITISH AND AMERICAN SCIENTISTS

Independent Variables	British		American	
	Regression Coefficient	R^2 Change	Regression Coefficient	R^2 Change
Sex status	-3.36	.01	2.52	.00
Prestige of BA institution	.80	.05	-0.53	.03
Predoctoral publications	-2.06[a]	.05	-0.35	.02
Predoctoral citations	2.88[a]	.00	.87	.00
Prestige PhD department/institution	.30	.00	1.16	.03
Prestige of current affiliation	3.41[a]	.06	1.71	.12
Professional age	-0.67[a]	.06	-0.42[a]	.00
Publications	1.04[a]	.54	.93[a]	.43
Awards	.42	.00	1.07	.00
Total R/R^2	.88/.78		.80/.64	
F	98.68		55.78	
Significance	.001		.001	

[a] Regression coefficient is more than twice its standard error.

Although Table 7 indicates the importance of particularistic variables, recall that this ordering, although sequential, is nevertheless somewhat arbitrary. Stepwise regression enters publications as the most important variable. Then, instead of 43 percent, publications explains 61 percent of the variation in citations. Prestige of undergraduate institution, PhD department, and current affiliation explain only 0.09 percent when they follow, rather than precede, publications in the regression analysis.

With the data on British and American scientists showing such similar universalistic results, it is difficult to declare which reward system has more universalism. One technique to assist in deciding is to separate performance variables (indicators of universalism) from ascriptive variables (indicators of particularism) and regress them at one time, as sets, on awards and citations as dependent variables (see Table 8). For awards the results are unambiguous: The reward system in the United States is more universalistic. Whether the total variation explained by performance variables (27 percent) is used as the criterion *or* the percentage of the total explained that is attributable to performance variables (87 percent), the reward system in American science is more universalistic. For citations, though, these results are somewhat indeterminant. The total percentage explained by performance variables in Britain is larger than the total variation explained by both performance and ascriptive variables in the United States. Nevertheless the portion of the total percentage explained by performance variables is larger in American than in British science.

The reward system in British science is characterized by virtually no interference with the universalistic allocation of recognition. Awards, as institutionalized recognition, are simply "delayed" recognition, not given too early in a scientist's career. This is probably a positive influence on science because of the potential for discontinuity of research if awards are bestowed early in one's career (compare Zuckerman, 1967). When publications, citations (as indicators of quality), and professional age are excluded, the total additional variation explained in awards is 7 percent (or in stepwise regression, only 2 percent); for citations, the total additional variation explained is about 17 percent (or in stepwise regression, only 5 percent). Citations, as general recognition, is also affected, as is awards by professional age, possibly because age enhances visibility through informal communication. Awards is included in all regressions on citations, but if having received awards increases visibility, awards does not improve one's chances of being cited when other variables are controlled.

The reward system in American science is similar to that in Britain. Publications explains most of the variation either for awards or cita-

TABLE 8   REGRESSION OF PERFORMANCE AND ASCRIPTIVE VARIA-
BLES ON AWARDS AND CITATIONS

Dependent Variable	Independent Variables Entered First	British % Explained/Total = % of Total	American % Explained/Total = % of Total
Awards	Performance[a]	26/36 = 72	27/31 = 87
	Ascriptive[b]	29/36 = 81	16/31 = 52
Citations	Performance[c]	74/78 = 95	62/64 = 97
	Ascriptive[d]	25/78 = 32	29/64 = 45

[a] Performance variables: predoctoral publications, postdoctoral publications, citations to predoctoral publications, citations to postdoctoral publications.

[b] Ascriptive variables: sex status, professional age, prestige of current affiliation, prestige of PhD department/institution, prestige of BA institution.

[c] Performance variables: predoctoral publications, postdoctoral publications, citations to predoctoral publications (excluded from total citations).

[d] Ascriptive variables: all in footnote *b* plus awards.

tions. And while variables other than publications show some independent effect, their influence is drastically reduced or eliminated when publications is first permitted to explain variation in either awards or citations. The only conclusion possible is that the reward system in science operates in a universalistic manner. For the 600 scientists there is little evidence of any advantage in being located at a prestigious institution. For British and American scientists separately, this is consistent evidence that the reward system operates according to norms of universalism. At this point the conclusion must be that any interference with the reward system caused by differences in the social organization of science in Britain and the United States is minimal, although the reward system in the United States appears almost to be slightly more universalistic. In any case the thesis that social organization affects the operation of the reward system needs further consideration within scientific communities in each country, and that must await examination of the reward system in biology, chemistry, and physics. In Chapter 6 I consider these three disciplinary communities first and then separate them within each country. The problem is whether cognitive development in a discipline or the social organization in a country affects the universalistic evaluation of scientific research in the allocation of recognition.

/ *THE REWARD SYSTEM*
IN BIOLOGY, CHEMISTRY,
AND PHYSICS

The reason for examining the operation of the reward system according to disciplines is that cognitive development, or codification of knowledge, in a discipline involves different degrees of agreement on the important problems in the field. There is consensus not only about the important problems in the field but also about criteria for evaluating research contributions. According to the evidence about these disciplines discussed in Chapter 3 biology is the least codified, chemistry is between biology and physics, and physics is the most codified.

The problem now is to examine the reward system for the three disciplines to see if there is any indication that their level of codification is related to the distribution of recognition for scientific research. The first section of this chapter ignores any effect that nationality may have on the reward system and considers the three disciplines separately. The second section introduces nationality and examines the disciplinary groups as representing separate social systems.

THE REWARD SYSTEM IN EACH DISCIPLINE

The previous chapter presented tables showing the percentage distribution of publications by awards within prestige categories for institutions or departments. That type of presentation becomes complex when several groups are involved. The logic of the presentation is to show that, after the level of prestige is *physically* controlled, there is a strong correlation between publications and awards, regardless of where scientists are located in the prestige structure. The gamma coefficients for the three disciplines, derived from percentage distributions (not presented) are shown in Table 9.

How do these correlations fit with the idea that cognitive development is related to the operation of the reward system? A first observation is that the relationship between publications and awards for biological scientists is not as consistently high as for chemists and physicists. The next to lowest prestige category has a very small correlation between awards and publications. If one averages the gamma coefficients, biology has a mean of .54, chemistry a mean of .80, and physics a mean of .75. Averaging coefficients really does not give much information, because the correlations have considerable variation.

In the highest prestige category biology has the largest correlation. It may turn out that, if biology really has the most particularistic reward system, it is not at the upper levels of prestige but in the middle ranges. Ambiguity about the quality of work in prestige categories might cause this. Perhaps one should expect deviation in the middle ranges because, at the lower end of the prestige structure, scientists are doing research that clearly is not important, and at the upper end, they are doing research that clearly is important. Only those in the middle categories are doing work that may or may not be important. Perhaps the research of those at middle ranges of prestige will turn out to be important, but it might turn out to be no better than that conducted at the lowest prestige levels. This is only a hypothesis and certainly cannot be tested without interview data.

If the average gamma coefficients are taken seriously, the biggest problem is explaining why chemistry is more universalistic than

TABLE 9   *GAMMA CORRELATION COEFFICIENTS BETWEEN PUBLICATIONS AND AWARDS, FOR CATEGORIES OF PRESTIGE OF CURRENT AFFILIATION*

	Prestige Categories				
Discipline	*0 (low)*	*1*	*2*	*3*	*4 (high)*
Biology	.64	.14	.34	.65	.95
Chemistry	.87	1.00	.86	.58	.67
Physics	.78	—[a]	.84	.56	.82

[a]Gamma not computed; only one row in pertinent table.

physics. When the cell with a coefficient of 1.00 for chemistry is omitted, the same cell not computed for physics, the average for the four categories shows chemistry to be the same as physics, but not lower as expected. One possible explanation is that cognitive development has no effect on the operation of the reward system. In that case chemistry, or any other field, could conform most to a universalistic model of reward allocation. Before concluding that, though, consider the second strategy for evaluating the reward system.

In the last chapter I described product-moment correlations in the text. With three groups it becomes too confusing, and so I show them in Table 10. The correlation matrices show consistently that the highest correlations are between publications and citations. For biology and physics the next highest correlations are between publications and awards; for chemistry the next highest correlation is between prestige of current affiliation and citations. These zero-order correlations do not inform us of the complete nature of the reward system. Prestige of current affiliation being controlled for, the partial correlations between publications and awards are only slightly reduced for each discipline.

Consider a different question. Suppose we want to know what the relationship is between prestige of current affiliation and awards, after controlling for number of publications? Does prestige help explain receipt of awards in addition to publications that have a strong impact? The partial correlations show a very small effect of prestige on awards and explain zero percent of the variance in awards for biology, only 1 percent for chemistry, and less than 1 percent for physics. Recall that the chronology of receipt of awards is not certain. Awards may precede current affiliation, but in the case of citations, to be considered next, the chronology is clear: Scientists were at their current affiliation before the 1972 citations were published.

Having one's work cited is probably more important for the maintenance of a reward system than the distribution of the much fewer awards. The relationship between publications and citations is very strong for each discipline and remains strong even after prestige of current affiliation is controlled for. Because the correlation between citations and prestige is higher for chemists, controlling for number of publications does not reduce the correlations between citations and prestige of current affiliation so much for chemists as for biologists and physicists. Remember that the reward system in chemistry appeared to operate more universalistically when I used gamma correlations to show the relationship between awards and publications. With the more precise technique of product-moment correlations it turns out that chemists, after publications is controlled for, have the largest partial

TABLE 10 CORRELATION MATRICES FOR THREE DISCIPLINES (DECIMALS OMITTED)

	Biology				Chemistry				Physics			
Variables	1	2	3	4	1	2	3	4	1	2	3	4
1. Prestige of current affiliation	—	—	—	—	—	—	—	—	—	—	—	—
2. Publications	27	—	—	—	53	—	—	—	30	—	—	—
3. Awards	16	46	—	—	35	52	—	—	23	51	—	—
4. Citations	29	75	31	—	59	84	45	—	29	83	41	—
Partial correlations												
$r_{23.1} =$	44				42				48			
$r_{13.2} =$	04				10				09			
$r_{24.1} =$	73				77				81			
$r_{14.2} =$	14				31				08			

correlation between prestige and awards (.10) and prestige and citations (.31). For chemists 9.6 percent of the variation in citations is explained by prestige of current affiliation, after the number of publications is permitted to explain all it can. That is not a large percentage, but it is more than the 2 percent for biology and the 0.6 percent for physics.

At this point it appears that the reward system involving receipt of awards is universalistic in each discipline, although the degree of universalism is not the same for all disciplines. In fact the pattern predicted for the rank order of universalism (lowest in biology, next for chemistry, and highest for physics) does not turn out to be the actual pattern. Before any explanation is offered for this pattern, it is necessary to see if the regression analysis also shows this deviant pattern.

The advantage of regression analysis is, of course, that many variables can be considered simultaneously. It is possible to see what the independent effect of a specific variable is after the effect of all the other variables in the analysis is taken into account. This technique was used to arrange the variables in their approximate chronological or sequential order and to maintain this order in subsequent analyses so that the reader can compare the equations across each various group of scientists. It is possible that professional age should have been entered last in the analysis because this is, of course, a constantly increasing variable. I placed it before publications, however, because the total career publications (excluding predoctoral publications) is also a measurement at the last point in the case of consistent producers, and I wanted every other variable to have a chance to explain as much variation as possible before the publications variable was introduced.

The regression, with the variables ordered as presented, shows a very interesting result. The amount of variation in awards explained by the independent variables is very similar for each discipline (see Table 11). Although there are only 22 women scientists (14 biologists, 5 chemists, 3 physicists), sex status has a statistically significant positive regression coefficient for awards in biology, but it explains only 1 percent of the variation in awards.

Compare the regression coefficients and the percentage of variation explained in the three disciplines. In all three instances, even after professional age has explained a large percentage of the variation, publications still explains much of the variation. In spite of the fact that the publications variable is entered into the regression next to last, the regression coefficients for professional age and publications are the only ones that consistently are twice their standard errors. Not shown is a stepwise regression that enters the variables into the equation in order

TABLE 11 REGRESSION ANALYSIS ON AWARDS FOR THREE DISCIPLINES

Independent Variables	Biology		Chemistry		Physics	
	Regression Coefficient	R^2 Change	Regression Coefficient	R^2 Change	Regression Coefficient	R^2 Change
Sex status	.48[a]	.01	-.02	.00	-.24	.00
Prestige of BA institution	-.02	.00	.02	.02	-.00	.01
Predoctoral publications	.12[a]	.02	-.09	.00	.05	.00
Predoctoral citations	-.03	.01	.12	.00	-.02	.00
Prestige PhD department/institution	.01	.01	-.08	.01	.01	.01
Prestige of current affiliation	.03	.02	.09	.10	.04	.04
Professional age	.02[a]	.15	.03[a]	.12	.02[a]	.13
Publications	.01[a]	.09	.01[a]	.09	.01[a]	.13
Citations	—[b]	—[b]	.00	.00	-.00	.00
Total R/R^2	.56/.32		.59/.35		.57/.33	
F	10.30		10.61		9.16	
Significance	.001		.001		.001	

[a] Regression coefficient is more than twice its standard error.
[b] Program eliminated variable from further consideration because of no impact.

of importance at that step. As expected, publications in each case was entered first in the regression equation. In the stepwise regression for biology, publications explained 21 percent out of the total 32 percent, and professional age next explained an additional 4 percent. For chemistry, publications explained 27 percent out of the total 35 percent, and professional age then explained 5 percent more. For physics, publications explained 26 percent out of the total 33 percent, and then professional age explained an additional 4 percent.

What the data in Table 11 show is that, when given an opportunity to explain any variation they can before the powerful variables are entered, those variables entered before professional age and publications explain very little of the variation in awards. The largest deviation from a virtually completely universalistic system occurs in chemistry, where prestige of current affiliation, entered before publications and professional age, explains 10 percent of the variation in awards. Nevertheless prestige of current affiliation is entered fourth in a stepwise regression equation, after publications, professional age, and citations, and then it explains only 0.6 percent of the variation in awards.

For scientists to have their work cited, it must have some visibility to other scientists in the appropriate community. If a scientist refers to another's work, which gives the other a citation, and this is done without consideration of where the other is located—"who" that scientist is, in other words—then it follows that the number of publications scientists have accumulated over a career should be strongly related to the number of citations they receive in any given year.

Scientists in this study, grouped by discipline, have just this type of strong relationship between publications and citations (see Table 12). The variables used show that number of career publications explains more of the variation in citations than any other variable considered in spite of its being entered at step seven of the analysis. In a stepwise regression publications is entered first and explains 56 out of 64 percent for biology, 71 out of 79 percent for chemistry, and 69 out of 71 percent for physics.

If there is any idea that having received awards prior to 1972 makes scientists more visible and therefore more likely to be cited in 1972, these data categorically negate it. Entered last in the regression, awards explains none of the variation in citations received. In three separate stepwise regressions biology does not enter awards at all in the equation, chemistry enters awards seventh when it explains no variation, and physics enters number of awards seventh also when it also explains none of the variation.

Which discipline appears to be the most universalistic when one is

TABLE 12 REGRESSION ANALYSIS ON CITATIONS FOR THREE DISCIPLINES

Independent Variables	Biology		Chemistry		Physics	
	Regression Coefficient	R^2 Change	Regression Coefficient	R^2 Change	Regression Coefficient	R^2 Change
Sex status	4.36	.01	-5.49	.01	-2.34	.00
Prestige of BA institution	-1.31	.00	.35	.02	-0.20[a]	.02
Predoctoral publications	-1.81	.03	-1.45	.07	-0.39	.02
Predoctoral citations	2.54[a]	.02	4.17[a]	.02	.73	.00
Prestige PhD department/institution	.03	.02	.84	.02	2.57[a]	.02
Prestige of current affiliation	1.55	.07	4.16[a]	.26	.43	.05
Professional age	-0.57[a]	.01	-0.60[a]	.00	-0.17	.05
Publications	1.09[a]	.49	.88[a]	.39	1.07[a]	.54
Awards	—[b]	—[b]	1.03	.00	-0.78	.00
Total R/R^2	.80/.64		.89/.79		.84/.71	
F	40.23		73.92		45.88	
Significance	.001		.001		.001	

[a] Regression coefficient is more than twice its standard error.
[b] Program eliminated variable from further consideration because of no impact.

93

looking at citations as a form of recognition? If the stepwise regression is used, the question may be answered by looking at the particularistic variables to see what they explain after publications has explained all it can. The most popular variables to examine are prestige of doctoral institution and prestige of current affiliation. Those two variables combined explain 0.5 percent for biology (doctoral institution is not entered in the regression, however), 2.5 percent for chemistry, and 1.0 percent for physics. Clearly these figures show that universalism exists, but they do not provide an unambiguous ranking. Biology is the most universalistic, but chemistry is not between biology and physics, as would be expected in a positive or negative linear relationship between cognitive development and universalism.

If we look to Table 12 to answer the question of which discipline is most universalistic in allocating recognition through citations, one method is to examine the amount of variation prestige of doctoral institution and prestige of current affiliation explain before publications is entered. In that approach biology has 9 percent, chemistry 28 percent, and physics 7 percent. Again this does not rank the disciplines unambiguously in a linear relationship, positive or negative, between cognitive development and universalism. Another method for the data in Table 12 is to examine the amount of variation explained by publications after the other variables have explained all they can. That shows chemistry to be the lowest in universalism, biology next, and physics highest, but this again is not the order predicted.

In Chapter 5 I showed that entering performance variables as a set in a regression analysis and then entering ascriptive variables produced a result that did not obtain for entering the sets of variables in the reverse order. This procedure provides a comparison between the relative effect of performance and ascriptive influences. The same type of analysis used in comparing British and American scientists is possible for the three disciplines (see Table 13).

Consider first recognition indicated by awards. The amount of total variation explained for awards is 32 percent for biologists, 35 percent for chemists, and 33 percent for physicists. This ordering is different from the predicted order if *total* variation explained is used to determine the degree of universalism. The ranking of disciplines, when only variation explained by performance variables is used, turns out to be biology, physics, and chemistry, but the differences among them are extremely small.

When I used this method to decide whether British or American science was more universalistic, I relied on the proportion of percentage of the variation explained by performance compared to the total

TABLE 13 REGRESSION OF PERFORMANCE AND ASCRIPTIVE VARIABLES ON AWARDS AND CITATIONS

Dependent Variable	Independent Variables Entered First	Biology % Explained/Total = % of Total	Chemistry % Explained/Total = % of Total	Physics % Explained/Total = % of Total
Awards	Performance[a]	23/32 = 72	28/35 = 80	26/33 = 79
	Ascriptive[b]	15/32 = 47	24/35 = 69	16/33 = 48
Citations	Performance[c]	59/64 = 92	74/79 = 94	70/71 = 99
	Ascriptive[d]	18/64 = 28	43/79 = 54	23/71 = 32

[a] Performance variables: predoctoral publications, postdoctoral publications, citations to predoctoral publications, citations to postdoctoral publications.

[b] Ascriptive variables: sex status, professional age, prestige of current affiliation, prestige of PhD department/institution, prestige of BA institution.

[c] Performance variables: predoctoral publications, postdoctoral publications, citations to predoctoral publications (excluded from total citations).

[d] Ascriptive variables: all in note b plus awards.

percentage explained. Using that decision criterion, I concluded that American science is slightly more universalistic. The results for these three disciplines are mixed but in almost the predicted order. For recognition through awards the pattern goes from biology to physics and then chemistry. For citations as recognition the ordering is precisely that predicted based on cognitive development: Biology is the least universalistic, chemistry is next, and physics is most universalistic.

As scientific communities these three disciplines show that cognitive development affects the operation of the reward system, at least to the extent that disciplines are not exactly alike. The data on the scientists grouped by nation (Chapter 5) suggested that the degree of centralization affects the reward system, although the direction of that effect was different from what I predicted.

It is clear that aggregating the scientists according to nationality or to discipline creates different patterns. These 600 scientists are, in fact, representatives of six different scientific communities. While I am not suggesting that it is inappropriate to examine scientists aggregated in groups in some instances, it can result in misconceptions that scientists are all alike and can be lumped together. Theoretical considerations suggest that different disciplines and specialties have unique characteristics. I consider now the 600 scientists in their disciplinary and nationality groups comprising 100 scientists each.

THE REWARD SYSTEM BY COUNTRY AND DISCIPLINE

Previous research and writings suggest that the degree of cognitive development and the degree of centralization are positively related to the operation of the reward system. On the basis of the ideas about codification and centralization it is impossible to predict how the six groups should rank on a scale of universalism. It is possible, on the one hand, that all American groups are less universalistic than all British groups. That would mean that social organization (centralization) is a stronger influence than codification. On the other hand, if both physics groups are more universalistic than biology groups, then codification is more powerful than social organization. Any other pattern than these means there is interaction between cognitive development and social organization in the operation of the reward system.

Previously I discussed the reward system by presenting data with increasing sophistication in their analysis. The tables became problematic quickly because of empty cells, and cross-tabulations within six groups each involving 100 scientists present serious problems. I am tempted, therefore, to omit presentation of gamma coefficents and the zero-order correlation coefficients, but because this study proposes to present a critical test of the reward system, I shall not omit data that other scholars might wish to use in their research or to evaluate my conclusions.

The first step is to examine the gamma correlations for tables constructed by cross-tabulating awards and publications, controlling within categories of prestige of current affiliation (see Table 14). Most of the coefficients are large, but they vary considerably because the number of cases in the tables becomes quite small and erratic. Among British scientists the pattern that arises shows consistently high correlations at the extreme categories of prestige but mixed correlations in the middle three categories. Earlier I suggested that, for biology at least, scientists at high- and low-prestige institutions may be known to be doing excellent or ordinary work respectively. Uncertainty exists at the middle ranges. Among American scientists there is not a similar pattern, and the only pattern imaginable is that, as one goes up the prestige ladder, the correlations tend to be higher. If it were not for the .25 correlation in the next to highest category for chemists, that description would seem perfect. Why this is the case is not obvious, except one could hypothesize that uncertainty about the quality of work simply corres-

TABLE 14   GAMMA CORRELATION COEFFICIENTS BETWEEN
PUBLICATIONS AND AWARDS, FOR CATEGORIES OF
PRESTIGE OF CURRENT AFFILIATION

Country and Discipline	Prestige Categories				
	0 (low)	1	2	3	4 (high)
British					
Biology	0.00[a]	−.10	.12	.39	1.00
Chemistry	1.00	1.00	.89	1.00	1.00
Physics	1.00	−[b]	.84	.42	1.00
American					
Biology	.70	1.00[c]	.68	.75	1.00
Chemistry	.85	−[b]	1.00	.25	1.00
Physics	.66	−[b]	.78	1.00	.86

[a] Only one scientist (out of five in table) in "wrong" cell, produced this gamma.
[b] Only one row in table.
[c] Only one scientist in "correct" cell produced perfect correlation.

ponds to the level in the prestige ranking. I am not proposing that as
the explanation, because gamma coefficients are unstable bases for
such conclusions.

The next strategy looks only at a few important zero-order and partial correlations (see Table 15). The relationship between publications
and awards is remarkably similar for the six groups with the possible
exception of British biologists, whose correlation is about half that of
the other groups. American biologists have the highest correlation, and
this suggests immediately that there is some interaction between social
organization (centralization) and cognitive development.

The correlations between citations and publications are much more
consistent among the six groups, ranging from a low of .70 to a high of
.88, and so the earlier correlations on aggregated data have not been
reduced by looking within these six communities. Of considerable interest are the zero-order correlations between publications and awards
and citations and awards. These indicate that only for American physicists is *quality* of research (with citations as the indicator of quality)
more important for awards than *quantity* of research is. Cole and Cole

TABLE 15   CORRELATION MATRICES FOR COUNTRY AND DISCIPLINE
(DECIMALS OMITTED)[a]

Variables	British											
	Biology				Chemistry				Physics			
	1	2	3	4	1	2	3	4	1	2	3	4
1	—	—	—	—	—	—	—	—	—	—	—	—
2	05	—	—	—	42	—	—	—	22	—	—	—
3	04	30	—	—	28	55	—	—	21	55	—	—
4	13	80	18	—	52	82	49	—	24	88	39	—

Partial
correlations

$r_{23.1} =$	.30	.50	.53
$r_{13.2} =$	.03	.06	.11
$r_{24.1} =$	.80	.78	.87
$r_{14.2} =$	.15	.34	.10

[a]Variable 1 is prestige of current affiliation; variable 2 is publications; variable 3

(1967:385) also found this for a sample of American physicists. For all the five other groups, quantity of research output is more important for awards than quality is (measured by citations).

For a first attempt at ranking these groups, take the value of the partial correlations involving the relationships between prestige of current affiliation and awards, controlling for publications ($r_{13 \cdot 2}$). This shows the effect of prestige on awards after the quantitative performance of scientists is controlled for. The largest partial correlation is among American physicists and the least is among American biologists. The British partial correlations are very small; none explains more than 1 percent of the variation in awards.

For partial correlations between prestige of current affiliation and citations, publications being controlled for ($r_{14 \cdot 2}$), two groups of British scientists are among the top three with highest partial correlations. That contrasts to one British group among the highest three partial correlations for *awards*. These partial correlations, which show effects of prestige, do not provide a basis for ranking the six communities on universalistic tendencies. All six groups show remarkable univer-

				American							
Biology				*Chemistry*				*Physics*			
1	2	3	4	1	2	3	4	1	2	3	4
—	—	—	—	—	—	—	—	—	—	—	—
47	—	—	—	57	—	—	—	34	—	—	—
29	60	—	—	42	53	—	—	32	48	—	—
37	70	45	—	57	84	45	—	31	77	50	—
	.55				.39				.42		
	.01				.17				.19		
	.64				.76				.74		
	.07				.20				.08		

is awards; variable 4 is citations.

salism, but additional variables are also important. Only in British chemistry, however, does prestige of current affiliation explain more than 10 percent of the variation in either of the recognition measures.

Every way of examining the data to this point has been directed ultimately toward comparing the six groups to determine how they rank as a universalistic community in the operation of the reward system. I turn now to each of these scientific communities to see what determines the allocation of recognition, through both receipt of honorific awards and having one's career publications cited in 1972.

Recognition in the Six Communities: Awards

If anyone ever doubted that disciplinary communities are different, then the data on these scientists should remove that doubt. I focus on a simple question: What are the variables that predict (or explain) the number of awards a scientist has received? There are, of course, influences on the receipt of awards that I have not measured. For instance, it is possible that certain specialties or research problem areas have been more favored with awards than others. Awards are subject to the limitations of the 41st chair phenomenon I discussed earlier, and so it is not surprising if it is impossible to explain completely the receipt of awards. To show that universalism is important in the allocation of awards, it is not necessary to explain all the differences in the distribution of awards; it is necessary only to *eliminate* the possibility that commonly noted ascriptive factors such as sex, race, religion, and social prestige are not important. I have no measures for race or religion, but there are no studies suggesting that either race or religion is a major influence on the operation of the reward system (see Cole and Cole, 1973:123–160). There are, no doubt, untested suspicions about this. Look first at British biologists (see Table 16). With the variables entered in this order, professional age is the strongest variable in explaining awards. The same pattern exists for British chemists, for whom almost twice as much variation in awards is explained by professional age. And among physicists still more variation in awards is explained by professional age. In all instances publications explains very little of the variation in awards when professional age has been permitted to explain all it can before publications is entered in the equation.

The impact of publications is not changed by looking at the data with stepwise regression, which was not the case when the disciplines were described. For biologists professional age is entered first, explaining 13 percent, and publications is entered second, explaining 4.0 percent. For chemists, in contrast, publications is entered first, explaining 30

TABLE 16 REGRESSION ANALYSIS ON AWARDS FOR BRITISH SCIENTISTS

Independent Variables	Biology		Chemistry		Physics	
	Regression Coefficient	R^2 Change	Regression Coefficient	R^2 Change	Regression Coefficient	R^2 Change
Sex status	.57	.02	-1.13	.00	-.02	.00
Prestige of BA institution	-.03	.00	.14	.07	.09	.02
Predoctoral publications	.05	.01	-0.06	.03	.04	.01
Predoctoral citations	.00	.00	$.18^a$	.01	-.03	.02
Prestige PhD department/institution	.02	.01	-0.13	.00	.01	.01
Prestige of current affiliation	.00	.00	-0.07	.03	.07	.03
Professional age	$.03^a$	.14	$.05^a$	.27	$.05^a$	.35
Publications	.01	.04	.00	.05	$.02^a$	.03
Citations	-.00	.00	.01	.01	-.01	.02
Total R/R^2	.46/.22		.68/.47		.70/.49	
F	2.41		8.05		8.07	
Significance	.05		.001		.001	

[a] Regression coefficient is more than twice its standard error.

percent of the variation in awards, and then professional age is entered, explaining only 7 percent (contrasted with the 27 percent shown in Table 16). For physicists, who in this case are similar to biologists, professional age is entered first, explaining 37 percent, and publications is entered second, explaining 6 percent.

It should be no surprise that professional age is important in the distribution of awards in Britain. I mentioned this aspect of the reward system when discussing the study by Blume and Sinclair (1973) and when pointing out that *honorific* awards are different from other measures of recognition. Honorific awards do not—partly because they cannot—go to the deserving scientist as an immediate feedback process as other kinds of more flexible and informal types of recognition can. Let us not, however, lose sight of the problem of particularism; recall that, in both Table 16 and the data on stepwise regression (not shown), little variation is explained in addition to publications and professional age. Only for chemistry is there any strong suggestion of particularism operating, the prestige of BA institution. But chemistry's stepwise regression showed it to be the only one of the three groups in which publications entered the equation first as having the strongest impact on awards. In that equation prestige of BA institution entered sixth and explained only 0.8 percent of the variation in awards. For awards, therefore, British chemistry is more universalistic than either biology or physics. Is this true for American scientists as well?

The data in Table 17 indicate that only for American biology is professional age, entered prior to publications, more important in explaining awards. Some particularistic variables, entered before publications and professional age, suggest that the reward system in these three disciplines in the United States may be operating less universalistically than they appeared to be when grouped with their British colleagues.

The stepwise regression provides another view of these American disciplines: Biology has 36 percent of the 47 percent total variation explained by publications, the first entry in the equation; chemistry has 28 percent of the 36 percent total, also the first entry in the equation; but physics has only 2 percent of the total 30 percent explained by publications, which is entered third in the equation. The first variable entered is citations, explaining 25 percent of the total 30 percent. (In Table 17, citations is able to explain 3 percent, even after being entered ninth in the equation.) The second variable entered is prestige of current affiliation, which explains only 3 percent but is nevertheless more important at that stage than publications.

It is clear that the British and American groups differ. For allocation of awards in Britain the most important variable is professional age in a

TABLE 17 REGRESSION ANALYSIS ON AWARDS FOR AMERICAN SCIENTISTS

Independent Variables	Biology		Chemistry		Physics	
	Regression Coefficient	R^2 Change	Regression Coefficient	R^2 Change	Regression Coefficient	R^2 Change
Sex status	.39	.00	.10	.00	-.19	.00
Prestige of BA institution	-.01	.00	-.06	.01	-.01	.02
Predoctoral publications	.20[a]	.04	-.13	.01	.01	.01
Predoctoral citations	-.11	.02	-.05	.00	-.00	.00
Prestige PhD department/institution	.01	.02	-.09	.02	.02	.05
Prestige of current affiliation	.03	.07	.16	.16	.04	.05
Professional age	.02[a]	.18	.02	.04	.00	.01
Publications	.01[a]	.12	.02[a]	.11	.00	.14
Citations	.01	.01	.00	.00	.00	.03
Total R/R^2	.68/.47		.60/.36		.55/.30	
F	8.53		5.51		4.13	
Significance	.001		.001		.001	

[a] Regression coefficient is more than twice its standard error.

sequential ordering of the variables (Table 16), and the same results, except for chemistry, obtained in the stepwise regression. Publications in the stepwise regression was the most important. For allocation of awards in the American disciplines professional age was the most important for biology, publications was the most important for physics, but prestige of current affiliation was the most important for chemistry—according to the data in Table 17. In the stepwise regression biology and chemistry showed publications to be the most important, while physics showed citations to be the most important. In none of these methods did professional age prove to be the most important. But with awards only, it is not possible to rank the six groups on a universalism scale. I defer any attempt toward that until the citations variable is examined.

Recognition in the Six Communities: Citations

The important question is to what extent citations in 1972 to career publications was influenced by particularistic criteria. For British scientists publications is the largest influence on citations. Professional age is least important for biology, but awards is a factor in physics, according to the regression ordering the variables chronologically (see Table 18). The stepwise regression does not alter that pattern very much. For all three disciplines the first variable entered is publications, explaining 66 out of the total 74 percent for biology, 67 out of the total 79 percent for chemistry, and 78 out of the total 82 percent for physics. For biology and physics the second variable entered is predoctoral citations, a measure of the quality of the research early in one's career, and it explains an additional 5 and 2 percent respectively. For chemistry the second variable entered is prestige of current affiliation, which explains an additional 4 percent. These data suggest a pattern in British disciplines that chemistry is not as universalistic as the other two disciplines.

For American disciplines, publications is also the strongest influence on citations (see Table 19). Except for physics, prestige of current affiliation appears to be important also, but publications explains a very large percentage even after these other variables have been able to explain all they can. Awards, entered last, still explains some variation for biology and physics. The stepwise regression shows this same pattern for American disciplines, with publications entered first in all cases. The percentages increase from those shown in Table 19 to 47 out of the total 55 percent for biology, 71 out of the total 78 percent for chemistry, and 59 out of the total 59 percent for physics. The second variable entered is, respectively, professional age (4 percent), predoctoral citations (4 percent) and awards (2 percent).

TABLE 18 REGRESSION ANALYSIS ON CITATIONS FOR BRITISH SCIENTISTS

Independent Variables	Biology		Chemistry		Physics	
	Regression Coefficient	R^2 Change	Regression Coefficient	R^2 Change	Regression Coefficient	R^2 Change
Sex status	2.10	.01	-24.15	.01	.35	.02
Prestige of BA institution	.44	.00	1.00	.09	.99	.05
Predoctoral publications	-0.71	.03	- 3.67[a]	.04	-0.43	.05
Predoctoral citations	2.42[a]	.04	4.28[a]	.00	1.62	.00
Prestige PhD department/institution	-0.77	.01	.44	.00	1.47	.04
Prestige of current affiliation	2.92	.02	6.13[a]	.18	1.51	.00
Professional age	-0.58[a]	.02	- 1.00[a]	.04	-0.11	.17
Publications	1.25[a]	.62	.92[a]	.42	1.16[a]	.47
Awards	-0.83	.00	2.49	.00	-4.42	.01
Total R/R^2	.86/.74		.89/.79		.91/.82	
F	25.37		35.33		38.62	
Significance	.001		.001		.001	

[a]Regression coefficient is more than twice its standard error.

105

TABLE 19 REGRESSION ANALYSIS ON CITATIONS FOR AMERICAN SCIENTISTS

Independent Variables	Biology		Chemistry		Physics	
	Regression Coefficient	R^2 Change	Regression Coefficient	R^2 Change	Regression Coefficient	R^2 Change
Sex status	5.11	.01	2.11	.01	1.57	.00
Prestige of BA institution	−1.21	.00	−0.07	.06	−0.61	.03
Predoctoral publications	−2.39	.05	1.25	.02	−0.87	.01
Predoctoral citations	2.17	.01	5.29[a]	.05	.06	.00
Prestige PhD department/institution	−0.02	.01	.18	.05	2.56	.05
Prestige of current affiliation	.52	.12	2.78	.22	.18	.04
Professional age	−0.61[a]	.00	−0.35	.00	−0.22	.00
Publications	.88[a]	.34	.91[a]	.36	.92[a]	.47
Awards	3.70	.01	.78	.00	11.93	.02
Total R/R^2	.74/.55		.88/.78		.79/.62	
F	11.75		34.16		15.44	
Significance	.001		.001		.001	

[a]Regression coefficient is more than twice its standard error.

It is no simple matter to rank these six groups on a universalism scale, primarily because all six groups show strong adherence to universalism norms in the allocation of recognition. I turn now to the final strategy in this process, which separates performance and ascriptive variables, to see their relative effect on the reward system.

Social Organization and Codification in Six Groups

In this section I deal with the effect of social organization and codification of knowledge on the operation of the reward system. The six groups should be compared for relative universalism in the allocation of recognition, including awards and citations to published work. By dividing performance and ascriptive variables into two sets, and regressing these sets of variables separately on awards and citations, the groups can be compared. The total amount of variance explained is the same, whether performance variables or ascriptive variables are entered first. The strategy is to see how much more variation is explained by introducing the second set of variables, after the first set has explained all the variation it can (see Table 20). This strategy would ideally rank the six groups in terms of how universalistic their reward systems are, but unfortunately, no unambiguous ranking occurs.

The pattern for awards is different from that for citations. This problem was, of course, encountered in previous instances when this procedure was used. From the previous discussion about the different patterns for awards and citations—the fact that different independent variables explain more of the variation in one than the other—it is necessary at this point to separate discussion of universalism in the six groups into (1) universalism and awards and (2) universalism and citations.

Any arbitrary decision criterion to differentiate these groups would be subject to severe criticism. Other scholars may wish to assess universalism according to procedures that will appear more appropriate to them. It is tempting to try to find a procedure that results in rank ordering the groups according to the predictions discussed earlier. Even if I could do that, it would be difficult to justify on intuitive grounds. What is desirable is a formula that would array the groups onto a continuum and one that would be simple enough to define. The formula that seems most suited is this:

$$\frac{P-A}{T} = universalism \; statistic$$

where P equals performance, A equals ascriptive, and T equals total. Take the percentage of variation explained when performance variables are entered first in the regression, subtract the amount explained

TABLE 20   REGRESSION OF PERFORMANCE AND ASCRIPTIVE VARIABLES ON AWARDS AND CITATIONS

Country	Dependent Variable	Independent Variables Entered First	Biology % Explained/Total = % of Total	Chemistry % Explained/Total = % of Total	Physics % Explained/Total = % of Total
British	Awards	Performance[a]	11/22 = 50	34/47 = 72	34/49 = 69
		Ascriptive[b]	16/22 = 73	35/47 = 74	42/49 = 86
	Citations	Performance[c]	71/74 = 96	71/79 = 90	80/82 = 98
		Ascriptive[d]	9/74 = 12	42/79 = 53	31/82 = 38
American	Awards	Performance[a]	38/47 = 81	31/36 = 86	27/30 = 90
		Ascriptive[b]	18/47 = 38	23/36 = 64	13/30 = 43
	Citations	Performance[c]	48/55 = 87	76/78 = 97	59/62 = 95
		Ascriptive[d]	29/55 = 53	43/78 = 55	29/62 = 47

[a] Performance variables: predoctoral publications, postdoctoral publications, citations to predoctoral publications, citations to postdoctoral publications.

[b] Ascriptive variables: sex status, professional age, prestige of current affiliation, prestige of PhD department/institution, prestige of BA institution.

[c] Performance variables: predoctoral publications, postdoctoral publications, citations to predoctoral publications (excluded from total citations).

[d] Ascriptive variables: all in note *b* plus awards.

when ascriptive variables are entered first, and then divide that figure by the total percentage explained. The computed values range from −1.00 to 1.00. A −1.00 indicates that the performance variables explain zero while the ascriptive variables explain, and are equal to, the total. Conversely a 1.00 indicates that the performance variables explain, and are equal to, the total, while ascriptive variables add nothing to the explanation. Any minus statistic indicates that particularism is initially strong, while any positive statistic indicates that universalism is initially strong. A statistic equal to 0.0 indicates equivalency between the percentage of variation explained when each set of variables is introduced first into the equation.

Consider these statistics first for awards (see Table 21). In American disciplines universalistic variables are much stronger, relative to ascriptive variables, than they are in Britain. Indeed ascriptive variables in Britain explain more variation when entered first than performance variables do when entered first. (The universalism statistic for British scientists as a group, discussed in Chapter 5, Table 8, is −.08 and, for Americans, 0.35.) These figures should not lead one to conclude that particularism is rampant in the allocation of awards in Britain, because the most important ascriptive factor is professional age, a problem I discuss later.

The rankings, shown in the column next to awards, show the order of the disciplinary groups to be different from what I expected. (Another way to compare groups is to look at the ratio of performance to ascriptive variables, and in Table 21 the rankings would be identi-

TABLE 21   UNIVERSALISM STATISTICS[a] FOR AWARDS
IN EACH DISCIPLINARY GROUP

Country	Discipline	Statistic	Rank
British	Biology	(11−16)/22 = −.23	6
	Chemistry	(34−35)/47 = −.02	4
	Physics	(34−42)/49 = −.16	5
American	Biology	(38−18)/47 = .42	2
	Chemistry	(31−23)/36 = .22	3
	Physics	(27−13)/30 = .47	1

[a] Universalism statistic = percentage of variance explained by performance variables entered first minus percentage explained by ascriptive variables entered first divided by total variation explained by both.

cal.) It was not possible to predict in advance how the rankings would turn out for all six groups. The presumption was that British physics would be the most universalistic because there would be more universalism in Britain and more universalism in physics. At the other end of the spectrum American biology would be the least universalistic, the other four groups possibly overlapping to some extent. Within countries the ranking should have been from physics to chemistry to biology. The American disciplines capture the first three of the six ranks, but not in the order predicted. In the British disciplines chemistry and physics are in reverse order.

If cognitive development of the disciplines strongly influences the extent of universalism, one conclusion is that the ranking of disciplines on a "cognitive development" scale is obviously incorrect. If the rankings were similar in each country, even if different from the order predicted, then there would be strong evidence that the expected ranking of biology, chemistry, and physics was unjustified. But because the ranking within countries is different and because there is a general consensus about the level of cognitive development of these three disciplines, the conclusion must be that something in addition to cognitive development is influencing the results. If American chemistry is less universalistic than American biology, but chemistry has more cognitive development, then some other influence must account for this. Before possible explanations are discussed, consider a second way of looking at universalism in the distribution of awards.

Professional age is important in the allocation of awards. Following standard sociological practice, I have used professional age as an ascriptive variable in looking at the six disciplinary groups in Britain and the United States. In spite of debates on the question of age and productivity, present in the literature over a long period, little attention has been focused on the question of age and recognition. Zuckerman and Merton (1973a) are exceptions to the general neglect of age and aging in science, although they devoted only a few paragraphs to the subject in their review, a consequence more of the lack of previous work that could be reviewed than of their lack of interest in the subject.

Is age an ascriptive variable in the sociology of science? My view is that in some circumstances age may be, but it may not be ascriptive in others. A simplistic view is that age is an ascriptive variable only if it is considered without any other evaluation of the merits of the situation. For example, suppose an older and a younger scientist both apply to a funding agency for research support. If the older scientist has accomplished very little over a career but nevertheless is the successful one because the decision is made on the basis of age alone, then age is an ascriptive factor in that case.

If professional age is removed from the set of ascriptive variables and entered by itself as a third step, after ascriptive and performance variables have explained all the variation in awards they can, professional age still has an effect in most groups. In British groups it is 6.6 percent for biology, 10.3 percent for chemistry, and 12.3 percent for physics. For American groups it is 6.6 percent in biology, 2.1 percent for chemistry, and 0.2 percent for physics. If I compute the same universalism statistic for these groups, on the basis of the smaller total of explained variation (using the total variation explained before professional age is entered), the results (see Table 22) are different. For British disciplines the ranking turns out to be the same as for cognitive development. Physics is the most universalistic, biology is the least, and chemistry is in the middle.

American disciplines do not have the pattern of the British. Biology is the American group most affected by professional age, and professional age being excluded, it turns out that biology is the most universalistic, followed by physics and then chemistry. Biology is relatively unaffected by other ascriptive variables, such as prestige of current affiliation. This is shown in Tables 21 and 22, where the amount of variation explained by ascriptive variables drops from 16 percent to only 3 percent after professional age is removed from the equation. With universalism based on awards, cognitive development correlates strongly with universalism in Britain, and it would in the United States if it were not for the anomalous case of biology.

I can summarize briefly the distribution of awards among these six groups of scientists. With professional age included as an ascriptive var-

TABLE 22   UNIVERSALISM STATISTICS[a] FOR AWARDS IN
EACH DISCIPLINARY GROUP WITH PROFESSIONAL AGE
REMOVED FROM THE ASCRIPTIVE VARIABLES

Country	Discipline	Statistic	Rank
British	Biology	$(11 - 3)/15 = .53$	4
	Chemistry	$(34 - 11)/37 = .62$	3
	Physics	$(34 - 6)/37 = .76$	1
American	Biology	$(38 - 9)/40 = .73$	2
	Chemistry	$(31 - 18)/34 = .38$	6
	Physics	$(27 - 13)/30 = .47$	5

[a] Universalism statistic = percentage of variance explained by performance variables entered first minus percentage explained by ascriptive variables entered first divided by total variation explained by both.

iable, American scientific communities are clearly more universalistic. All three British groups have negative universalism statistics. Excluding professional age from the total variation explained and considering only the other variation explained by ascriptive and performance variables result in British disciplines' capturing three out of the first four ranks. Clearly professional age (or age, which is highly correlated with professional age) is more important in Britain than in the United States. This is partly because there are fewer awards for scientific productivity in Britain. The rate of scientific productivity for each year of professional age, divided by the average number of awards is .195 for British scientists, while the same figure is .265 for American scientists. There are more awards available in the United States for similar productivity. With this situation scientists in Britain have to wait longer to receive awards than their American colleagues. In addition to merit, based on scientific productivity, scientists in Britain have to be old to receive awards. Age is not a sufficient condition but it is a necessary condition.

When professional age is not considered as an ascriptive variable, as in Table 22, the British disciplines have higher universalism scores than their American colleagues. The average of these scores for British scientists is .64, but for American scientists the average is .53. Professional age is not really an important ascriptive variable when awards are considered. There is no reason to believe that allocating awards after a scientist has spent considerable years in a career is detrimental to the morale or is indicative of particularism, certainly as long as the ultimate allocation is not based on criteria such as where the scientist took undergraduate and research training or where the scientist is currently located in the institutional pecking order.

On the assumption for the moment that my arguments vindicate professional age as a criterion for partially determining who shall receive awards, then it is possible to see that the social organization of science, that is, whether it is centralized or decentralized, appears to influence the relative amount of universalism. British science is slightly more universalistic because not only is the average of all universalism statistics higher in Britain, but also three of the first four ranks are held by British disciplines.

Before final assessments are made about the relationship between universalism, cognitive development, and social organization, it is necessary to consider the influence of ascriptive and performance variables on citations (see Table 23). Citations are a better test of universalism than awards because citations are not limited in number the way honorific awards are. Conceivably everyone's work can be referred to

TABLE 23 *UNIVERSALISM STATISTICS^a FOR CITATIONS IN EACH DISCIPLINARY GROUP*

Country	Discipline	Statistic	Rank
British	Biology	(71– 9)/74 = .84	1
	Chemistry	(71–42)/79 = .37	5
	Physics	(80–31)/82 = .60	2
American	Biology	(48–29)/55 = .35	6
	Chemistry	(76–43)/78 = .42	4
	Physics	(59–29)/62 = .48	3

^{a}Universalism statistic = percentage of variance explained by performance variables entered first minus percentage explained by ascriptive variables entered first divided by total variation explained by both.

with some frequency, even that of the youngest scientists, who have insufficient years spent in a career and who may, therefore, be virtually ineligible to receive honorific awards.

The universalism statistics within countries should be considered first. In American disciplines the rank order is precisely the predicted order. In British disciplines biology is first, not physics, and chemistry is third. With universalism based on citations, cognitive development correlates strongly with universalism in the United States, and it would in Britain if it were not for the anomalous case of biology.

I computed the universalism statistic for citations by omitting professional age, but only in British physics and American biology does professional age have any influence. (Stephen Cole, 1970, suggests that the rate of diffusion of scientists' work is not affected by age, and diffusion is measured, as recognition is here, by citations.) While the universalism statistics increased a few points for these two groups, the overall ranking, and the within-country ranking did not change.

By this time the data and interpretations have become complex, and so a combined summary of awards and citations should simplify the situation. Ranking can cause the reader to perceive the differences between groups to be equivalent to the differences in ranking, but the differences are not nearly so equivalent. One way to summarize the ranking of groups is to take several possible measures of universalism, rank all groups on each measure, and then finally get an average ranking (which can then be ranked). On the one hand this removes dependence on one or two measures, but on the other hand it assumes all measures are equally important. I ranked (1) percentage of variation in awards explained by performance variables only, (2) percentage of variation in awards explained by ascriptive variables only (including professional age), (3) universalism statistics for awards (including professional age), and (4) universalism statistics for awards (excluding professional age). To these I added the four similar rankings for citations. (Only the data for the eighth measure are not presented in a table.) The eight combined ranks produced totals, in increasing order of magnitude and consequently decreasing rank order:

British physics	23.5
British biology	24.5
American physics	25.5
American biology	27.0
American chemistry	33.5
British chemistry	34.0

The reader will note quickly that the total of the ranks equals 168 (8 times 21—the total of 1 plus 2 plus 3 and so on through six ranks). The within-country rankings for each country show biology and chemistry in reverse order. Recall earlier that, in the case of the universalism statistics for awards (Table 22), the British groups were aligned according to cognitive development, while biology was anomalous in the United States. In the case of universalism statistics for citations, the American groups were aligned according to cognitive development, but biology was anomalous in Britain. When all these data are combined, biology does not take over the most universalistic position in either country, but chemistry takes the anomalous position of third place in each country.

There are many different ways that these data should have been examined to achieve a ranking. Indeed some readers may wish to rearrange the data by using methods different from mine. It turns out that, regardless of the methods I used, these rankings were the most consistent.

On the assuption that these rankings are valid indications of the relative universalism in each group, there is support for the idea that universalism is related to social organization. The first two ranks are British groups, the next three are American groups, and the last is a British group. In spite of the British chemistry group's being ranked the least universalistic, this does not mean there is much particularism, certainly not to the extent reported by Blume and Sinclair, 1973.)

There is some support also for the contention that universalism is related to cognitive development. In each country physics is the most universalistic, biology is next, and chemistry is third. This similarity suggests that cognitive development is influencing the extent of universalism.

There is also interaction between cognitive development and social organization. While the centralized system captures the first two ranks, the decentralized system captures the next three, and the centralized system captures the last rank. This leaves the questions of why chemistry is less universalistic than biology, and how interaction occurs between cognitive development and social organization. I discuss the former question first.

One possible explanation for why biology is more universalistic than chemistry is that these samples happened by chance to select highly codified specialties in biology but much less codified specialties in chemistry and thereby inadvertently rearranged the order of cognitive development. If specialty identification were known for these scientists, and if there were some consensus about the level of cognitive development of all the specialties in biology and chemistry, then that hypothesis could be tested. Unfortunately no data are readily available to do so.

Another possibility is that measurement error caused these differences. Indeed, because the results were different from what I expected and from what I thought others would expect, I did a variety of checks on the coding, on the keypunching, and on the computer analysis to be certain there were no systematic errors. I believe the results could not be the consequence of measurement errors.

Another possibility is that cognitive development does not enhance the possibility of more universalism in science. In this case physics would appear to be more universalistic only because it just happened to be ranked first. In any ranking, if the groups are not tied, something has to be first. The dimensions of cognitive development, such as agreement on significant problems and consensus on criteria for evaluating results, are not powerful influences—indeed, are not influential at all—in promoting the universalistic allocation of recognition. This would mean that the extent of universalism in a scientific community is not a direct function of the nature of the research but rather depends more on the personal qualities of individual scientists. The extent of universalism would be a function of the socialization process and the individual integrity of scientists. I would have a difficult task to argue that the socialization process in physics and biology is superior to that in chemistry. The first question requiring an answer would be what makes physics and biology superior in conforming to norms in the first place. That would require an infinite search back into history, to trace the founding scientists' influence on subsequent normative behavior of their scientific progeny. That would take also an infinite stretch of the imagination to believe that such effective socialization would survive the ages, without some kind of structural support within science to sustain it. I am not inclined to argue that universalism is prevalent as a function of ethical and conforming individuals. Rather, I see universalism as a function of effective social control enhanced by the scientific discipline or specialty.

All these explanations fail to show why biology would be ranked over chemistry in the universalistic allocation of recognition. I suggest, therefore, a bold, but tentative, hypothesis that would explain the disciplinary ranking within countries: *Chemistry ranks third within each country because the original hierarchy of cognitive development, with physics, chemistry, and biology in that order of development, was incorrect.*

Proposing that biology has a higher level of cognitive development is risky. In the first place it is different from the consensus held by scholars. But evidence for the consensus, much of it described in Chapter 3, is not based on much empirical data. One may ask what data are there, beyond that in this study, that support the possibility that chemistry is less codified than biology. Admittedly the evidence is scattered and unsystematic, but some items can be mentioned.

For *item one,* in Chapter 3, I mentioned Zuckerman and Merton's (1973b) survey of the rejection rates of scientific journals in several fields. Although the study was not comprehensive in breadth or intensive in depth, the results ordered scientific fields along a continuum that intuitively seems correct. I used their results to exemplify the kinds of data that support the notion of the hierarchy of disciplines, but I noted carefully that *chemistry was out of order.* When rejection rates are used to indicate consensus both on importance of problems and criteria pertinent to evaluate the research product, physics has a rejection rate of 24 percent, biological science has 29 percent, and chemistry has 31 percent. If these results reflect reality, then there is less cognitive development in chemistry. Zuckerman and Merton did not, nor would I, propose that journal rejection rates are purely a function of consensus in a field. Indeed Zuckerman and Merton (1973b:474–475) discussed the possibility that available journal space might have some influence on rejection rates. What I am proposing is that their data, ranking chemistry lower than biology, might not require explanation. Rather, what does is why we have assumed so long that chemistry's cognitive development was second to physics.

For *item two* Hagstrom's (1967) survey of American scientists had several questions that provide comparison of these three disciplines.

Hagstrom's data do not prove that chemistry is less cognitively developed than biology, but they show that, on several dimensions, physics and biology are more similar to each other than chemistry is to either. For example, about 46 percent of the chemists collaborate with persons of faculty or equivalent rank, but 66 percent of the physicists and 61 percent of the biologists have such collaboration (Hagstrom, 1967:29). The percentage of scientists engaged in research who said that junior scientists usually or frequently avoid collaboration with senior faculty was 30 percent for chemists, but only 10 percent for physicists and 13 percent for biologists (Hagstrom, 1967:39).

For *item three* Hargens (1971) surveyed scholars in mathematics, chemistry, and political science. Whereas neither physics nor biology was included in the study, and direct comparisons are not possible, some of Hargens' data suggest that cognitive development is not as high in chemistry as one might suspect. For example, scientists were asked about experiencing difficulty in formulating research questions. Of the chemists, 7 percent responded they always had difficulty and only 10 percent of the political scientists responded similarly. At the other extreme 30 percent of the political scientists indicated they never had difficulty, but only 38 percent of the chemists responded similarly (Hargens, 1971:41). Of course, there are real differences between the responses of political scientists and chemists, but the differences are not so great as most of us would have expected.

When asked about the agreement among scientists about the relative importance of research questions, only 3 percent of the chemists and 1 percent of the political scientists responded there was a high degree of agreement. At the other extreme 8 percent of the chemists said there is little agreement on the relative importance of various research (19 percent for political scientists). Furthermore 33 percent of the chemists (and 47 percent of the political scientists) said there was some agreement on a few major questions but *little agreement about the rest* (Hargens, 1971:37). Hargens, (1971:36) asked scientists about the existence of major schools of thought, and 12 percent of the chemists saw no major competing schools of thought involved in their discipline, and a much smaller 1 percent of political scientists responded similarly. The fact that political science shows less cognitive development is not the point here. The existence of considerable disagreement on problems and the prevalence of believing there are schools of thought in chemistry are pertinent.

Hargens also asked whether there was disagreement about the validity of published results in the discipline. Of the chemists 51 percent said there is disagreement often, or almost always, about published results, while political science had a large 83 percent (Hargens, 1971:35). If 51 percent of the chemists believe that often or almost always there is disagreement about the validity of published results, it remains difficult to characterize chemistry as a field in which there is a general consensus not only about the important problems in the field but also about the criteria used to evaluate research results. (On his page 43 Hargens refers to Zuckerman and Merton's data in an early version of the paper reporting journal rejection rates. The later version I referred to, which ranks biology closer to physics, is undoubtedly a more accurate estimate of journal rejection rates.)

For *item four* information published by the National Science Board (NSB) (1973) shows some changes in support of biological research that are much different from the trends in physics and chemistry. These changes do not characterize biology as being similar to physics, but they offer some possible reason why biology during the last 15 years could be more developed than commonly thought. For example, while financial support for chemistry and physics in universities has increased in real (1961) dollars between 1964 and 1972 by approximately 7 percent and 2 percent respectively, the equivalent increase is about 40 percent in biology (NSB, 1973:118). For only federal expenditures in universities, a part of the total just described, the figures for changes between 1964 and 1972 are plus 2 percent for chemistry, minus 9 percent for physics, but a plus 35 percent for biology (NSB, 1973:119).

Probably as a consequence of changing support arrangements, the percentage of PhD academic staff receiving federal support for basic research has decreased 10 percent for physics (from 84 to 74) between 1964 and 1970, 14 percent for chemistry (from 74 to 60), but only 6 percent for biology (from 77 to 71). And approximately the same percentage differences have resulted for the percent of senior PhD academic scientists receiving federal support for basic research (NSB, 1973:121). This information does not prove, of course, that biology is more cognitively developed than chemistry. It does, however, suggest the possibility that changes in the financial support for biological research over the last 15 years may have had considerable impact on its cognitive development. Moreover this information pertains only to American biology, and while comparable data do not exist for British biology, there is little reason to believe that developments in American biology have not been closely paralleled in Britain.

Whatever the eventual disposition of the hypothesis that biology is probably at a higher level of cognitive development than chemistry, there is still the question of the effect of social organization on the reward system. The facts that British groups have the two top ranks on universalism but the third British group (chemistry) occupies the lowest rank indicate that interaction occurs between cognitive development and social organization. Any overlapping in fact between national groups would indicate interaction between these two dimensions.

Because the British groups, for the reasons predicted, showed more universalism than the American groups, no further explanation is required. Why British chemistry ranked last, and lower than American chemistry, appears to require some explanation. The best explanation is that the two groups are so similar as to be virtually identical. In the total of eight rankings used to summarize the universalism measures, recall that American chemists had a total of 33.5 while British chemists had a total of 34.0, and this difference of one-half rank was the smallest difference between any adjoining ranks. In the eight individual rankings the two groups had adjoining ranking, first one group being ranked higher and then the other. This one-half difference only appears precise. The fact is the differences are too close to permit distinguishing between the two groups.

What the ranking of both chemistry groups suggests is that cognitive development is more influential than social organization in determining the operation of the reward system. That is to say, the social organization of research in Britain and the United States does not influence the operation of the reward system nearly so much as the cognitive development of the disciplines in which the reward system operates. The implications of this require much research. In the future, research may determine how and under what conditions this hypothesis is correct.

The question of the effect of cognitive development and social organization has been settled for the data examined in this study. No doubt many questions will be raised as other scholars examine this problem, and the results, in all probability, will be modified as we learn more about the reward system in all kinds of scientific communities and in countries with social organizations much different from Britain and the United States.

In Chapter 7, I address the problem of the allocation of recognition, and the questions connected to the fact that, in spite of the unusual amount of universalism in these scientific communities, there are still scientists whose recognition is not commensurate with their performance. Some appear to gain more recognition than they seem to have earned. Conversely some fail to achieve the recognition they seem to deserve. That leads me to Chapter 8, in which I discuss the differences in scholarly productivity and try to deal with the question of why there always seems to be enormous variation among scientists in the number of research papers they publish.

Chapter 7 / THE MATTHEW AND OTHER
            EFFECTS IN THE ALLOCATION
            OF RECOGNITION

Compared to the reward system in other social institutions, that in science works unusually well. It rewards scientists according to how they perform their role as discoverers and creators of new knowledge, the evidence of such performance being papers published in scientific journals. It operates in a social context in which stratification exists among institutions where scientists are trained and where, subsequently in the same or other institutions, they themselves train another generation of scientists. There are many stages in the research process where the social context could adversely affect the way the reward system operates, but the unwritten norms of science are obviously strong influences ultimately on the allocation of recognition and social status.

Scientific productivity and acknowledgement by the community of that performance are the two most important parts of the reward system. They both vary considerably in any scientific community. Every study I have seen shows that a relatively small percentage of the scientists are responsible for the lion's share of the publications produced, a problem I discuss in Chapter 8 (see also Price, 1963:41–50). An even smaller percentage of the scientists receives the lion's share of recognition.

That scientists receive different amounts of recognition is exemplified in the present study. In the three disciplinary groups, although there is variation between countries, biologists received, on average, .30 award (with a standard deviation of .76); chemists, .48 (S.D. = 1.25); and physicists, .24 (S.D. = .67). For the same three groups, citations being taken as a measure of recognition, biologists received an average of 21.5 citations (S.D. = 26.3); chemists; 35.2 (S.D. = 36.2); and physicists, 26.6 (S.D. = 31.8).

That scientific recognition is distributed in such a highly skewed fashion is not surprising. If productivity is skewed, and if the reward system operates to allocate credit where it is due, then it follows that recognition will be unequally distributed. Explaining the general distribution of recognition is not difficult, because research contributions, more than any other variable, explain the variation of recognition among scientists. The zero-order correlations between scientific productivity and recognition are high in most studies. For example, in this study, for all scientists, the correlation is $r = .51$ for total publications and awards, and .82 for total publications and total citations in 1972. Cole and Cole (1967:385) found that, among elite American physicists, $r = .46$ for number of papers and number of awards. Among British high-energy physicists, I found $r = .69$ for number of papers and a recognition index (Gaston, 1970:724). Among a sample of American biologists, political scientists, and psychologists, Crane (1965:702) found gamma= .48 between the productivity and recognition indices. Finally, among British chemists, Blume and Sinclair (1973:132) found gamma = .66 for the number of papers published in a five-year period and recognition scores.

That the correlations are not perfect means that there are some additional influences (including measurement errors, of course) on the allocation of recognition. The deviation from perfection requires some explanation, and the explanations tend to deal with the groups with either high or low recognition. One explanation for scientists with high recognition is the *Matthew Effect.* The explanation for those with low recognition tends to focus on a process that has not been labeled, and so I shall do so here. It is the *Podunk Effect.* While both of these effects offer some insight into the less-than-perfect distribution of recognition based on merit, I show after the next section that other considerations seem also to be appropriate for dealing with problems of the allocation of recognition.

THE MATTHEW AND PODUNK EFFECTS

The Matthew Effect is an explanation for the differences in recognition among scientists whose contributions are approximately equal (Merton, 1973:443–447). By now this famous "effect" can be quoted by almost anyone, even those who have not read the original text in Matthew (25:29, which is, of course, similar to Matthew 13:12), but it bears repeating: "For unto every one that hath shall be given, and he shall have abundance; but from him that hath not shall be taken away even that which he hath." In modern language it is the observation that those with a lot get more, and those with little have a hard time holding on to what they have.

The Matthew Effect on the reward system works to favor already well-established scientists by causing them to get more recognition from a specific contribution than others would obtain for the same or "equivalent" contribution. Of course, the Matthew Effect has long been observed in other social situations—it has been captured in verse and song—the rich get rich, and the poor have children, is one popular lyric. And it has been acknowledged more than once by people who allude to the fact that it takes money to make money.

In some ways it is unfortunate that the Matthew Effect has been taken as one, if not the best, explanation for differences in scientific recognition. In the first place, although I believe that Merton does not subscribe to this view, the Matthew Effect is invoked to argue that science is probably no more universalistic than other social institutions. This is unfortunate because Merton's observations did not originate with a total scientific community, but rather primarily with Nobel laureates, a very small elite group. Moreover, Merton's original discussion of the Matthew Effect dealt primarily with the dysfunctions of the process for certain individuals, as in the cases of collaborators of unequal social standing or of scientists making independent, simultaneous discoveries. While on the one hand the Matthew Effect might be dysfunctional for individuals, it can be functional for science generally, especially in the communication system, by focusing scientists' attention on work by individuals known to be worth looking at and thus saving needless reading of all possible papers (see Merton, 1973:447–450; Cole and Cole, 1973; Chapter 7).

The Podunk Effect is a hypothesis often alluded to as an explanation for the disadvantage caused by scientists' location in the institutional stratification system. This effect is a consequence of being affiliated with a low-prestige institution, an institution at the periphery, and an undesirable place for a scientist to be. Rothman (1972:103) mentions this as a problem when he reports that, in 1965 for example, only 10 universities received 25 percent of the federal money going to university researchers. He acknowledges that this distribution of funds can be explained partially by the concentration of better scientists at such schools, but nevertheless he believes that institutional affiliation is decisive. "A number of applicants report being rejected because the referees assume that the employing institution does not have the 'appropriate atmosphere' for research, or other non-scientific criteria" (Rothman, 1972:103–104). The significance of this quotation is not only that it conveys incomplete data, but also that Rothman's footnote at the end of the statement refers the reader to Klaw's (1968) book, *The New Brahmins*, where there is reported *one* such instance of an unfunded scientist.

Mulkay (1976:643), in a discussion of the norms of science, also mentions a problem with obtaining recognition when one suffers from the Podunk Effect. Mulkay (1976:643) admits that what is known about the way rewards are distributed substantiates the importance of universalism, because

> the quality of the information furnished by accredited members of the scientific community appears to be judged by criteria which are largely independent of such particularistic factors as social class, educational background, and so on. But even this modest argument is subject to considerable limitation. In the first place, the distribution of recognition *is* noticeably biased in favour of those at elite universities, irrespective of their work [his italics].

The significance of this quotation is twofold. In the first place it is not clear that the general statement—recognition is biased in favor of elite universities—is accurate. In the second place, for his evidence, Mulkay refers in a footnote at the end of this quotation to the study by Blume and Sinclair (1973), which I have discussed earlier and have rather conclusively shown to be extremely problematical. Suffice it to say that, if Mulkay's statement is accurate, the study he refers to does not support it unambiguously.

In a group of scientists it is difficult to locate those who have benefited from the Matthew Effect. By most procedures those who benefit by receiving unusual increments of recognition would show up as having received much recognition based on what is indeed outstanding performance. For example, if a scientist has already achieved widespread acclaim, receiving one more honor or additional kind of recognition will not change the statistical relationship between his performance and recognition. The result will continue to show a very high positive correlation between contributions and recognition. Indeed the Matthew Effect, insofar as it is prevalent, operates at the highest levels of scientific accomplishment. Even then the most severe problem faced by disadvantaged scientists is that recognition will more likely be delayed rather than never received at all. Scientists who are doing work that results in simultaneous discovery with other, more eminent scientists may, as Merton points out, suffer in the short run from failure to receive appropriate recognition. It is improbable that such scientists —capable of doing work equivalent to the quality of eminent scientists—will not receive ultimately their just recognition. Merton (1973:445) describes one such case, among others, that shows precisely this career pattern. And delayed recognition may be very good for scientists, and consequently for science (see Zuckerman, 1967, for potentially negative impact of rapid fame in the life of Nobel laureates).

The Matthew Effect has interesting implications for the advancement of science and for professional careers, but I do not present any systematic data on its effect among the 600 scientists in this study. The Podunk Effect is the more interesting for the moment because of the idea that real suffering takes place when that effect operates.

In discussions of the inability of scientists to achieve recognition because of the Podunk Effect, the impression is that *unrewarded* performance is mostly at low-prestige institutions. Furthermore it is presumed that scientists at these institutions are the ones who cannot achieve appropriate recognition while those at high-prestige institutions are not only able to achieve recognition when it is earned but also more likely to obtain it when they do not deserve it. This notion has been strengthened, more than a little, by a paragraph from Crane's (1965:710) paper:

> Although the very productive were most likely to have won highest honors, highly productive scientists at the major university were more likely to have won recognition than highly productive scientists at a lesser school. The latter were, in fact, no more likely to win recognition than unproductive men at the major school. Evidently, productivity did not make the scientist as visible to his colleagues in his discipline as did a position at a major university.

I contend that, for a thorough understanding of the reward system, one must consider not only the scientists who achieve the level of recognition commensurate with their performance but also those who failed to achieve recognition or who achieved more than they apparently deserve. One way to do this is to examine individual deviant cases. Examples of this procedure are presented in the next two sections (drawn, in part, from unpublished Chapter 10 in Gaston, 1969; see also Gaston, 1975).

DEVIANT CASES IN THE REWARD SYSTEM: BRITISH HIGH-ENERGY PHYSICISTS

Previous studies are excellent sources for seeing the extent of the problem in obtaining more or less recognition than scientists apparently deserve. The first problem in looking at deviant cases is to determine which individual cases are deviant. One procedure that can be used is to arrange scientists into all possible combinations of productivity and recognition. Assuming that the divisions between high and low recognition and productivity are meaningful (a risky assumption of course), one can place scientists into four discrete categories. These should not be confused with Cole and Cole's (1967) categories, which are different. The four theoretical possibilities, and the labels describing them are as follows:

PRODUCTIVITY

RECOGNITION	LOW	HIGH
LOW	Spectator	Loser
HIGH	Winner	Competitor

Once the scientists are described, it is possible to look at the frequency of these categories in previous studies while seeing to what extent the Podunk Effect is prevalent.

Competitors are scientists with high status in the scientific community. They have contributed to the community and have been rewarded for it. They are competitors because they have entered the competition and won. *Spectators* are scientists who have contributed little and have received little recognition. They are spectators in the sense that they mostly observe science as it progresses around them. Both Competitors and Spectators receive the appropriate amount of recognition, and they best exemplify the ideal reward system. In a perfect world, and in a twofold classification scheme, these would be the only cells containing scientists. The others would be empty, but clearly the world does not work like that.

Losers are scientists who have contributed a great deal to the community but have not received much recognition. These scientists are, to some extent, supposed to be the greatest victims of the Podunk Effect. By all outward appearances Losers should have received recognition from the scientific community. Why they have not is the problem to be explained. *Winners* are scientists who have contributed few papers but have received high recognition. Losers and Winners are deviant cases.

Scientists from any study may be placed into one of these four categories for any prestige category being considered. Because of too few cases in most studies it is necessary to divide institutions only into low and high prestige. For the five previous studies discussed in this book some alterations must be made from the methods the original papers used to present the data. These adjustments are described in the notes to the table (see Table 24).

The data do not completely discount the Podunk Effect, but some interesting observations may be noted. In all studies some Losers are at low-prestige institutions, which by itself would support the prevalence of the Podunk Effect. Unfortunately for scholars committed to that interpretation, Losers are also at high-prestige institutions. Winners are also at both high and low-prestige institutions.

The data in Table 24 do not show the percentage distribution for each category of prestige, because the purpose of this presentation is not to show that *relatively* more or less Losers and Winners are at low- or high-prestige universities. The reader can determine that by converting the percentages. The purpose is to show that in all studies there are scientists who do not conform to the ideal pattern of prestige and recognition and who are deviant cases. In Crane's study 34 percent are deviant; in Hargens and Hagstrom's study 40 percent, in Cole and Cole's study 29 percent, in my study 32 percent.

Although these are necessarily only approximate percentages, little attention has been given to these deviant cases. I shall use the 203 scientists in my study to show that the 32 percent who appear deviant, from a statistical perspective, do not in fact prove that the reward system is not operating equitably. If other studies did the same type of deviant case analysis, they might also find that most of the deviant cases could be explained.

Losers and Winners do not differ in social class backgrounds, type of secondary school attended, prestige of undergraduate university, and prestige of PhD university. One explanation must be that Winners' research contributions are of greater quality therefore worth more to the scientific community, while Losers have produced trivial or less worthwhile research. Unfortunately, because I had no precise data about the quality of the scientists' research, I cannot eliminate that possible explanation.

I did have an indirect measure. The usual career grade of scientists in British universities is lecturer, because promotion to professor is not a career expectation of most scientists. Professors are appointed on the

Paper[a] (N cases)	Category Label	Possible Combinations of High and Low Productivity/Recognition	Prestige of Current Affiliation[b] High	Low
Crane (121)	Competitor	High/High	15	7
	Loser	Low/High	7	8
	Winner	High/Low	8	11
	Spectator	Low/Low	12	31
Hargens and	Competitor	High/High	17	11
Hagstrom (464)	Loser	Low/High	8	10
	Winner	High/Low	8	14
	Spectator	Low/Low	7	25
Cole and Cole (120)	Competitor	High/High	19	14
	Loser	Low/High	3	4
	Winner	High/Low	14	8
	Spectator	Low/Low	10	27
Gaston (159)	Competitor	High/High	5	13
	Loser	Low/High	4	12
	Winner	High/Low	6	10
	Spectator	Low/Low	21	30
Blume and Sinclair	Competitor	High/Low	5	9
(861)	Loser	Low/High	1	7
	Winner	High/Low	3	8
	Spectator	Low/Low	8	58

[a]Crane (1965:711). Prestige is high for the major university and low for the minor universities.

Hargens and Hagstrom (1967:34, derived from Table 4). Recognition is having a position in the top categories of the upper or lower half of the prestige structure; prestige of academic affiliation is a position in the upper half (high prestige) or the lower half (low prestige) of the prestige structure.

Cole and Cole (1967:386, derived from Table 5). High prestige is appointment in a department ranked among the top 10 departments; high recognition is high quality of research (60+ citations).

Gaston (1970:722, Table 2, and Gaston's unpublished data). Medium- and low-prestige categories combined into "low" prestige; recognition is based on recognition index.

Blume and Sinclair (1971:135, Table 8). Productivity is quality of research (high plus low = high, zero = low). While not directly comparable to productivity, they use it to determine the extent of particularism. Recognition based on index (high = high, low plus zero = low). High prestige is Oxbridge and London; low prestige is all others.

[b]Total for sample in its eight cells equals 99-101, depending on rounding.

basis of outstanding research contributions, and whereas factors in addition to research quality may be involved, appointment to professorships results from open competition. Not only are applicants subjected to scrutiny by scientists at the appointing university, but also opinions about prospective professors may be sought from wherever they are needed. One might predict that rank would be related to the type of scientist outlined in the four categories, and the data provide some support for this contention. Professors (and laboratory scientists holding the highest position possible) are much more likely to be Winners or Competitors. Competitors are recognized for producing many publications (presumably of high quality) and Winners are recognized presumably for few but high-quality papers. Whereas only 28 percent of the lecturers are either Competitors or Winners, 74 percent of the professors are. The comparable figure for senior lecturers and readers, the middle ranks, is 42 percent.

I found also that theorists are more likely to be recognized than experimentalists, presumably because their research is worth more to the scientific community. This suggested that theorists, more than experimentalists, should be Winners. Theorists indeed are more likely to be either Competitors or Winners (47 percent compared to 28 percent for experimentalists). Theorists are also least likely to be Losers (8 percent compared to 18 percent). While the presumed quality of research does not explain every deviant case, it does add to the explanation. Of the scientists working on problems defined by them as among the three most important areas in high-energy physics, 42 percent are Competitors or Winners, whereas among those not working in such important areas, only 21 percent are either Competitors or Winners.

The number of different institutions at which a scientist has been located is related to this typology. Competitors and Winners held more positions than Spectators or Losers. This suggests that scientists with low productivity, Winners, are able to obtain recognition because of the increased number of different people they have come in contact with in the scientific community. This does not necessarily mean that they compensate their low productivity by becoming personally acquainted with scientists who help allocate rewards, but mobile scientists are able to bring their high-quality papers to the attention of those who might otherwise not see them, and they may be mobile to begin with because of the quality of their research.

Quality probably accounts for most apparently unmerited recognition obtained by Winners, but it does not account for all the deviant cases. Although theorists are more likely to be Winners, some experimentalists are also Winners and some theorists are Losers. When all variables that help explain being either a Winner or Loser are controlled for, such as type of scientist (theorist/experimentalist), rank, number of positions held, and whether the scientist works on an important problem area, it is then possible to examine the cases that require further explanation for their deviant status.

There are four theorists who are Losers and who require explanation. The others do not work on problems they consider among the most important. One was almost rated "high" on recognition, but his score was just under the cutoff point between high and low recognition. The three others are affiliated with institutions where there are eminent theorists whose presence may have a limiting effect on obtaining invitations to give guest lectures at other institutions, an item that constituted one of the components of the recognition index. Because this group situation was not true for the Winners, that explanation seems plausible.

Experimentalists who are Losers need less explanation because the scientific community places more value on theoretical contributions, but some explanation is in order. Eight of the 21 do not work on one of the most important areas. Of the other 13 experimental Losers, 9 are lecturers, 5 of whom have been in only one institution and 4 have been at two institutions. They are members of large research groups and are thus overshadowed both by numbers and the eminence of others. The remaining four, though they have been at more than two institutions, also work in groups comprised of some of the more eminent researchers in this specialty in Britain.

The 14 theorists who are Winners need little explanation because theoretical work is highly valued. Only 2 do not work in one of the most important areas, and 1 of those has held four different positions. The other is the leader of a small group of theorists without a colleague of professorial rank in the group, and this causes him to receive recognition that appears unmerited because he has leadership responsibilities. Such responsibilities were not part of the recognition index but perhaps should have been included.

There are 18 experimentalists who are Winners. Half hold either a readership or professorship. The other half (with one exception) are engaged in leadership activities at a laboratory or in a university group. The younger ones are not group leaders but in effect are leading groups who have rather inactive leaders, and this probably results in their receiving recognition that might normally accrue to the group leader. The one exception was categorized "high" on recognition, but he was barely above the cutoff point between low and high recognition.

My attempt to explain deviant cases might not be satisfactory to the most devout believer that particularism is rampant in science. Some of the specific cases might appear to be more of an excuse than an explanation. And, even if they sound plausible, some of the explanations actually may be considered evidence of particularism, such as the cases involving mobility and consequent visibility to other colleagues in the scientific community. Remember that quality was not measured directly, and if it had been, the situation might have required only little, if any, explanation at all.

DEVIANT CASES IN THIS STUDY

In the previous studies I mentioned it was possible to arrange the data so that there would be discrete categories of high and low recognition and high and low productivity for two levels of prestige. It would be possible in the current study to do that, but I use a better strategy to select deviant cases. I divided number of publications by professional age to obtain an average rate of publication per year for each scientist. I did this for each discipline and each country. The effect of this is to take what the pattern of publications is in each community without contaminating it with patterns in the other disciplines or country. Next, I regressed the individual rates of publication on their citations in 1972. The residuals from that regression give estimates of scientists who received more or fewer citations than "expected," based on publications. I could have looked at awards, but the modal number of awards is zero, and so a scientist receiving even one award is already "over" recognized according to a regression equation. In such a situation the scientists with the largest number of awards are going to show "over" awards, irrespective of how truly the awards are deserved, even if they have produced dozens of papers.

For each of the six groups I selected the three scientists with the highest positive residuals and the three with the highest negative residuals, making a total of 36. That I am using citations, rather than some recognition index, means that this approach is not precisely comparable to the previous studies. The question is whether scientists who appear to have received more recognition than deserved (Winners) will be in high-prestige institutions and whether those who appear to have received less than deserved will be in low-prestige institutions (Losers). The Podunk Effect predicts this pattern.

Citations are, of course, an appropriate measure of quality, as well as a form of recognition. If, through this approach, Losers are found at low-prestige institutions, one could argue that what is really at work is not the Podunk Effect but rather the process whereby recognition goes where quality is indicated. More importantly I contend that the Podunk Effect is not a serious threat to the reward system in science. The best evidence is to discover instances of the converse of the Podunk Effect, the Knudop Effect (Podunk spelled backwards). The Knudop Effect is the process whereby scientists at low-prestige institutions receive more recognition than they apparently deserve. If there is a process opposite from the Podunk Effect, then one must think of the scientists at high-prestige institutions who fail to receive recognition, at least their "share," as experiencing something almost opposite from the Matthew Effect. Let us call it the Wehttam Effect (pronounced wet-tem).

To see if the 36 scientists are experiencing these effects, I combined the top two and the bottom three prestige categories to report the affiliation of the deviant cases. Of the 18 Winners 9 are in the top two (Matthew Effect) and 9 are in the bottom three prestige categories (Knudop Effect). Of the 18 Losers 2 are in the top categories (both in the highest category), indicating the Wehttam Effect, and 16 are in the bottom categories, indicating the Podunk Effect. While the Podunk Effect has a large percentage of the total, the proponents of this hypothesis cannot dismiss the fact that, of the 18 winners, half are experiencing the Knudop Effect. Certainly more scientists are in low-prestige than in high-prestige departments, and so out of pure chance it would be expected that more would be in that category.

The kind of argument that supports the Podunk Effect promotes the argument that scientists in low-prestige institutions suffer while those in high-prestige institutions do not. The fact is that scientists in prestigious departments also fail to get recognized (Wehttam Effect) and those in low-prestige departments also gain recognition when their productivity would suggest they do not deserve it (Knudop).

I am not arguing that any scientist should receive undeserved recognition—indeed I suspect that rarely happens. My contention is that, to understand the reward system, it is necessary to investigate both the Losers experiencing the Wehttam Effect and the Winners experiencing the Knudop Effect. Is it not as important, sociologically, to learn under what conditions scientists in low-prestige departments gain significant recognition, in spite of low productivity, as it is to point an accusing finger at the lack of universalism in science when data are interpreted to suggest that scientists obtain recognition only because they are affiliated with high-prestige institutions?

In contrast to the deviant cases among British high-energy physicists, I cannot explain in detail those in this study. I do not have the qualitative data and other information about the particular circumstances of these scientists that personally interviewing the high-energy physicists provided. I am unable to argue that there is no injustice in these 36 extreme cases of overrecognition and underrecognition. The step-wise multiple regression indicated that prestige of current affiliation had almost no impact on the distribution of citations. Specifically the percentage of variance explained by prestige of current affiliation for each group, after several other important variables were controlled for, turned out to be only 1 percent for British biologists, 4 percent for British chemists, zero percent for British physicists, zero percent for American biologists, 4 percent for American chemists, and zero percent for American physicists. Those figures indicate that prestige of current affiliation has little impact on the distribution of citations, after other variables also related to receiving citations are controlled for. Putting a group of scientists into categories and cross-classifying them will usually generate deviant cases, but the more sophisticated analysis shows how negligible the effect of prestige really is.

Recognition may appear difficult to explain completely, but overwhelmingly recognition is explained by the research productivity of scientists. Explaining productivity is more difficult than explaining recognition. I discuss that problem in the next chapter.

Chapter 8

/ *CUMULATIVE ADVANTAGE,*
REINFORCEMENT, AND
RESEARCH PRODUCTIVITY

Scientific recognition can be explained almost entirely by the amount of publications scientists produce. As Price (1963:41) puts it, ". . . although there is no guarantee that the small producer is a nonentity and the big producer a distinguished scientist, or even that the order of merit follows the order of productivity, there is a strong correlation. . . ." And while some might wish to argue that considerations other than productivity are equally important for the allocation of honorific awards, those scholars are a minority.

Even if there is some disagreement on the bases for the distribution of awards, there is absolutely none on the fact that the number of publications scientists produce varies enormously, whether one looks at a year's production, or a five-year period, or a lifetime. And most of this variation has never been explained in any published paper on the subject. That situation makes scientific productivity one of the most difficult and perplexing problems in the sociology of science. The purposes of this chapter are to illustrate this variation, to discuss the hypotheses advanced to explain it, and to propose a different interpretation for some of those hypotheses.

VARIATION IN SCIENTIFIC PRODUCTIVITY

There are so many studies of scientific productivity that I cannot mention all of them, but several examples will document the problem. Price (1963), observing long-term historical patterns in individual productivity, refers to various historical studies of scientists. One study of a group of eminent scientists shows that their range of lifetime publications is from 27 to 768 papers. Another study shows a range from 7 to more than 140 papers. Consistent observations show, that in any group, the number of publications is small for most scientists and extremely large for a few. This led Price (1963:43) to suggest that scientific productivity conforms to an inverse-square law of productivity. Price believes the law takes this form: "The number of people producing n papers is proportional to $1/n^2$. For every 100 authors who produce but a single paper in a certain period, there are 25 with two, 11 with three, and so on." (There is some disagreement on the implications of this "law." See Allison et al., 1976:269–276.)

In one study of productivity Babchuk and Bates (1962:344) looked at sociologists who received their PhDs between 1945 and 1949 to see what they had published during the years 1940 to 1959. They found enormous variations: 95 of the 262 sociologists had published no articles, 60 had published 1 or 2, 35 had published 3 or 4; at the upper ranges 1 had published between 21 and 30 articles, and finally, 1 had published more than 30 articles. Although they did not take into account the differences in time the sociologists had to publish their total number of articles, controlling for those years "at risk" for publication probably would not have resulted in substantial changes in the *form* of the distribution.

Lightfield (1971:128–133) reports a study designed similarly to that of Babchuk and Bates. He studied sociologists who received their PhD degrees between 1954 and 1963 and who were members of departments offering graduate degrees. He looked at their publications for the period 1953–1968 in the *American Sociological Review,* the *American Journal of Sociology,* and *Social Forces.* These journals are not the sole publication outlets for sociology, and this sample does not represent the universe of American sociologists. The publication data are, therefore, conservative, representing the elite part of the sociology profession that publishes in elite journals. This reduces the variation in productivity that one would expect to find. Lightfield gave each 100 pages of a published book a value of one article, except that he gave any book of more than 400 pages a maximum equivalency of four articles. Nevertheless, counting six or more publications as "high" productivity and fewer than six as "low" and not taking professional age into account, Lightfield (1971:131) reports that 48 percent had high and 52 percent had low productivity. On the average, with professional age not being taken into account, 52 percent had published *no more than* the equivalent of 0.33 article each year (five articles/15 years); many no doubt published fewer.

Babchuk and Bates (1962:344) also discuss several other studies. They note that their percentage distributions are generally consistent with those reported for other disciplines. They mention Logan Wilson's report of a survey of 35 institutions, not in the prestige elites, where only 32 percent of the faculty had any publications over a five-year period, and of those, the median number was only 1.3 papers. They quote Wilson's report of a survey by the American Historical Association showing that only 25 percent of the doctorates in history consistently produce publications. And, finally, they mention Wilson's report of a survey of nearly 3000 mathematicians who took a PhD between 1862 and 1933. The survey showed that only 54 percent had published; 19 percent published only 1 paper; 8 percent, 2 papers; 11 percent 3 to 5; 6 percent, 6 to 10; 2 percent, 21 to 30; and 2 percent, more than 30 papers.

Babchuk and Bates (1962:345) refer also to a study of psychology graduates from the University of Michigan. The survey included 296 alumni receiving doctorates in the postwar period. Of the 85 percent who responded, about 27 percent had published no articles; 43 percent, one to four; and 30 percent, five or more.

Meltzer (1956:35) reports a study in which more than 75 percent of the physiologists in the United States responded to a survey. They answered a question about the number of research papers they had published during the past three years. Although Meltzer did not report the distribution for zero, one, two, and so forth, about half of the physiologists had published five or more papers, and the other half had published four or fewer.

Crane (1965:702) measured the productivity levels of her biologists, political scientists, and physiologists with an index of productivity that allowed for the length of time scientists had held the PhD. According to the index 36 percent of her sample are "high" producers and 64 percent "low". Although high and low is an arbitrary and somewhat crude classification, her data show wide variations in levels of productivity.

Cole and Cole (1967:381) report the productivity levels of their sample drawn disproportionately from eminent physicists. The specialties these scientists represent are approximately the same (except for solid-state physics) as the distribution then among university physicists. Their sample of physicists is more homogeneous than Crane's sample, which included three disciplines. It is also more homogeneous than a random sample of all university physicists would be. Nevertheless, in spite of the homogeneity, Cole and Cole (1967:381) report that 45 percent of their scientists have produced more than 30 papers while 55 percent have published fewer than 30. These categories reflect arbitrary cutting points, but they still indicate wide variation.

Zuckerman (1967) studied the most eminent group of scientists. She interviewed 41 of the 55 Nobel laureates at work in 1963 in the United States, (Zuckerman, 1967:393) comparing them with a sample matched on several dimensions, and concluded:

> The laureates not only start to publish earlier and continue longer; they also publish at a much higher rate, with a median of 3.9 papers each year since they began their careers compared with 1.4 papers per year by the matched scientists. The most prolific laureate has managed to get out 10.4 papers annually—one every five weeks—for more than twenty years. Only one laureate has published less than one paper annually as against twelve men in the [matched] sample.

Nobel laureates do not exemplify low levels of publishing activity, but the difference between the group's mean of 3.9 papers annually and one of the individual's mean of 10.4 papers annually indicates there is considerable variation even in a highly prolific group.

Hagstrom (1967) reports means and standard deviations of articles published in several disciplines during the five-year period prior to his survey of faculty in doctoral granting departments. For our purposes the pertinent comparisons are not differences between disciplines. Explaining these differences is not the problem I am discussing, although it is, of course, interesting. The important comparison is the mean and its standard deviation. Hagstrom's (1967:114) figures are as follows:

Discipline	Mean	Standard Deviation
Mathematics	6.30	6.67
Theoretical physics	9.96	9.03
Experimental physics	7.39	8.24
Chemistry	12.41	13.47
Experimental biology	11.63	10.82
Other biology	11.59	11.74

Reskin's (1976a,b,c, 1977) data on chemists are more appropriate to illustrate the variation in productivity than most of the other studies.

For example, based on a systematic random sample of 238 chemists obtaining their PhD between 1955 and 1961, her data support the general observation that most scientific publications are produced by a small percentage of scientist. Reskin (1977:496) notes that, after she had followed the careers of these scientists through the first decade after their PhD, 7.5 percent did not publish at all and another 11 percent published only one article. Furthermore, 15 percent contributed about half of the total papers published (2000) by the sample during that cumulative period of 2380 years (238 times 10 years) of scientific activity, or in some instances, inactivity. Reskin (1977:496) also notes the distribution by year after PhD, so that, except for 1 of the 10 years, more than 60 percent of the chemists did not publish in any single year.

The American Council on Education (ACE) conducted the largest and most nearly comprehensive survey of American academics, one in 1969 and one in 1972–1973. The survey asked faculty to indicate their career publications, and although the results are not given for faculty according to professional age, one question in the 1972–1973 surveys permits interpretation according to a specified time. The question asked for the number of published writings in the previous two years. Of faculty in universities (excluding four-year colleges and lesser institutions) 37.2 percent published no papers in the previous two years; 45.6 percent published one to four; and 17.22 percent, five or more. This variation over a short period gives sufficient reason to report the distribution of career publications, because it is clear that variations over a career are not simply a function of professional age. For the two surveys, article production is the following (Bayer, 1970:15; 1973:28):

Number of Publications	1969	1972–1973
None	29.5	24.0
1– 4	29.7	25.9
5–10	14.1	16.1
11–20	10.3	14.0
21+	16.3	19.9
	99.9	99.9

These studies also give publication data by type of institution and by sex, but the data I showed for universities are most appropriate for this discussion because research is more likely to be an appropriate activity in universities than in other institutions of higher education (see also Fulton and Trow, 1974).

To this point I have mentioned survey data only for American scientists. That does not mean that large variation in scientific productivity is peculiar to the United States. Some examples from British science—not the data on the 300 British scientists described in this book—confirm that, even in a much more homogeneous system of higher education, there is much variation in scientific productivity. For example, Blume and Sinclair (1973) asked chemists about productivity over the five-year period prior to their survey. Of 791 chemists 44 percent published fewer than 10 papers in the period; 42 percent, 11 to 30; and 14 percent, more than 30. These figures are probably much higher than those Reskin (1977) reports, although the format each uses does not facilitate comparability. And even if Blume and Sinclair's are higher (British chemists are more productive than American chemists in the samples studied for this book), that does not reduce the problem of explaining intragroup variation.

I asked British high-energy physicists (Gaston, 1969:383) about their career publications and found the following distribution: 1 percent published nothing; 21 percent, 1 to 4 papers; 22 percent, 5 to 9; 32 percent, 10 to 20; and 25 percent, 21 or more. (The 101 percent total results from rounding.) This distribution does not take professional age into account. Dividing the 203 scientists into categories of chronological age (highly correlated to professional age), I found that there is still considerable variation. For example, for the scientists 30 to 34 years old, the comparable percentages for numbers of papers are 2, 13, 22, 41, and 22. For scientists 40 to 44 years old, the comparable percentages are 0, 6, 0, 31, and 63. Regardless of whether one looks at the total scientists or within age groups, there is large variation in scientific productivity.

Blume and Sinclair's chemists and my high-energy physicists do not represent nearly the total faculty in British universities, but Halsey and Trow (1971) conducted a large survey of a representative sample of British academics. Wolinsky and I (1977) took their data and computed the means and standard deviations for three primary academic groups. We combined books and articles according to a formula that gave arts faculty the benefit of higher value for books and social scientists somewhat less. It turned out that books for natural scientists were equivalent to papers, as others have intuitively suspected. By taking the number of publications as the midpoint of the coded categories and dividing that by the number of years since the first degree, to allow for years "at risk," we arrived at the following data:

Faculty Group	Mean Rate	Deviation Standard
Arts faculty	1.16	1.37
Social sciences	1.00	1.07
Natural sciences	1.08	0.81

I have focused only on the studies dealing with individual variations in productivity, because that is the problem I am discussing here. This exclusion omits the extremely important problem of the possible variations among nations. Those studies try to account for national differences in terms of institutional structure, support for science, competition, and other sociological variables. Some of those important studies include work by Price (1969) and Ben-David (1960, 1964, 1971). Although the ultimate explanation of individual productivity may tie in with the explanation of national differences, that problem is not my major interest for this chapter.

If there was any question about the assertion that scientific productivity varies, the preceding examples should be enough evidence. The studies I referred to are limited, of course, by incomparability and by the fact that they are only a sample of the large universe of such papers. But the inevitable conclusion I reach after reading these studies is that scientific productivity varies considerably, and so I deal now with some of the hypotheses advanced to explain the variation.

SOME EXPLANATIONS FOR SCIENTIFIC PRODUCTIVITY

Whether one approaches the problem from a sociological or psychological perspective, one of the first things that come to mind is the possibility that scientific productivity varies because scientists' ability varies. Surely some scientists, on the basis of evidence, are *able* to produce more publications than others. The problem is that being able to do something is not the same kind of *ability* that I am talking about.

Cole and Cole (1973:68–72) discuss the role of measured IQ in scientific performance, and IQ is what most people think about when one mentions ability. The available data are clear that scientists have mean IQs that are above average, and so, whether scientific training requires some minimum threshold of ability or whether brighter people self-select scientific careers, scientists originate from the highest levels of intelligence in the population. For trained scientists there are conflicting data on the relationship between IQ and performance. For example, Bayer and Folger (1966) found a negative correlation ($r = -.05$) between IQ and scientific achievement (measured by citations). Cole and Cole (1973:69) report that their data on 499 scientists in various disciplines produced a correlation of only $r = .05$ between papers published and measured IQ. They also discussed other possibilities such as motivation and self-discipline, but they had no data to test them. Roe (1952), who studied eminent scientists, suggests that individual characteristics, such as being the oldest or only child, are related to eminence. One cannot have much confidence in her conclusions, because of the design of the study and because of the problem that prevalence of such factors in a sample must be compared to the prevalence in the total population.

Other personal characteristics include variables such as creativity, for example, (Kubie, 1954; Roe, 1952) and motivation (Cole and Cole, 1973). Creativity is such an elusive concept that it has been unfruitful to this point in explaining differential productivity. Motivation intuitively seems to be a perfect candidate for explaining it, at least to some extent, but so far as I know, no one has developed a good measure for motivation. Cole and Cole (1973:115) describe one version of motivation as the "sacred spark" hypothesis:

> Adherents of this theory would argue that scientists do science not because they are rewarded but because they have an inner compulsion to do so. Certainly the history of science offers many examples of men like Cavendish who shunned external rewards but continued throughout their lives to do a great deal of excellent science. According to the sacred-spark theory scientists who are rewarded and continue to be productive would be productive even if they were not rewarded.

That quotation mentions the motivation based on rewards for scientific contributions (described by Merton, 1957, and Hagstrom, 1965, and slightly revised by Storer, 1966). It is commonplace in the sociology of science to assume that scientists are motivated by the possibility of obtaining scientific recognition for their research contributions. And there is little evidence, if any, to negate this assumption. What sociologists of science have not done to this point is measure the degree to which some scientists are more motivated to seek rewards than others. On the assumption that the amount of motivation varies, it would be possible to determine whether or not, as scientists' motivation for rewards increases, their productivity increases also. It is possible, because almost anything is sometimes plausible, that we have the best explanation for differential productivity right under our noses! Motivation probably changes for many scientists during a career, and if so, the methodological difficulty inherent in measuring motivation would be increased by trying to measure it after the fact. (See Zuckerman and Merton, 1973a:497–559, for discussion of career changes.)

Some variables pertaining to individual characteristics, or specific to an individual, that correlate with productivity include sex, age at PhD, year between BA and PhD degrees, age at first publication, publication before the PhD degree, time devoted to research, a research versus a teaching orientation, and of course, professional age. (Studies dealing with these and other variables, especially sex differentials, are Clemente, 1973; Cole and Cole, 1973; Cole, forthcoming; Reskin, 1977; and Zuckerman and Cole, 1975.) There are generally small but positive zero-order correlations between most of these variables and scientific productivity.

Scientific productivity is related also to variables measured by their connections to scientists. For example, scholars have measured the relationship between individuals' scientific productivity and the quality of their undergraduate institutions, PhD departments, eminence of thesis directors, prestige of first positions after leaving graduate school, and prestige of current affiliations. These variables generally have low to moderate zero-order correlations with scientific productivity. And for some of the variables it is not altogether clear which precedes and which succeeds productivity. (This problem was noted for some of the variables in this book.) Many of the zero-order correlations are reduced, however, when controls are introduced.

As Hagstrom (1967:61–62) notes:

> The data from this study, then, suggest that superior productivity of scientists in high prestige departments is a consequence of their superior skills and greater motivation to do research. Of course, the association that does exist is not great; knowing the departmental prestige of each member of a sample of scientists enables us to account for only 6 per cent of the variance in their productivity.

Because scientific productivity cannot be explained easily by available measures of presumably pertinent variables, two other plausible hypotheses have been suggested. Not unlike much scientific development these are difficult to test. It is not that they are untestable, but they require considerable ingenuity and resources to test adequately, and there are likely to be differences of opinion about the adequacy of any test, at least in the near future. These potentially fruitful hypotheses are "reinforcement" and "cumulative advantage."

Scientific Productivity and Reinforcement

The basis of the reward system is that scientists receive recognition according to their performance as scientists, and this requires producing work *publicized* primarily through publications. Because receiving recognition is a basic assumption about the reward system, the notion of reinforcement weaves a thread throughout studies of the system.

But what is reinforcement? Cole and Cole (1973:114) indicate that reinforcement is simply this: ". . . scientists who are rewarded are productive, and scientists who are not rewarded become less productive." It is a simple hypothesis, but its simplicity should not deceive one about the complexity in discovering how much variation in productivity can be explained by reinforcement.

How then does reinforcement work? Consider an example of two scientists, Jones and Smith. Jones completes training for the PhD and tries to publish a paper from his recently accepted thesis. He prepares a paper and submits it to a journal. After some time the editor sends the paper back to Jones with a form letter stating that the paper might have been publishable some time ago, but the referees believe the substance of the paper is now well known. The editor states that the journal would appreciate seeing future papers that Jones might wish to submit. What does Jones do now? He turns to his current research and most likely has some doubts about his worth as a scientist.

Scientist Smith is a graduate school colleague of Jones. Smith completes a thesis about the same time as Jones and takes a position similar to the one taken by Jones. Soon he prepares a paper and submits it to a journal. In due course the editor notifies Smith that his paper will be published in a forthcoming issue of the journal. Smith is pleased to have his work accepted and continues to work on the research initiated soon after arrival in his department. He enters his laboratory cheerfully, smiles at his colleagues, and in general, feels very good about himself. He is optimistic that his current research will turn out to be important, if not significant, and he moves along with his work, even on those days when everything seems to go wrong.

These hypothetical descriptions do not include much detail, because fictional illustrations, at least in the hands of a nonfiction writer, cannot do justice to the whole range of human characteristics existing in real life. But in a simple way these descriptions illustrtate the *potential* importance of reinforcement. Certainly it is possible that, even with the rejection of Jones's first paper, some other conditions might be present to keep him from feeling too bad about his poor "luck." And these conditions could maintain his sense of worth. Perhaps he received notice of a research grant before the paper was rejected; perhaps he had just been invited to spend the next summer at a prestigious laboratory; or perhaps he had made good progress on his current research and it had won the approval of his departmental colleagues, along with their wise assurances that his current research was better than merely important. Because of the social–psychological context in which positive and negative reinforcement occurs, it is difficult to predict accurately what the outcome would be for Jones. And his social context is much more complicated than the situation in which pigeons, rats, and monkeys are studied.

In spite of the difficulty in making a critical test of the reinforcement hypothesis some attempts have been made to assess its potential. Cole and Cole (1967:388–390; 1973:110–116) report two of these attempts. First they examined early publication activity of physicists and citations in their early work. Scientists whose early work was cited were much more likely to be highly productive later in their careers. Because this particular test involved some methodological problems, they tried a different method and explain (1973:113–114):

> We took a random sample of fifty physicists who received their Ph.D.s from American universities in 1957 and 1958. We then looked up in *Science Abstracts* the number of papers each had published in every year from the time they received their degree through 1969. We were thus able to compare productivity in the first five years after the Ph.D. with productivity in the last five-year period (1965–69). We were able to use citations received in 1961 as an indicator of recognition received for early work. . . . The later productivity of physicists was substantially influenced by recognition received by their early work. Those men who produced the best work were rewarded and continued to be highly productive. The productivity of those who were not rewarded dropped off.

Lightfield (1971:128–133), examining reinforcement in 83 sociologists who obtained PhDs between 1954 and 1958, traced their publication records for the first 10 years after the PhD. He examined their citations in the *American Sociological Review, American Journal of Sociology*, and *Social Forces* to determine which papers had been cited. He found that 36 of 49 who published and received citations to their work in the five years immediately after receiving the PhD continued to be active in publication and to be cited during the second five-year period. In contrast, only 3 who published and were cited in the first period dropped out of "professional" sight. Only 1 "bloomed" late, in the second period. Most importantly, of the 21 who published but did not receive any citations during the first five years, only 1 received any citations during the second five-year period. Lightfield (1971:133) notes that "Unless a person achieves a qualitative piece of research during his first five years as a sociologist, therefore, it seems unlikely that he will do so during his next five years—if at any time during his career." Because he did not control for any other variables when he presented these results of his study, it is not clear whether originally being cited might resulted from potentially particularistic considerations or whether simply, in the absence of such possibilities, the research publications were not worth citing.

Both Reskin (1977) and Allison and Stewart (1974) discuss tests of reinforcement as a hypothesis to explain scientists' differential productivity over time. Although they mention reinforcement, they suggest that other factors could explain their results as well as reinforcement. They argue that reinforcement cannot be ruled out by their particular analyses.

A major problem in these studies is the lack of conceptual separation between reinforcement and cumulative advantage (which I discuss in the next section). As I understand the two hypotheses, reinforcement deals with *why* scientists continue in research activities and successfully produce scientific publications, but cumulative advantage deals with *how* some scientists are able to obtain resources for research that in turn leads to successful research and publication. Clearly the two are not unrelated, but as long as they are treated as saying somewhat the same thing in different ways, it will be impossible to separate them. For example, let us return to Jones and Smith. If Jones does not get positive reinforcement, and if there are no other forces operating to assist him, he will not accrue any advantages in obtaining resources for his next series of research projects. Smith obtained some positive reinforcement (not honorific recognition, but I will deal with that later), and in contrasting the two cases, one has to admit that Smith received *some* reinforcement. But if circumstances do not provide Smith with continued or additional resources for research, then the reinforcement may not account for much. In other words reinforcement is a process whereby one is encouraged to continue research, but cumulative advantage is the process whereby one is enabled to continue research. And there is nothing to guarantee that advantage will accrue. There can be positive reinforcement without cumulative advantage, but there can hardly be cumulative advantage without prior positive reinforcement.

Scientific Productivity and Cumulative Advantage

In modern times it is clear that scientists must have resources to do their work. Even those who are essentially "pencil and paper" theorists must have time and library resources. Few scientists being independently wealthy, their personal resources cannot provide for all their needs. I discussed the Matthew Effect in Chapter 7 as an outcome of incremental growth in scientific recognition for those who had established themselves and as a consequence seemed to gain additional recognition because of prior recognition. The Matthew Effect does not result in undeserving scientists' being recognized for work they did not do, and it does not negate a universalistic reward system. Rather, it works simply to facilitate future recognition.

Merton sees the Mattew Effect as a special case of the process of cumulative advantage, and I think it can be seen also as a process that explains the increasing personal resources allocated to individuals because of demonstrated success in research. Nothing about cumulative advantage necessarily means it is inequitable. If scientists receive additional resources because they have used previous resources wisely and efficiently, both society and science are better served by allocating them to scientists with proven track records, as long as the outcome does not shut off resources completely from people whose track records have not had time, because of youth, to develop (see Merton, 1975, for descriptions of countervailing mechanisms that prevent increasing concentration of resources).

How does cumulative advantage work? Merton (1977:89) briefly describes the history of the concept and then outlines its major idea in this way:

> Processes of individual self-selection and institutional social selection interact to affect successive probabilities of access to the opportunity-structure in a given field of activity. When the role-performance of the individual measures up to demanding institutional standards, and especially when it greatly exceeds them, this initiates a process of cumulative advantage in which the individual acquires successively enlarged opportunities to advance his work (and the rewards that go with it) even further. Since elite institutions have comparatively large resources for advancing work in their domains, talent that finds its way into those institutions has the heightened potential of acquiring differentially accumulating advantages. The systems of reward, allocation of resources, and social selection thus operate to create and maintain a class structure in science by providing a stratified distribution of chances among scientists for enlarging their role as investigators.

Cumulative advantage at this point is still an hypothesis, albeit an intuitively appealing one. Cole and Cole (1973:237–247), discussing many aspects of how it could account for differences in scientific careers, indicate why it is not a negative outcome for science or society.

But in spite of its being generally well understood, little attention has been given to dealing empirically with the process, and what has been done is less than satisfactory (including what I describe in the next section). The most serious problem is in obtaining data that bear directly on the process and that can be used definitely to rule out alternative explanations.

Allison and Stewart (1974:596–606) set out deliberately to examine several hypotheses, including cumulative advantage, using the data collected by Hagstrom (1967). The data from almost 2000 scientists are cross sectional and according to the hypothesis should be longitudinal, but they made a case for assuming cohort characteristics by dividing the sample into age groups. Their central hypothesis was that productivity among scientists increasingly becomes more unequal as careers develop. They used a Gini index, which is a measure of group inequality. Allison and Stewart (1974:605) conclude:

> The hypothesis of accumulative advantage in science implies that the distribution of publications and citations will exhibit increasing inequality as a cohort passes through its career. In the absence of cohort differences, this same pattern should be observed in a cross-sectional sample stratified by age. Our data corroborate this consequence for three disciplines: physics, chemistry and mathematics. Specifically, when productivity inequality is measured by a Gini index of publications or citations, there is a substantial, nearly-linear increase from younger to older career-age groups.

The fourth discipline, biology, did not conform to the same pattern for reasons they believe are caused by the presumed inefficiency in the system of communication and rewards in biology. They have no empirical test of their explanation, however, and if they are correct, then the major conclusions I reached in Chapter 6 are in error. Future research will have to appraise our conflicting interpretations.

While Allison and Stewart are successful in demonstrating that quasi-cohorts increasingly differ in the production of scientific papers and in the receipt of citations, they cannot rule out other hypotheses. Allison and Stewart (1974:605) carefully note: "This evidence in support of the accumulative advantage hypothesis does not disconfirm the heterogeneity hypothesis, however. In fact, our analysis still leaves a major source of inequality unaccounted for: that which is observed among the youngest age strata." The heterogeneity hypothesis refers, of course, to the presumed tendencies for scientists to be differentially motivated from the beginning of their careers. And it is confounded by additional situational factors, such as initial resources and research opportunities at post-PhD positions.

In another study of cumulative advantage Faia (1975:825–829) takes Allison and Stewart to task because of their methodological problem of using cross sectional data. Then Faia uses cross sectional data (referred to earlier in Bayer, 1973) and reaches substantial agreement between the Matthew Effect and cumulative advantage, and his data are more restrictive than Allison and Stewart's because he had only categories of productivity, not counts of publication. Nevertheless he too could not eliminate the cumulative advantage or the heterogeneity hypothesis.

In a recent study using longitudinal data Reskin (1976:5) comments on the Cole (1973:110–115) findings that physicists, cited more in their first five postdoctoral years, produced more papers in later years. She maintains that ". . . their weak control for early productivity and their failure to control other potentially confounding variables imperils their conclusion that early recognition encourages later productivity." Reskin (1977:501), applying a stricter definition to cumulative advantage than most others, concludes:

> Without data on the chemists' research resources, I cannot directly test the accumulative-advantage hypothesis, which predicts both a direct reinforcement effect of citations as well as indirect effects from early productivity and early recognition mediated by the resources both can attract. Since research resources vary considerably by organizational context, a crude test of the hypothesis might use decade context as a proxy for resources. University employment at the end of the decade significantly increased decade productivity ($b^* = .280$), which is consistent with the accumulation of advantages. However, the selection hypothesis remains a viable alternative.

No doubt future research will settle some of the issues involved in reinforcement and cumulative advantage, and these concepts will be used to explicate other observed phenomena in science (for a recent attempt at the latter, see Price, 1976). I did not set out initially to test the hypothesis of either reinforcement or cumulative advantage, but fortunately my data were collected and coded in a way that provides limited assessments of these hypotheses. Some of my data approximate more closely the ideal type of data to test these hypotheses because my data are longitudinal, not cross sectional, they represent three disciplines and two countries, productivity is measured by counting abstracts of papers in the relevant disciplines (they are not self-reported), and my citation data take into account co-authorship.

SCIENTIFIC PRODUCTIVITY AND THE 600 SCIENTISTS

The previous section began with a discussion of the reinforcement hypothesis, but I discuss cumulative advantage first in this section. The cumulative advantage hypothesis says that scientists' productivity varies because of the differential resources that accrue to them from their early productivity. Scientists, successful early in their careers, are able to command, obtain, or receive increased time for research, increased facilities, or increased support. Before it is possible to move to the second step of assessing the impact of access to differential resources, variability in research productivity must be established.

Cumulative Advantage

There are various ways to measure productivity variability in a cohort of scientists. Allison and Stewart (1974) used the Gini index, which is one way to measure group inequality; Faia (1975) used the variance, which is a more commonly understood measure. I did not use either of these measures, because the Gini index is less common and no more appropriate than a simpler measure. The variance is an unstandardized measure that is not comparable across groups. I used the coefficient of variability, which is computed by dividing the variance by the mean. The variance fluctuates widely if there are a few extreme cases. Dividing the variance by the mean has the effect of reducing the measure and makes it somewhat more conservative, but it also standardizes the statistic so that comparisons are appropriate.

The first problem is to determine appropriate cohorts and measure their publication variability through time. I did this by using the date that scientists received their PhDs, or in a few instances when they did not have PhDs (mostly British scientists), I used the date of their most recent degree. I grouped the scientists into dates of PhD, using a five-year interval. Those receiving PhDs from 1930 through 1934 comprised one cohort, and those receiving degrees from 1935 through 1939 comprised another cohort, and so forth (see Table 25). For each cohort I looked at the number of predoctortal publications and the number of publications in subsequent five-year periods. Unless the postdoctoral period extended completely through a five-year time period, the scientist and his publication data for that time period were excluded. For example, a scientist receiving a PhD in 1959 is included in the first and second time periods only. The third period would have required publication data for years more recent than are included in the study. This procedure means that the statistics for each five-year period cover all scientists with five years of experience in that period.

*TABLE 25   COEFFICIENT OF VARIABILITY OF PUBLICATIONS
BY TIME PERIODS FOR COHORTS, ALL SCIENTISTS*

Year of PhD	Pre-PhD	First 5 years	Second 5 years	Third 5 years	Fourth 5 years	N^a
1965-1972	2.32	5.03	30.84	—[b]	—	47
1960-1974	2.14	4.89	10.49	—	—	132
1955-1959	2.31	6.18	10.54	13.21	—	126
1950-1954	2.88	3.11	9.92^c	9.42	13.51	114
1945-1949	2.44	4.94	13.15	18.29^c	17.78	54
1940-1944	2.77	5.83	8.31	8.35	17.61	35
1935-1939	2.49	3.15	7.94	9.33	25.21	30
1930-1934	1.28	4.79	7.19	11.16^c	10.23	29

[a] The total is 567, because some lacked information or received PhD before 1930.
[b] Blanks indicate insufficient cell size for meaningful computation.
[c] Linear increase is not consistent.

There are eight cohorts in Table 25. Three experience one five-year period in which the coefficient of variability is larger than a subsequent five-year period, but in all three instances the differences are very small. These data show that, as scientists go through their career, their inequality or variability steadily increases. With samples of scientists that are not real cohorts the inequality exists according to age groupings, but here they certainly exist in real cohorts.

An idea of cohort differences is available from inspecting the columns in Table 25. Except for the earliest cohort, variability in predoctoral publications is small. There are several cohort differences in the second five-year periods; few in the third period, but several large differences in the fourth period.

The heterogeneity hypothesis says that scientists are different from the beginning, but this does not seem a likely hypothesis unless one can explain the lack of heterogeneity for those completing their degrees before 1935. If the heterogeneity hypothesis can be rejected, the cumulative advantage hypothesis becomes a more likely candidate for explaining differential productivity. Because I do not have data on resource allocation to scientists, it is not possible to test directly the cumulative advantage hypothesis, but one thing is clear: It cannot be rejected, because there is an almost perfect linear relationship between time and increased variability. This is an appropriate set of data to establish that fact because these are real cohorts. Further studies will have to design appropriate measures of career resource allocations and other factors as administrative diversions. But any further study can have a high level of confidence that it will find a similar linear relationship between elapsed time and variation in scientific productivity.

I computed the coefficient of variability for each discipline and for British and American scientists separately (see Tables 26 and 27). The general results are similar. There is increasing variability through time for all scientists, British and American scientists, and disciplinary groups. These disaggregated data suggest that the cumulative advantage is as appropriate for British as for American scientists and that the process probably exists in all disciplines. There are insufficient cases for examining disciplinary groups within the countries because the number of scientists in each cohort is too small for meaningful statistics. Possible interaction effects, unfortunately, cannot be assessed.

TABLE 26   COEFFICIENT OF VARIABILITY OF PUBLICATIONS BY TIME PERIODS FOR COHORTS, BRITISH AND AMERICAN SCIENTISTS

Year of PhD	*Pre-PhD*	*First 5 years*	*Second 5 years*	*Third 5 years*	*Fourth 5 years*	N^a
British:						
1965-1972	2.53	4.43	$-^b$	—	—	31
1960-1964	1.70	4.57	11.28	—	—	72
1955-1959	2.19	7.19	11.18	10.17	—	66
1950-1954	3.32	3.93	6.80	7.01	—	53
1945-1949	1.96	5.34	16.15	22.85^c	19.46	27
1940-1944	3.48^c	1.89	3.00	6.50	7.20	10
1935-1939	1.55	3.40	7.55^c	7.35	11.74	11
1930-1934	0.75	1.92	7.33^c	4.58	6.32	5
American:						
1965-1972	2.11	6.14	—	—	—	16
1960-1964	2.87	5.01	7.06	—	—	60
1955-1959	2.39	5.22	9.61	16.65	—	60
1950-1954	1.21	2.62	11.79^c	11.68	15.02	61
1945-1949	3.26	2.67	4.21	6.76	8.43	27
1940-1944	1.59	6.59	10.88^c	9.54	23.08	25
1935-1939	3.51^c	2.87	6.47	11.02	37.28	19
1930-1934	1.39	3.96	7.27	13.06^c	9.78	24

[a] The British total is 275; the American total is 292 because some lacked information or received PhD before 1930.

[b] Blanks indicate insufficient cell size for meaningful computation.

[c] Linear increase is not consistent.

TABLE 27 COEFFICIENT OF VARIABILITY OF PUBLICATIONS BY TIME PERIODS FOR COHORTS, FOR DISCIPLINES

Year of PhD	Pre-PhD	First 5 years	Second 5 years	Third 5 years	Fourth 5 years	N^a
Biology:						
1965-1972	2.64	5.56	$-^b$	—	—	18
1960-1964	3.29	3.35	6.84	—	—	36
1955-1959	1.50	4.21	10.66^c	8.53	—	45
1950-1954	1.63	2.79	4.95	7.52^c	6.02	41
1945-1949	1.33	3.09	2.75^c	5.86^c	4.88	14
1940-1944	3.10	4.57^c	4.54	5.43	8.65	17
1935-1939	—	—	—	—	—	8
1930-1934	—	—	—	—	—	8
Chemistry:						
1965-1972	1.56	3.30	—	—	—	10
1960-1964	1.33	6.32	14.02	—	—	48
1955-1959	2.59	8.20	9.08	10.24	—	35
1950-1954	4.19	4.43	9.45^c	7.76	14.06	33
1945-1949	2.56	4.55	14.56^c	11.65	17.54	24
1940-1944	1.60	7.72	14.31^c	11.76	27.37	11
1935-1939	3.23	3.54	8.71	11.78	26.86	14
1930-1934	1.08	2.95	4.78	10.42^c	5.40	12
Physics:						
1965-1972	1.20	5.94	—	—	—	19
1960-1964	1.81	4.66	5.48	—	—	48
1955-1959	2.79	5.47	12.01	18.55	—	46
1950-1954	1.32	2.48	10.72	11.55	15.87	40
1945-1949	2.50	5.21	5.79	32.26^c	18.54	16
1940-1944	—	—	—	—	—	9
1935-1939	—	—	—	—	—	8
1930-1934	—	—	—	—	—	9

[a] The biology total is 187; the chemistry total is 187; and the physics total is 195 because some lacked information or received PhD before 1930.

[b] Blanks indicate insufficient cell size for meaningful computation.

[c] Linear increase is not consistent.

Reinforcement

The data on reinforcement are more interesting than those on cumulative advantage. Although they do not provide critical tests to eliminate competing explanations, they are consistent regarding some aspects of reinforcement. Early positive reinforcement is essential to the notion that scientists continue to do and publish good research, but previous studies discussing reinforcement usually examined only citation data (see for example, Cole and Cole, 1967; 1973; Lightfield, 1971). With the present analysis of my data I cannot eliminate all possible competing hypotheses from consideration when examining the reinforcement hypothesis, although I shall pursue this line of research in the future. It is possible to examine a series of correlations to see what variables are related most to productivity over periods of time. According to the reinforcement hypothesis a scientist produces something at one point in time. The amount of recognition received for that contribution will influence the amount of productivity at a second point in time. Thus early publications and their recognition should influence future publications. That can be examined in statistical terms by looking at the correlation between predoctoral publications, citations to predoctoral publications, and publications and citations at a later point in time.

Recall that these citation data came from 1972, but the citations were coded according to the published date of the papers being cited. This procedure stemmed from the idea that, whereas citations to a paper in one year are not of the same magnitude as in a different year, yearly rates are stable. Papers cited in 1972 to work published 10 or 20 years previously would in most instances (the rare exceptions are probably random fluctuations) signify a high probability that the work had been cited soon after it was published (see the work of Reitz mentioned in Cole and Cole, 1967:381). Testing that assumption would be almost impossible and certainly tedious, because systematic citation data are available only from 1961. On the basis of the research of Cole and Cole (1967:380–381) I did not weigh the citations according to the publication date of the paper being cited. In other words, if a scientist received a PhD in 1960, with 1972 citations to predoctoral publications printed between 1957 and 1959, his citations should probably carry less weight than 1972 citations to another scientist's predoctoral publications printed in 1947–1949. While I recognize the potential problem, I admit to having no rational bases for determining how I should have assigned heavier weights to the very old, compared to the recent, predoctoral publications.

The basic question is this: What influences publication efforts more in successive time periods—recognition of early efforts or some other factor? I cannot eliminate all other factors, but the correlation data suggest that recognition, *evidenced by citations,* is not the most important influence (see Table 28). A consistent pattern shows up in rows 3, 5, 7, and 9. In all instances the correlations are stronger between the publications of the previous period and those of the succeeding period than the correlations between the recognition given to work (citations) in the previous period and publications in the succeeding periods. Correlations between citations and publications in any period, except the predoctoral period, where $r = .41$, are consistently at least .70 or above. While the correlation of .41 is respectable in social research, those above .70 are high and consistent.

These correlations do not prove that prior productivity is more important for future productivity, but they suggest it. This possibility should be considered in future research. If this is correct, does it mean that recognition is unimportant for reinforcing a scientist's feeling of worth and importance? I think not.

Because Reskin (1977:502) anticipates me in this line of argument, I present her interpretation:

> The hypothesis that collegial recognition in the form of citations influences later productivity was supported, but to a smaller extent than past research on university scientists would suggest. This is not due to the heterogeneity of the sample: the effect of citations on decade productivity was *weaker* [her emphasis] for those in contexts that emphasize research. In such contexts, immediate, informal recognition from research-oriented colleagues may be more important in maintaining productivity than the formal, but delayed recognition that citations provide. This is consistent with the greater direct effect of early productivity on decade productivity among university chemists than those employed in other contexts. Given the reward structure of most university departments, the act of publishing—signalling both successful professional performance and a variety of forthcoming rewards—may be especially reinforcing to university scientists.

I came to this conclusion some time ago, but it is convenient to have a published source to quote. The germ of this idea is present in the hypothetical case of scientist Smith I described earlier. *Notification* of acceptance of his paper, not to mention the immediate gratification of mailing it off to the journal in the first place, was the first formal indication to him that his work was worthwhile. If the journal was refereed, and since I made up the story, let us say it was, not only did the referees agree on its value, but also the editor endorsed their opinions.

TABLE 28 CORRELATION MATRIX FOR 10 VARIABLES

Variables	1	2	3	4	5	6	7	8	9	10	X	S.D.	N[a]
1. Predoctoral publications	—										.79	1.58	600
2. Predoctoral citations	.41	—									.54	2.03	600
3. 1st 5-year publications	.29	.22	—								4.97	5.18	600
4. 1st 5-year citations	.19	.24	.70	—							4.82	9.39	598
5. 2nd 5-year publications	.19	.12	.59	.48	—						7.78	9.40	531
6. 2nd 5-year citations	.18	.14	.50	.58	.75	—					8.21	15.35	527
7. 3rd 5-year publications	.16	.10	.53	.45	.76	.56	—				9.19	11.19	398
8. 3rd 5-year citations	.09	.12	.36	.37	.52	.56	.73	—			8.58	13.51	389
9. 4th 5-year publications	.08	.02	.47	.36	.65	.56	.77	.59	—		9.87	12.78	273
10. 4th 5-year citations	.09	.07	.36	.35	.46	.59	.52	.59	.75	—	10.21	17.76	267

[a]Correlations are pairwise.

At least two or three independent judges gave him significant reinforcement. Furthermore, as Reskin implies, and with the risk that I may sound too anecdotal, receiving notice that a paper is to be published is important news. It is news that, in a well-integrated department at least, travels faster than some of the best gossip. All one's colleagues offer their congratulations, and the recently annointed colleague basks in the sunshine of positive reinforcement.

Some months later the article appears in print, which again elicits some congratulations, but by then major reinforcement by one's colleagues has been exhausted. And much later our colleague sees that someone, whom he would never suspect of having seen the paper, actually refers to it in the text or a footnote, and it shows up, with all the bibliographical trappings, in the list of references. I do not want to underestimate the importance of recognition that accrues at this point—rather, one's satisfaction at this point is more personal and private because colleagues are much less likely to see work cited, and therefore to comment on it, than they are to offer congratulations on hearing about the editor's letter and knowing that the major hurdle toward publication has been crossed.

This is not to cast doubt on the validity of Cole and Cole's (1973:114) assessment of the reinforcement hypothesis. They do not, however, state whether publications in the first and second periods are more strongly related to each other than citations to papers in the first period and publications in the second period are. Lightfield (1971) also does not reveal the relationship.

These data and interpretations do not cast doubt on the *importance* of early recognition and positive reinforcement. They do acknowledge that recognition through citations is delayed recognition, and even if citations are more rapid than honorific awards, they are still delayed. Because they are delayed, some of the impact may be lost when compared to immediate reinforcement. And of course, after our fictional scientist Smith has crossed the hurdles a few times, collegial congratulations may become less important, because time has passed, and he has sufficient publications to provide a reasonably steady stream of citations. But even among scientists who publish prolifically and who receive few, if any, citations, one must conclude that something is probably reinforcing their behavior. The simple event of having a paper accepted, not to mention actually seeing it in print, must be important to them.

The University of Chicago Press is not unaware of this phenomenon. Although I cannot find it now, and so it must remain uncited, they once had a little booklet that, distributed to potential authors, functioned to notify an author that personal feelings then being felt were quite normal, because everyone experiences them to some extent. The message came through clearly when one read what historical figures had to say about seeing their first work in print. One story was about a noted author who confessed to carrying a copy of his new book around in his pocket, checking periodically to make sure the ink had not vanished from its pages.

There is the lingering problem about the timing and amount of reinforcement. Because my data are from a representative cross section of scientists, at least these data on 300 American scientists, I may have sampled scientists from different types of important reinforcement systems. The same sampling possibility could account also for Reskin's (1977) findings. Cole and Cole (1973:115) mention that in some universities people are likely to be rewarded more for quantity than quality of productivity, and they suspect that lower prestige departments operate in this fashion. For those of their 120 physicists working at distinguished departments (and remember that their sample represents eminent physicists more than the "average" physicist) the correlation between quantity and quality of publications was $r = .71$; in the other departments it was $r = .42$. Because of coding procedures I am not able to distinguish the scientists' locations at the various points in time between their PhD institution and current affiliation (something I shall correct in the future). I cannot determine whether or not the correlations in Table 28 are influenced by departmental quality. But that possibility is an alternative hypothesis.

These data suggest that future research in explaining scientific productivity should examine the role of early recognition, especially situational recognition, on subsequent scientific productivity. Cole and Cole (1973) suggest the possibility of two or more strata that may incorporate differential forms of recognition for positive reinforcement. Hargens and Hagstrom (1967:33–34) suggest this too in their study of mobility. The upper and lower strata institutions appear to use different criteria for placing scientists in desirable departments. Hagstrom (1965:22) remarks that the socialization of scientists leads them to expect that recognition will not be equitably distributed.

Studies I used to formulate the research for this book, including of course, my own, included only formal honorific recognition. It became clear to me that other types of recognition, in the form of citations, are important. Moreover many others already referred to have identified citations as a form of recognition, and so I included citations in this study as a measure of recognition that is less formal and less delayed. It is probable that formal honorific awards and formal acknowledgments (citations and otherwise) are probably not widely distributed quickly enough to provide positive reinforcement, even for mature individuals who do not require *instant* reinforcement but who certainly need some kind. When I interviewed the 203 British high-energy physicists, there was a specific scientist who had published frequently and consistently over the years. But he had no indications of any kind of recognition. It was then a mystery to me how he would keep on and on doing things that everyone seemed to ignore. He told me he did research for the fun of it. Either there has to be recognition accruing to him in some fashion, or we have to rethink the conditions under which recognition is *not* necessary, or we have to modify our notions about the functions of the reward system and the processes inherent in it. Cole and Cole (1973:53–56) acknowledge not only that the formal reward system does not include most scientists but also that many scientists are not even aware of the potential awards available.

It may be that highly visible and formal honorific awards may be necessary for continued reinforcement of outstanding scientists, for if they are not appreciated, they probably could make outstanding contributions in fields other than science—even at age 40 and with PhDs in physics rather than business or economics. Scientists may, contrary to popular and stereotypical views, have a highly developed sense of reality. Brilliant scientists know they deserve awards, they receive them, and everything is good. Ordinary scientists know they deserve only ordinary recognition, that is what they get, and they are satisfied. Indeed, one scientist, in as many words, says just this when he discusses inequality among scientists and the fact that members of the community recognize inequality. There are the Einsteins of this world, and there are the dullards, and, he says, "One would not be human if one did not listen rather more carefully to the former than to the latter, nor if one did not seek to be heard *at least in proportion to one's estimate of one's own standing on this scale*" (emphasis added; Ziman, 1968:133).

Something that could be included in a mail or interview survey to elicit data on scientists' self-perceptions might be a simple question that asks scientists to rate, on a scale, from 1 to 10, first, how much recognition they have received, and second, how much they think they deserve. The results could be astounding.

Recently various scholars have written about the ethos of science, and many studies, such as the present one, have focused on one or more of the institutional norms of science. Increasingly, these norms, their relevance, and scientists' actual conformity to them have been questioned. The norms are at the core of the studies of the reward system in science. I focus on these norms and their critics in the next chapter.

Chapter 9

DISPUTES AND DEVIANT VIEWS
ABOUT THE
ETHOS OF SCIENCE

Many social groups have a set of formal expectations about the way their members should act. Churches have rules, fraternities, voluntary associations, formal organizations, and cities have rules, and the most pervasive collectivity group—the state—has rules that cover most aspects of our lives. These various sets of rules are not equally elaborate, and nonconformity does not result in equally severe sanctions. But one thing is common about them: After the process of composing them is completed, they are public for everyone to see.

Groups that do not have such published rules nevertheless have specific expectations for their members. An informal group of neighborhood children preparing a "hideout" often seem to spend as much time on what is expected in intragroup interaction, and how nonmembers will be treated, as they spend on the actual building of the hideout. Whether groups have formal and published rules or informal and implicit rules, all groups have rules.

Where are the rules for the groups of people whose common interest is scientific research? Are not scientists subject to rules and regulations? Indeed they are. There are all kinds of rules codified by various organizations with overlapping memberships. Universities have rules that impinge on research: who will do it, how much time will officially be allowed for it, how necessary material will be purchased, who may be employed as research assistants and staff, what safety precautions will be observed, and so on. The (federal) state and the 50 states, all financially involved in research, have rules about research, similar in many ways to those issued by universities.

Federal science policies are directed toward maximizing the amount of knowledge (payoff) from funds allocated to research while minimizing the amount of graft, corruption, and nonperformance of the grants or contracts. Federal policies do not set out institutional rules (for the institution of science) that specify how scientists should react to other scientists' research and how the scientific community can collectively move science toward the ultimate goal of describing and explaining the physical and social worlds.

While there is consensus that scientific activity is a social activity and that research scientists comprise social groups, there is less consensus on what precisely the social nature of scientific groups is and on what the institutional norms are that orient behavior and achieve conformity to those norms. The paradigm for this study of 600 scientists is based on the norms of science described by Merton (1942; reprinted in Merton, 1973:267–278), and with an extended elaboration by Barber (1952; see the 1962 version, especially pages 95–135).

The set of norms consists primarily of four basic prescriptions. In order for science to progress most rapidly and efficiently in extending the frontiers of certified knowledge, the scientific community must adhere to (1) organized skepticism, (2) universalism, (3) communality, and (4) disinterestedness (see Storer, 1966:76–86). For a brief discussion of these, see Chapter 1.

Of the four norms universalism is the most important for the present study, but it is difficult to see how violation of one would not result in tendencies to violate the others. The norms form an ethos, and while one or another may be the most important, they are a set and are necessary for defining comprehensively the institutional requisites for extending certified knowledge.

If these norms had not been previously defined, they would have to be invented ultimately. The scientific community generally observes these norms, as the present study shows. The reward systems in Britain and the United States (in chemistry, biology, and physics) adhere remarkably to a model of science in which the norm of universalism is a predominant component. It is "remarkable," not because it is unexpected, but because some members in all groups deviate to some extent from the set of norms governing behavior. And in many groups, if not most, nonconformity is much greater than could possibly be the case in these scientific communities.

If scientists are not observing these norms, there must be some process other than conformity to group expectations to explain these results. But if that is the case, the process would have to be working in such a way as to result in the same outcome. No competing norms have been proposed that could explain outcomes similar to those resulting from universalistic practices. It is necessary to examine some of the criticisms of these norms because, if the critics are correct, the explanation for the results of this study is far from obvious.

QUESTIONING THE ETHOS OF SCIENCE: EXEMPLARS OF ORGANIZED SKEPTICISM

Some scholars have questioned the accuracy of the Mertonian norms of science. Others have suggested that, even if the norms are accurate, they are not observed. Still other scholars have attacked the set of norms because they believe the model of science from which the norms are allegedly derived is neither accurate nor the most appropriate. These categories of scholarly concerns are not mutually exclusive. Indeed there may be other ways of cataloging the concerns. My discussion is not intended to be a complete defense of the norms of science, but I shall attempt to discuss all the writings of which I am aware and which are generally available. My intention is also not to defend Merton or Mertonian sociology of science. Merton is more than capable of defending himself, and future research will resolve the appropriateness of Mertonian sociology of science. If the papers that criticize the validity of the norms of science are unconvincing, then the best explanation for the results in the present study is that the institution of science observes these norms.

In his original paper Merton systematically explicated the norms of science. Later criticisms have tended to deal with bits and pieces of his ideas about the normative structure. This makes comparative analysis of critical papers difficult, overly complex, and almost impossible. One way to order the discussion is to take parallel issues from each paper, but that requires evaluating a single paper several times if it includes one or more issues. A discussion that honors chronology remains the clearest way to organize the evaluation.

*Kaplan's "Science and the Democratic
Social Structure Revisited"*

Kaplan (1963) was one of the earliest critics of the Mertonian norms of science, but it is not easy to categorize his criticism. He believes the norms are problematic because they do not seem to account for what he perceived to be happening in European science. The purpose of Kaplan's paper was to examine the hypothesis that the European system of science is changing in some degree, " . . . because of (1) serious departures by scientists from the ethos of science as suggested by Merton; (2) the relative malintegration of this residual ethos of science with the values of the larger society" (p. 2).

Kaplan offers observations about how each norm is not pertinent for European science, but his paper is difficult to evaluate. On the one hand he suggests that universalism is not practiced in Europe, but on the other hand he shows that these problems, to the extent they exist, are largely outside the realm of the scientific community. "While in general," Kaplan (1963:4) says, "truth claims in Europe as elsewhere in the world of science continue to be subjected to the established, impersonal criteria, the European institutional arrangements for science have denied in practice and in principle completely free access to the establishment of truth claims." He saw this occurring on two levels. First recruitment to scientific careers has been restricted to a relatively small group in the population, especially the children of parents with money and respect. Kaplan is careful to indicate, however, that this process is largely the fault of society, and not of science. For the second level he makes a peculiar logical twist, saying that "But for all men who are already scientists, the growing insufficiency and inadequacy of the facilities and support provided, in effect denied them the possibility of establishing truth claims as effectively as they might otherwise have" (p. 4). And those who are admitted into science, from among the small group gaining access to the scientific career, are hampered in their career by the shortage of university posts. After some discussion of the lack of research opportunities Kaplan (p. 6) concludes "It might well be argued that the European university almost succeeded in stifling the continued growth of science because of its rigidities in structure and the incongruence of its value system with that of science."

This and similar statements do not make the case that science does not operate in a universalistic fashion. Kaplan argues that science has not been universalistic in Europe, but he presents no empirical evidence to substantiate that conclusion, and his observations are based largely on processes beyond the authority and control system of science.

Discussing the norm of communality, Kaplan suggests that the scarce positions led scientists to act secretively about their work until it was almost finished so that others could not use the work to their own competitive advantage. He recognized that "while it is true in general that substantive findings have been communicated openly within the European scientific establishment, it is also true that the recognition and esteem component was generally reserved to *the* professor, and much less frequently to his juniors" (p. 9).

For disinterestedness Kaplan uses the idea that intense competition is prevalent among all scientists, but especially among young scientists vying for the small number of possible permanent career positions. With a proliferation of publication outlets and the intense competition scientists have not demonstrated disinterestedness but have instead increased their "... number of somewhat less-than-disinterested publications of a trivial nature, designed almost entirely for self-aggrandizement" (p. 12).

Kaplan suggests that, unlike the other norms, organized skepticism does operate in European science but that this norm does not flow over into scientists' activities as citizens. Kaplan seems to think that this is not as it should be, but he suggests it never has been that way.

Kaplan summarizes his arguments by saying that in Europe only one of the four institutional imperatives, organized skepticism, correlates with norms in society and that some of the noncapitalistic societies stress universalism (in recruitment of scientists). Kaplan (1963:14, 15) concludes his paper with peculiar inconsistencies:

> ... our analysis of the European situation indicates that it is precisely its lack of encouragement in this universalism sector that has led to a breakdown of the old laissez-faire system of science. Merton's model of analysis is an excellent one, but his results fail to substantiate his own argument that science thrives best in a democratic society. Our own analysis indicates that of the four, universalism seems to be the crucial imperative for both science and society. To the extent that this is observed in both science and society we have considerable forward movement within science. The other three may or may not be significantly crucial elements of the current scientific ethos. In any event, they appear to be sufficiently insulated from rather than consonant with the general societal value system. Our own studies would indicate that the particular values posited by Merton are more likely to have been historically correct than contemporaneously so. It is most likely that there have been significant changes in the overall internal scientific institutional value structure.

One way to look at Kaplan's paper is to see it as an attempt to say that Merton's norms were correct for science at one time but that they are no longer applicable. He seems to accept the norms as important requisites, especially universalism, but he presents no data or evidence that tests the validity of the norms either "historically" or "contemporaneously." His sentence, "To the extent that this is observed in both science and society we have considerable forward movement within science," certainly does not suggest that universalism is unimportant. Indeed what I understand about the Mertonian norms of science is that *if* these norms are observed completely, science will progress faster. To the extent they are not observed, there will be negative consequences for the progress of science. What is unknown, of course, is what the precise conditions are under which norm violation produces various types of negative effects on scientific progress.

Perhaps Kaplan's last sentence about institutional *value* structure is the key to his apparent misunderstanding of the effect of the scientific ethos. Values are the preferred outcome(s), in this case, advancement of certified knowledge. Norms, in contrast, are the prescriptions for collective action to achieve the value. Either Kaplan does not understand the difference between norms and values, or he believes that institutional value structure has changed. If the value "achieving progress in certified knowledge" has changed, Kaplan did not mention it until the final sentence of the paper, and there is no evidence to suggest that the goal (objective, value, preferred outcome) of science has changed. Kaplan's paper suffers from raising questions about irrelevant aspects of the ethos of science and from suggesting that a particular situation exists without providing data to support his conclusion. Kaplan's paper, with all its inconsistencies and contradictions, cannot be considered a serious or important criticism of the norms of science.

Mulkay's "Some Aspects of Cultural Growth in the Natural Sciences"

Mulkay (1969) sets out to show that the Mertonian norms of science are unable to explain the growth of science over the last three centuries. He suggests there are no empirical studies to show that the norms of science are peculiar to the scientific community. "If the norms are equally common throughout the rest of the academic community then we would not be able to explain the uniquely rapid and continuous growth of the natural sciences in terms simply or even primarily of conformity to the Mertonian norms" (p. 27).

After summarizing some historical data dealing with the problems that new ideas have in becoming part of the culture of science, Mulkay writes:

> I would like now to demonstrate the inadequacy of this functionalist view by showing how scientific theory and methodological rules operate as *the dominant source of normative controls* in science and, in fact, as a basic hindrance to the development and acceptance of new conceptions (p. 30; his emphasis).

Mulkay is not arguing against the presence of norms in science; rather, he is saying that the rules that guide scientists' behavior are not social but technical norms. (This position, peculiar for a social scientist to take, is discussed in the last part of this chapter.)

The bulk of Mulkay's observations are based on the account given in a special issue of *The American Behavioral Scientist* (Volume 7, September 1963) devoted to aspects of Immanuel Velikovsky's work, especially *Worlds in Collision*. The extreme negative reaction toward Velikovsky and his work, by some members of the scientific community, is proof to Mulkay that scientists do not observe the norms of science. He believes that the reception of Velikovsky's work indicates that the norms do not govern scientists' behavior "to any noticeable degree." But he mentions that some people reacted to the negative reception by others in such a manner as to suggest that they believed in the norms and that observance of the norms was important for the benefit of the total scientific community. Mulkay (1969:35) notes, however, that

> what is particularly noticeable about the Velikovsky affair is not this mild and uncertain reaction against the widespread failure within the scientific community to conform to the Mertonian norms but the persistent tendency of scientists both in the United States and elsewhere, through the medium of published reviews as well as personal contacts, to justify rejection of Velikovsky's claims simply by indicating the latter's departure from established beliefs.

Mulkay believes that, from the perspective of Mertonian norms, scientists should have taken Velikovsky's work seriously and should have taken great pains to examine the potential validity of his ideas. "If any scientists had reacted publicly in an emotional and negative manner they would have been restrained by reaffirmation of the Mertonian norms by their professional colleagues. As we have seen, this did not happen" (p. 35).

The negative reaction of Velikovsky, according to Mulkay, was an example of scientists' showing the results of their socialization, a process designed to incorporate the technical aspects of science, not its social–behavioral aspects. Mulkay maintains that given this training and the presumed cognitive dissonance produced by Velikovsky's claims, scientists had to act to reduce the dissonance. The only way to do this was through reacting to the fact that Velikovsky's claims did not conform to accepted knowledge about the natural world.

Mulkay realizes, of course, that this paints him into a corner. If scientists were reacting to Velikovsky because of his introducing an element of cognitive dissonance into their lives, the same kind of response could be expected of other "radical" theoretical suggestions. He suggests, therefore, a different process producing cultural growth in the natural sciences. His idea is that paradigms (and scientists) from one area are absorbed into other areas which creates new problem areas. "Science tends to proceed therefore by means of discovery of new areas of ignorance" (p. 42) that are not considered to be in conflict with current paradigms, and therefore, there is little resistance to innovation.

Mulkay adds another dimension to his view of scientific growth by suggesting that "cross-fertilization" between fields increases the incidence of innovation. He uses Ben-David's (1960) comparative study of nineteenth-century medical research to exemplify the process of cross-fertilization (Ben-David's equivalent term is "role-hybridization"). Mulkay may be correct in his model of scientific growth and change. But the Mertonian norms of science could provide the normative structure in which Mulkay's process of cognitive development occurs. Mulkay does not consider this; he appears far too interested in claiming that the norms of science are not observed by scientists.

Mulkay obviously sees contradiction in his perception of the implications of the Mertonian norms of science and in the process of cultural growth (scientific change and development). His error about the implications of the Mertonian norms of science prevents his development of a potentially comprehensive and important sociological model of scientific growth. The Mertonian norms of science are not inherently inconsistent with his sociological model of scientific growth, but Mulkay's mistake was to conclude that the negative reaction to Velikovsky was appropriate evidence to demonstrate that the norms of science are not appropriate.

But was the scientific community's reaction to Velikovsky evidence against the observance of the norms of science? Consider several important points. First, at no time was there a significant number of scientists involved in rejecting Velikovsky, and so even if they were all deviating from the "civilized" process usually seen in observing the norm of organized skepticism, the lack of conformity to the norm did not reach crisis proportions. Second, it is naive to expect any scientific community to turn away from its own research program to test systematically all the ideas, even those that could be tested, presented by Velikovsky. The amounts of time, energy, and resources to do that kind of thing would be enormous.

A third consideration is that many scientists are routinely sent papers from all kinds of amateurs or other "outsiders," and it is unreasonable to expect the norm of organized skepticism to require them to spend time on such improbable theories. One could ask how it is known that they are improbable theories if scientists do not evaluate them. The answer is that even social scientists experience this. In social gatherings just about everyone propounds a favorite theory, but that does not mean that it should be considered a serious proposal and that one must run out to test it right away. Scholars have their own work to do, and there is hardly time to spend trying to satisfy all the personalities of this world who have personal (not scientific) whims and theories. The instances wherein serendipity is gained would be insignificant compared to those wherein it is impossible!

A fourth consideration is the principle of just rewards. No one seems to deny that Velikovsky violated the norms and standard practice of the scientific community in publishing his ideas first in popular magazines (for a fee?), and it is clearly the purpose of those magazines to publish sensational articles to expand and maintain circulation. Now, having done that, it is not unreasonable to expect scientists to resist taking the work seriously and to oppose any effort to give the scientific community's blessing for its subsequent publication as a scientific book. If Macmillan had wanted to publish the book without any scientific endorsement, the scientific community would not have raised a fuss. But it is in the interest of maintaining the norms of science to require active resistance to such official endorsement. For if Velikovsky and his publishers could get away with it, what would keep the potential flood of such people from drowning the whole scientific community with their books? I can say it somewhat differently. There is one view of justice stating that if a person transgresses the rules considered sacred, that person has no claim to being treated with the dignity and respect to which others, not deviant, have a claim. Although I do not claim that is a correct posture to take, it is understandable when some people operate from that position.

Mulkay's criticism of the norms of science is problematic. It neither casts serious doubt on the accuracy of the norms as an ethos nor provides convincing evidence that they are not observed by the scientific community. There may be data that could cast doubt on the prevalence of scientists' conformity to the norms, but the case of Velikovsky is not sufficient, for the reasons given, to conclude that scientists do not conform to the norms of science.

Barnes and Dolby's "The Scientific Ethos:
A Deviant Viewpoint"

Barnes and Dolby (1970:3–25) attack what they see as a "school" of thought in the sociology of science. The students in the school are the scholars influenced by Merton. They list several areas of study that have come out of the Mertonian school, and one of these is incorrect:

"The patterns of recognition and reward in the academic world are interpreted in terms of the norms of communality and disinterest[edness]" (p. 6). In fact the subject matter of those studies has not been predominantly these two norms. The focus has been universalism.

Barnes and Dolby, concerned that the norms of science are pertinent more for academics involved in "pure" research, see this situation as facing a rapid decline, but they also see this as the critical component of the Mertonian approach. They concentrate on showing that Merton has failed to identify a normative structure within which pure research occurs.

They do not accept the basis from which Merton derived the set of norms in the first place. They believe that one cannot obtain accurate indicators from what scientists write, how scientists behave, or what norms are theoretically necessary as requisites for achieving the institutional goal of extending certified knowledge. They eliminate the third source of the norms from their attention because "it rests upon the theory of functionalism which has achieved no consenus within sociology" (p. 7). Of course, Barnes and Dolby could be faulted because their assertion that functionalism has achieved no consensus is questionable, and secondly, even if it were true, that would not rule it out as a consideration.

Barnes and Dolby divide their criticism into three parts. In the first part they argue that it is not possible for skepticism, rationality, and universalism to represent statistical norms; in the second part they argue that professed and statistical norms in science vary throughout history; in the third part they criticize Merton's description of scientific ambivalence.

Barnes and Dolby argue that rationality is part of every society, not specific to science, and that everyone behaves rationally—according to some standard of what is rational. Deviations from rationality are defined as misunderstandings, not as irrationality (p. 9). They argue that universalism, as rationality, has the same problem of comparative standards.

> What society does not possess prior impersonal criteria for truth? Anything distinctively "scientific" must lie within the specific nature of the "impersonal criteria" used by scientists. Merton attempts to distinguish specifically scientific criteria for truth claims; he contrasts the requirements of scientists that truth claims be "consonant with observation" with criteria found in other parts of society or even within whole societies; criteria such as dogma or attributes of the person making the claims. This treatment is mistaken and rests upon a failure to distinguish between criteria of truth and indicators of truth (p. 9).

They are way off the mark because they do not deal with the actual meaning of universalism, and this causes their claim about universalism's not being peculiar to science to be almost outrageous. Their ideas about *criteria* of truth and *indicators* of truth are these:

> We would argue that when, for instance, a Nazi stated that non-Aryan science was bad he was making an empirical claim, not uttering a tautology. That is to say, he was using race as an indicator of bad science, which . . . he defined in terms of the same criteria of truth as anyone else. He was making a mistake, not using a set of separate standards. The form of this behavior is analogous to that of the scientist who scans the journals reading articles by "big names" only, or who learns to avoid the work of certain known incompetents (pp. 9–10).

That argument has many problems. I find it peculiar that scholars can set out to criticize a set of ideas because the ideas are not based on sufficient data and then use considerably lower standards for their own evidence. How prevalent is reading only the work of "big names"? (See Cole and Cole, 1973:191–215.) There are big names in most specialties, if not all, and scientists do not usually read much outside their own specialty. They are more likely to read the work of "little names" in their own specialties than big names in a different specialty.

In a most remarkable twist of logic Barnes and Dolby, discussing organized skepticism, argue that, because scientists appear to push for their favorite theories, they are not skeptical. Certainly scientists who have worked on their favorite research will try to defend it against other skeptical scientists. Mitroff (1974) uses that kind of data to suggest that scientists deviate from disinterestedness. Barnes and Dolby agree that scientists usually have viewpoints that make them skeptical of some results but not of others—this is the norm, they say. Having found themselves in a situation suggesting that scientists practice organized skepticism, they then argue (pp. 10–11) that, because others in society are skeptical—for example, religious fundamentalists about alternative interpretations of the Bible—the fact that skepticism is present in society means it is not *peculiar* to science and cannot therefore be a norm *of science*.

What Barnes and Dolby seem not to realize is that Merton never said that one of the set of norms could not exist in society. Indeed, to the extent that there is social support for the norms of science—at least for science to observe the norms—there is correspondingly a greater probability that sicence can progress harmoniously with society. What does seem to be special about the norms of science is that *as a set they are peculiar to science*. Religious fundamentalists may be skeptical about other interpretations of the Bible, but they have been neither "accused" of being universalistic nor expected to be skeptical about their own interpretation of religion. Scientists are often skeptical about interpretations in their own paradigm.

In the second part of their criticism, dealing with temporal changes in scientific norms, Barnes and Dolby (1970:14–18) argue that communality was not a norm in the early period, because Black and Cavendish did not feel required to publish and Lavoisier practiced secrecy by delivering a sealed note to the secretary of the French Academy in 1772 to establish priority and to avoid anticipation by others. Disinterestedness was not a norm, because there was little opportunity to gain financial advantage from scientific pursuits.

Barnes and Dolby, acknowledging that Merton's norms are more important for the next "professional" period of scientific development, admit that there are scientific pronouncements of disinterestedness, skepticism, and emotional neutrality in the writings of the period. But they indicate that an example, or two, exists to cast doubt about whether these norms reflect behavior in a statistical sense. In the recent and more modern period problems of big science and multiple authorship and the implied loss of autonomy suggest to Barnes and Dolby that the norms of science are problematic. This section of their paper appears to move quickly to their last substantive section of criticism dealing with ambivalence and the scientific ethos. Perhaps this brief treatment is a consequence of their inability to defend their position on the norms of science in the professional and modern periods.

In their last section (pp. 18–23) they criticize the idea that there can be pairs of norms that produce ambivalence in scientists. They suggest that, even with conflicting norms, scientists are not paralyzed to action, because there are technical norms to prescribe the appropriate line of action. That brings them to the ultimate conclusion in their paper: The scientific community does not require a set of social norms. In a differentiated society, which science exemplifies in terms of disciplines and specialties, social order can be maintained without normative consensus:

> Those groups of scientists showing the greatest degree of consensus are Kuhn's paradigm-sharing communities. The cohesion, solidarity and commitment within these stem from the technical norms of paradigms not from an overall scientific "ethos." Technical norms can be espoused without the adoption of a "scientific identity"; they are compatible with a wide range of religious, political or philosophical orientations; they can be sanctioned in a recognition system or by financial rewards; and a variety of legitimations is available for their associated activities (pp. 23–24).

Barnes and Dolby return to the approximate conclusion Mulkay reached. They are comfortable with the idea that technical norms are sufficient for social control and order in the social organization of science. They are sure science can exist and operate without social norms. Technical norms change frequently, but these replace social norms as a major force in directing the social behavior of scientists. Because growth and change are explained, science does not have a special ethos different from any other specific institution or society in general.

Rothman's "A Dissenting View
on the Scientific Ethos"

Rothman (1972:102–108) argues that the scientific ethos needs to be reexamined. The paper is brief, clearly written, and entirely unconvincing. His thesis is ". . . that a variety of evidence points to widespread deviation from the ideals embodied in the scientific ethos" (p. 103). His strategy is to take universalism, systematic skepticism, ethical neutrality, communalism, and disinterestedness and show how each of these components, of what he incorrectly calls the "system of values," is no longer appropriate.

The major problem with his argument is that he does not provide sufficient evidence to support his claims. For universalism he claims that elitism and particularism are rampant in the distribution of grant money because, in 1965, 25 percent of the federal funds for research went to researchers at 10 major universities. "While at least some of this concentration can be accounted for by the concentration of better scientists at such schools it appears that personal factors do enter in, and that the institutional affiliation is decisive. A number of applicants report being rejected because the referees assume that the employing institution does not have the 'appropriate atmosphere' for research, or other non-scientific criteria" (pp. 103–104). He cites Klaw (1968:120), for evidence, and Klaw reports one scientist who claims that, after leaving one institution to move to a more prestigious one, he immediately obtained a research grant. It is possible that what happened was this: As a consequence of completing important research at the first institution the scientists was invited to the prestigious one, and the same research success that permitted him to move was what resulted in the subsequent research grant. Whether that hypothesis is correct or not, this one case does not indicate the destruction of universalism!

For systematic skepticism Rothman mentions the case of Velikovsky, although he does not refer to Mulkay's use of the same case. (In fact Mulkay's paper is not cited.) I need not repeat the objections to that example. He admits that the Velikovsky case is only one instance, but he believes rejection of scientists' work is frequently based on nontechnical criteria. He refers only to three other sources, none of which actually provide evidence about organized skepticism.

For ethical neutrality, or "no-holds-barred" research, Rothman claims that this "value" is becoming obsolete because of problems such as sensitive research, which is being criticized frequently. Ethical neutrality is violated when research is criticized because it deals with unpopular subjects or findings, different from what groups in society want to believe. While this is certainly a matter for concern, regardless of whether it is a value or a norm or is simply desirable, Rothman is not clear about whether this is the fault of society or of the scientific community. In mentioning work on genetics and intelligence, he implies that scientists are the biggest obstruction to this research, but there are members of the scientific community on both sides of the argument. Indeed most scientists are in favor of no-holds-barred research, and only a small but vocal minority is intent on censoring other scientists' research.

For communality Rothman says ". . . at least one observer has claimed that scientists are as secretive as dress designers" (pp. 105–106). That amount of evidence hardly justifies comment, but Rothman also claims that "invisible colleges" are engaged in social processes that have the *potential* to deviate from the ideals of communality. That logic is analogous to asserting that, because there are married couples, there is potential for someone to commit adultery.

Finally, for disinterestedness, Rothman sees that the desire for professional recognition has become a matter of open competition and that scientists race to publish their work, if necessary even in newspapers, to circumvent slower publication in journals. He refers to James Watson's account of the discovery of the structure of DNA and Christiaan Barnard's heart transplants (few scholars would consider that *science*) as relevant evidence for scientists' attempts to gain prestige and success. He indiscriminately refers to (and incorrectly cites the pages of) Hirsch's (1968:24–27) report of National Opinion Research Center data: "Studies of scientists show that money and other extrinsic rewards are important." The data show that many scientists actually do think of their work as a chance to earn enough money to live comfortably, but here is how Hirsch (1968:21–22) originally interprets the tabular data cited by Rothman:

A recent study of graduate scientists and engineers allows us to generalize about attitudes toward work on the basis of a large national sample (over 50,000). In every discipline, concern with professional values is higher for those who are employed in academic settings than is the desire to make money, while the reverse tends to be the case for those who are employed in business and industry. This is in line, of course, with what we should expect. Academicians get a sort of "psychic income" in addition to their wages and they choose their occupational settings accordingly. Significantly, this is equally true for the younger and the older groups (covering the age range from 30 to 54)—in other words, a large-scale displacement of values is not supported by these data.

Hirsch states that scientists could, of course, be saying what they think people expect to hear, but the fact remains that they have stayed in academic settings although generally they could obtain higher salaries in industry. On the basis of lack of evidence, and with no other reason to accept his thesis, I conclude that Rothman's assertion that the scientific ethos ought to be reexamined is not convincing. Not only does he fail to provide any appropriate evidence, but also he does not understand the difference between values and norms.

Sklair's "The Political Sociology of Science:
A Critique of Current Orthodoxies"

Sklair (1972:43–59) writes that his purpose is to augment recent attacks on Mertonian orthodoxy and to see if it is true, as others say, that the orthodoxy is really bourgeois ideology claiming to be scientific sociology. Sklair's strategy is to discuss each of the four norms and then to indicate that they are not necessary for science. While Sklair's strategy promises to be systematic, his argument ranges widely and is actually unsystematic.

Sklair's discussion of universalism is peculiar because it does not deal with how Merton and almost everyone else defines universalism. He states that universalism is both the basis on which scientific results are evaluated and the opportunity to produce results. Sklair asserts that Merton had good examples of Nazi interference with science that caused Merton to believe that, if social forces reduce universalism in science, science will suffer. And Sklair believes that, when Merton reprinted the original paper in 1949, the situation of Soviet biology gave Merton another excellent case of the importance of universalism.

But after conceding the importance of the Nazi and Lysenko problems, Sklair reports that, at the meeting where Lysenko won out, only about 10 percent of the scientists present spoke against him, and by the end of the conference half of those showed their support for Lysenko's views. Sklair quotes one of those three who extolled the virtues of Lysenko's ideas for helping to build a communistic society. Then Sklair adds that he quoted the scientist, not to show how far science can decline in totalitarian societies, but to show that universalism is complex and that its implications are more than is usually thought. Sklair believes universalism is violated when science is specifically supported as a means of anything but the production of knowledge. "For universalism is held to exclude any extra-scientific criteria in the prosecution and evaluation of scientific work" (p. 44).

Sklair wants to convince others that, if universalism is to be included as part of the set of norms defining the ethos of science, its proponents are painting themselves into a corner. He does this by stretching the implication of universalism much further than any proponent has ever tried to do. Sklair implies that, if universalism is important, then it does not permit society to have an interest in the ultimate importance of science to that society.

Sklair continues this peculiar line of argument by relating an instance in which Castro criticized a Dr. Thomas Preston, the Director of the Institute of Animal Science in Havana (and a British scientist). It seems that Dr. Preston's research conclusions did not fit into the government's agricultural policy. Sklair reports that Castro issued a statement placing the research into a socioeconomic context. What Castro said was that people in positions of public responsibility should have enough knowledge to evaluate the results reported by scientists, technicians, and other specialists. Sklair notes that, subsequently, Castro and Dr. Preston apparently resolved their differences. But he adds a peculiar twist by saying that the Castro–Preston case suggests that the political control of science is linked with democratization, especially in contrast to the elitism involved in the ideology of pure science:

> This ideology of pure science means that only scientific considerations are ever relevant to scientific work. This would mean that medical science, for example, would advance at an even greater rate than it at present does, for the norm of universalism would ensure that no squeamish, unscientific rules prohibiting crucial experiments on human subjects would obstruct this advance. On this argument democratic societies, concerned with the rights of the individual and minority groups, appear to place obstacles in the way of scientific progress that could be and have been removed by totalitarian societies. Thus, as far as the norm of universalism is concerned in some respects, only in non-democratic societies like Nazi Germany and Stalinist Russia, is scientific research truly unfettered (pp. 45–46).

Sklair argues that it is not adequate to study science as a purely intellectual pursuit, because science is affected by society in many ways. "We must" he says, "continually be aware of the ways in which science is *not*

self-contained, and as I have indicated, a concentration on the institutional norm of universalism, paradoxically, can obscure them in certain
circumstances" (p. 46). Of course no one who has observed scientific
activity for more than a day would doubt that science is affected by its
social environment. Indeed that is one of the basic arguments in the
democratic-social-structure-and-science hypothesis. But to admit that
science does not operate in a vacuum does not at the same time mean
that universalism is unimportant or unnecessary. Sklair errs badly
when he says that universalism is violated because society does not want
its members to be used indiscriminately as guinea pigs, and I doubt
that any serious scholar would accept such an absurd interpretation it
its meaning.

But Sklair does not stop with universalism. He notes there are two
aspects of the norm of communism or communality. One is that science
is public knowledge, although his use of the term *public knowledge* is
much different from Ziman's (1968). The second is that communality
rejects secrecy in scientific matters. Everyone agrees on the second aspect, but just when Sklair has an opportunity to pursue a reasonable
argument, he fails, for in the sentence immediately following, he states:
"Let it be immediately and categorically stated that much if not most of
contemporary science is carried out under conditions of formal or informal secrecy, and that one has to restrict the notion of public knowledge in describing modern science in such a way that private knowledge will appear to be just as accurate a description" (p. 46). For that
wild assertion Sklair neither provides evidence nor refers to any.

Sklair's definition of "science" begins to show at this point: He believes that everything under the usual rubric of research and development (R&D) is science. It is his right to define science as he wishes, and
he could show that secrecy is rampant in research development and
nonresearch development, but most scholars in the sociology of science
do not accept such a broad definition of science *for purposes of the ethos of
science.* Who among us Mertonian sociologists of science has ever suggested that technologists (and that is the label appropriate for most
personnel in R & D) ought to be disinterested or that they should freely
give their information over to competitors? Indeed that would strain
the imagination to suppose that the thousands of technologists are not
interested in personal or corporate gain and that they should give over
their hard-won development projects to others without licensing fees or
patent rights. I cannot explain why Sklair would assume such a posture.

Although it is simple to dismiss Sklair's contentions about secrecy, it
is less easy to dismiss his claims about public knowledge. It might be
easy if it were clear exactly what his concerns are. His argument that

science is more like private than public knowledge takes this logic: There are too many journals for everyone to read; there is a crisis because of the publication explosion; scientists publish partly to establish priority because of the unnecessary struggle within science. *Therefore,* science must be private knowledge. It is difficult to enter an intellectual discussion with someone using that kind of logic.

Sklair takes disinterestedness to be bound up with communality, but scientists are not disinterested, for if they were, they would not engage in priority disputes. Sklair does not see the priority disputes as an instance of scientists' maintaining the normative structure of their community. What he does see is that Merton's explanation is geared to prop up a functional view of the world, and anything that is "tainted" with functional analysis cannot have even a shred of validity.

Sklair believes that organized skepticism is the boundary between sociological and philosophical accounts of the scientific enterprise, a boundary that has been "hotly attacked" and "stoutly defended" but that is now crossed more frequently, he believes, because of Kuhn's work. "But this norm and the important contemporary debates surrounding it fall outside the scope of my present limited purpose" (p. 56). Sklair concludes that the *necessity* of the other three norms has not been demonstrated, although he did not evaluate that problem systematically in his paper. He argues that the norms of science and the social organization of science implied by the norms have an important but only limited connection to science,

> but have a very great deal more to do with science as it is carried out in advanced capitalist society. . . . The orthodoxy that I have been criticizng would have us believe that these norms are indispensible to the survival of science as such, whereas if the criticisms in the previous pages are cogent then it is apparent that the Mertonian sociology of science is merely expressing the interests of particular sections of the scientific community in a liberal democratic social order (p. 56).

My conclusion is that Sklair neither demonstrates the invalidity, unimportance, and noncomformity to the norms nor does anything except attempt to destroy a model created by his false image of what Mertonian sociologists of science are talking about when discussing science.

Mitroff's "Norms and Counter-Norms in a Select Group of the Apollo Moon Scientists"

Mitroff's (1974:579–595) paper is based on a longitudinal study of 42 "moon" scientists, including those among the elite of all scientists studying the moon. Mitroff's starting point was Merton's early and later writ-

ings on the norms of science and Merton's ideas about sociological ambivalence. Mitroff focused mostly on sociological ambivalence and tried
to crystallize from his interviews the essence of what counternorms
would be like and how they would work.

There are several problems with Mitroff's approach, and at least two
authors have discussed them (Merton, 1976; Mulkay, 1976). Without
repeating their criticisms, my view is that Mitroff has taken the position
that scientists sometimes adhere to institutional norms *positively* and at
other times *negatively*. Stated somewhat differently, what Mitroff
defines as norms is simply the way scientists behave. If they deviate
from the Mertonian norms, instead of calling it *deviance*—and specify-
ing under what (extenuating) conditions they deviate form the
norms—he sees their behavior as conforming to counternorms.

It may be that a philosopher is not accustomed to thinking in terms
of conformity and noncomformity. Indeed he set out to show that science does not work like the "story book" image or textbook image that
many people have of science. Consequently he is interested in reinter-
preting what science actually is and what scientists actually do, instead
of what philosophers usually describe as a model of the process of
scientific inquiry.

Mitroff argues (pp. 593–594) that science would probably suffer if
there is consistent conformity to the Mertonian norms, because he sees
positive functions of the counternorms. Of course it is a risky business
to generalize to "all of science" from data on only 42 scientists—those
who represent an unusual and exotic specialty. It may very well be that,
to the extent Mitroff observed counternormative behavior, the same
behavior could be explained simply by deviance, and any claim that
deviant behavior has positive functions for the institutional goal of science seems extremely speculative, if not illogical. He claims secrecy has
a positive function because, instead of distracting from scientific progress, it helps avoid consuming time and energy over priorities. He goes
on to say that "Without secrecy, science would degenerate into a state
of continual warfare. A certain amount of secrecy *is* [his emphasis] rational since scientists are not always able to acknowledge the source of
their ideas" (p. 593). Mitroff suggests that "While stealing may be more
difficult than secrecy to make into a counternorm, . . . stealing and ap-
propriating may be important ways of informing a scientist and his
peers that his work is significant" (p. 593).

An example of the responses that Mitroff used to base his conclusions involves a scientist who said " 'You know you're doing something
significant when people want to steal it' " (p. 593), but if that statement
is considered carefully, the scientist could have meant that you know

you are doing something significant when people want to emulate you! If a scientist wants to initiate research along the same line as someone else, that could also be called "replication." Surely science can benefit from replication, but Mitroff is unconvincing in his argument that science can benefit from stealing, even on a small scale. Published statements about stealing before Mitroff's viewed the determination of real theft of ideas as problematical, but real theft was viewed as an extreme case of normative deviance.

Mitroff's paper is different from the other papers reviewed because he is not trying to argue that the Mertonian norms are invalid, irrelevant, unnecessary, or some combination of these. He was apparently initially concerned because of the enormous personal commitment to their own ideas that scientists had, and this conflicted with the idea that scientists should be emotionally neutral about their research. One hypothesis to explain this strong personal commitment is that commitment is inversely related to cognitive ambiguity in a research area. Indeed Mitroff (p. 586) seems almost ready to propose this but does not. He reports in a footnote about the three scientists who were overwhelmingly identified by their peers as the most committed and whose reputation did not change over the three-and-a-half-year period:

> At the one extreme, are the three highly committed scientists who wouldn't hesitate to build a whole *theory* of the solar system based on no tangible data at all; they're extreme speculative thinkers." At the other is the data-bound experimentalist who "wouldn't risk an extrapolation, a leap beyond his data if his life depended on it." Whereas the three highly committed scientists are perceived as biased, brilliant, theoretical, as extreme generalists, creative yet rigid, aggressive, vague, as *theoreticians,* and finally as extremely speculative in their thinking, the opposite extreme are seen as impartial, dull, practical, as specialists, unimaginative yet flexible, retiring, precise, as *experimentalists,* and extremely analytical in their thinking (p. 586, fn. 11; emphasis added).

Mitroff suggests that, contrary to Merton's view, some of these attributes help explain, at the psychological level, why some scientists are more contentious than others and thereby more prone to priority disputes. Although Mitroff agrees with Merton that science does not recruit more contentious people than other areas of life, he believes that "some kinds of scientists are more contentious than others and thus quicker to initiate and press their claims for priority" (p. 587).

Mitroff's hypothesis is testable by empirical data, but I suggest that the real hypothesis is that certain areas in science, theoretical areas, for example, are more likely to self-select certain types of scientists but that the important variable is the type of research in which the scientists are engaged. A modest example is the simply documented but enormous difference between theoretical and experimental scientists (see Gaston, 1973; and White et al., 1976). Certainly, among the moon researchers, experimental scientists' research was structured, partially owing to the available experimental moon samples; theoretical scientists' research, in contrast, was much less structured. Their research interests involved explaining all manner of phenomena, from speculating about the origin of the moon to wondering why material found on the moon might differ by location. Experimentalists had to focus on more or less standard analytic problems, but theoreticians had no such focus, since their territory covered virtually any questions about the moon. What Mitroff does not seem to suspect is that the reason why experimentalists could not be so personally committed to a particular notion is that evidence, if available, could be relatively definite; theoreticians' notions, if testable, could still be open for alternative, untestable possibilities. Thus, while Mitroff believes that some psychological differences may explain commitment to a scientific notion, my view is that the social structure of research and the division of labor in science is a serious alternative hypothesis.

Mulkay's "Norms and Ideology in Science"

In Mulkay's (1969) previous paper he argued that the norms of science are not observed, and even if observed, they would not explain the growth and change in science. Rather, he believes, science grows by finding new areas of ignorance that are not threatening to the commitment scientists have for established paradigms. In this later paper Mulkay (1976:637–656) talks about the "supposed norms of science" (p. 637).

Mulkay states that the idea of norms in science is more than a mere assertion that they exist; rather, he cites Storer (1966) as claiming "that widespread conformity to the norms is maintained by an effective system of social control" (p. 638). Without this claim Mulkay believes one could not argue that norms have a positive function for science.

> In other words, it is suggested that certified, reliable scientific knowledge will be produced only insofar as these, and not other, norms actually guide scientists' action. This assumption plays a crucial part in Merton's initial discussion of the norms, where it is argued that scientific knowledge develops more effectively in democratic societies because such societies are more willing to allow the institutionalization of a set of norms in science which parallel those operant within the political system (p. 638).

Mulkay explains that those who argue that scientists generally conform to the norms focus on the negative consequences of deviant acts. And he agrees that it is easy to see that deviance might interfere with creating certified knowledge. And from that perspective he understands how the norms could be important to science. "It is assumed," he writes, "that considerable conformity to these norms is maintained; and the institutionalization of these norms is seen as accounting for that rapid accumulation of reliable knowledge which has been the unique achievement of the modern scientific community" (p. 638).

But that is as far as Mulkay will go. He refers to recent criticism of this "functional" view by noting that studies by historians and sociologists show frequent disregard for these norms in their actual behavior. The problem is that for support of this assertion he refers to his earlier paper (Mulkay, 1969) and Barnes and Dolby's (1970) paper, discussed earlier. Those papers raised questions about the prevalence of conformity to the norms, but it is not correct to say they demonstrated frequent disregard of one or several of the norms.

Mulkay, assessing Mitroff's (1974) paper, finds it interesting because he believes the data indicate prevalent disregard for the norms of science. Of course, it requires a certain stretch of the imagination to believe that data on 42 scientists could indicate widespread deviance. Mulkay dismisses Mitroff's findings, nevertheless, by saying these norms originate from scientists who say what they believe people want to hear (that scientists are honorable, that scientists are really human, as evidenced by deviant behavior) or what people need to hear (that science has lofty moral principles and deserves special consideration).

To Mulkay, then, the scientific ethos is purely a public relations exercise. Scientists say things that suggest they observe scientific norms, and they talk about the special nature of science, but it is all window dressing, camouflaging what really goes on in science.

Mulkay summarizes his thesis in three points (pp. 653–654). First what previously has been thought of as the norms of science are really "vocabularies" of justification. Their function is justification, evaluation, and description of the professional actions of scientists, but the norms are not institutionalized as behavioral norms in the scientific community; they are only an ideological posture. Second these vocabularies have been used by scientist-statesmen to argue for and justify special status for scientists. Third scientists have presented a view of sicence to gain social and financial support for research activities. Scientists use this ideology in the same way that other occupational (and professional) groups use ideology: to protect and enhance their status.

Mulkay's thesis is interesting and provocative, and it is based on a series of assumptions that I can make explicit. First Mulkay acknowledges that scientists are aware of the idea of conforming behavior, for they talk about it. Second he admits that a set of norms would indeed support the creation of reliable knowledge. But Mulkay, after accepting the validity of these two assumptions, asserts that there is widespread deviance from the norms, and so they cannot be institutionalized. If scientists are aware of the behavior prescribed, and if they recognize the positive aspects of conforming to the behavioral guidelines but do not conform, Mulkay believes that makes the validity of the norms questionable; but because they are generally recognized and verbalized, they must be serving some *function* (an ironic conclusion from an antifunctionalist). The function they serve is occupational ideology. The key to his whole argument is, of course, the belief in widespread disregard for the norms of science. That belief is not supported by evidence from Mulkay or from anyone else. Without evidence Mulkay's thesis is pure conjecture.

REAFFIRMING THE ETHOS OF SCIENCE: THE POWER OF EVIDENCE

My discussion and evaluation of the criticism of the Mertonian–Barber norms of science should not be construed to mean that viable alternative interpretations of the scientific community are not possible or acceptable. The most serious problem with all the papers reviewed is the lack of evidence. They show a tendency to leap from a single or a few observations of deviance to a wholesale dismissal of the validity and effectiveness of the norms in guiding scientists' behavior. Perhaps some explanation other than conformity to norms could produce my findings on the 600 scientists. Perhaps the correlations between productivity (role performance) and recognition are not explained by the hypothesis that scientists generally conform to the norms of science, producing outcomes that must be characterized as "universalistic." But if there are alternative explanations, they cannot be gleaned from the papers reviewed in this chapter. (For some different criticisms of the "Mertonian" sociology of science, see Collins, 1977; King, 1971; Whitley, 1972. For another view, see Wunderlich, 1974.)

I would be surprised if some of the 600 scientists have not suffered from particularistic evaluation of their work. Surely the reward system is not completely universalistic, if only because human beings are involved. But it is remarkably universalistic in spite of the several stages in a career where there is an opportunity for particularism to enter and eliminate or reduce any recognition accrued for prior achievements.

But these data on 600 scientists represent, with considerable statistical confidence, many hundreds of scientists in physics, biology, and chemistry. The data fortunately are a random sample from major lists of scientists, not a purposive sample of a small group or a simple enumeration of some esoteric specialty.

The recent attack on the norms of science calls for some explanation. First there is the problem of the nature of this concern. Second there is the problem that scholars appear to resist the possibility that scientists are guided by social norms. Third there is the resistance of scholars to the possibility that science as an institution may be different from other social institutions. These problems are no doubt strongly related.

One conceivable hypothesis to explain the origin of the attack on the norms of science is the indisputable phenomenon that, in spite of differences, scholars from various perspectives (or paradigms) in sociology share at least one common characteristic. They think that representatives of other perspectives are not attending to the "real concerns" of sociology and are consequently wasting their time. They imply that others are wasting time because they fail to address the proper questions. It may be that different perspectives are relevant and potentially important, but scholars seem to strive for some monolithic perspective. If that is generally true for sociology, it is no less true for sociology of science. Scholars who criticize the normative structure of science should consider either focusing on problems within their specific perspectives or designing studies that would provide critical tests of the accuracy of the views they do not accept (for whatever reasons).

The second problem, resistance to the idea that scientists' behavior is not guided by social norms, is difficult to explain. If sociologists assume that all groups have norms, and if scientists comprise a group (or groups), then it follows that scientists have norms. Mulkay (1969) claims that scientists observe technical, not social, norms. Even if this is so, there is still the problem of identifying the social norms that scientists observe, in addition to the technical norms. If scientists do not observe social norms, then what regulates their social activity as scientists? Do they have guiding principles for behavior no different from any other person? And are those principles sufficient to maintain a scientific community? Scholars who denounce the Mertonian norms without suggesting alternative *social* norms must realize this is a problem. It becomes a more serious problem for their own ideas based on the false claim of widespread disregard for the Mertonian norms. If their ideas are based on false claims, and they propose no convincing alternative norms, one must conclude that the scientific community is without norms. For sociologists to argue seriously that a community without norms is a view of reality is, quite simply, remarkable.

The third problem, resistance to the idea that the institution of science is different from other social institutions and has a specific ethos, fails to acknowledge the one fact that no one in the anti-Mertonian tradition has criticized: No institution other than science has as little fraud, dishonesty, and chicanery. And even when those infrequent acts occur, a scientific peer is most often the one who exposes the culprit.

The lack of negative evidence about the norms of science puts the critics in weak positions. Moreover, there has been one study that attempted to determine the prevalence of scientists' acceptance of the norms. The usual criticisms may be invoked to question the quality of the argument based on these kind of data. The most popular one is this: Scientists would say only what they thought people wanted to hear. The next most popular criticism is this: There is a big difference in what people say and what they actually do!

(Permit me to inquire of my reader: Have you ever noticed the difference in the reaction to surveys showing that people did something that might be valued as "good" in contrast to surveys showing that people did something that might be valued "bad"? About the first there is a tendency for cynics to say people just respond with what is expected as "appropriate" responses. About the second people are likely to accept the deviance as having been correctly reported and to believe that surely the respondents are telling the truth. People in general, and sociologists in particular, seem willing to believe the "bad" things people say they do but are very skeptical about believing the "good" things people say they do.)

Blissett's (1972:72–73) survey, involving more than 800 scientists, asked scientists to indicate whether they agreed, disagreed, or were undecided about various statements. The statements about the norms were not worded in a parallel fashion, and he offered three statements each about universalism and communism, and one statement each about the other norms. He tried to tap various dimensions of universalism and obtained different responses to the three statements. For the statement about whether acceptance or nonacceptance of scientific evidence depends on the social positions of scientists providing the evidence, 33 percent agreed, 60 percent disagreed, and 7 percent were undecided. Of course, these data could be interpreted to mean that, whereas scientists' work is not evaluated by particularistic criteria, work at certain places is known for its high quality. But this would not mean that particularism was involved. Blisset's statement that "Scientists must adhere to a common set of objective standards by which proof can be demonstrated" showed 64 percent in agreement, 29 percent in disagreement, and 7 percent undecided. His statement that scientists anywhere in the world can communicate with each other because the terms used for communication have precise meaning, showed 72 percent in agreement, 22 percent in disagreement, and 6 percent undecided. Even without my reinterpretation of the meaning of the first statement, it is hardly correct to conclude there is widespread disregard for universalism among scientists.

Blissett's statement that "Only those scientists who have high standing, or work or associate informally with those who do, have the kind of information that lies at the cutting edge of inquiry" received 57 percent disagreement (showing support for communality), 30 percent agreement, and 12 percent undecided. For the other two statements dealing with communality (1) that the communication of results is necessary, and that (2) in fundamental research areas scientists regard their ideas as common property, there was 97 percent in agreement with the first and 82 percent in agreement with the second.

For disinterestedness Blissett stated that "Science differs from other professions (medicine, law, etc.) in that there is less chance that a scientist would take advantage (financial or otherwise) of the layman." Without knowing what the response was to that, one would have to think this statement does not relate very much to disinterestedness. The statement received 47 percent in agreement, 30 percent in disagreement, and 23 percent undecided. Because this statement received the largest percentage of undecided responses, it must be too ambiguous. On its face the statement could easily appear to be asserting that scientists as a group are more honest than doctors and lawyers, for it is clearly demonstrable that scientists do not have the same relationship with the "layman" as doctors and lawyers do.

Finally, for organized skepticism, Blissett again offers a statement that does not relate to the usual meaning of organized skepticism. He states that "Scientists are skeptical even about their own findings until other scientists have evaluated them." Surely organized skepticism as an institutional norm requires that scientists be skeptical about findings, but especially about those of others, not necessarily skeptical about their own, because others will provide that skepticism. The percentage of agreement and disagreement with that statement was split 44 and 45 percent, respectively, with 11 percent undecided.

Blissett's study generally lends strong support for the norms of science. If what scientists say about such statements can be interpreted as their actual support for the norms, one must conclude that, contrary to the papers reviewed, and generalizable of course only to the 800 scientists in his study, the norms seem to have been institutionalized. Blissett's study cannot be construed as indisputable evidence about the norms, but his is the first, and as yet, only study that tries to obtain the quality of empirical evidence that might be used to evaluate the presence of norms in the scientific community. Final answers must await the properly designed studies that would include refined statements similar to Blissett's, and also statements that would assess the critics' views. Perhaps one or more of them will put their proved intellectual talents to work on this problem.

Chapter 10 / *COGNITIVE DEVELOPMENT,*
SOCIAL ORGANIZATION
AND THE REWARD SYSTEM

This study set out to determine how the reward system in science is influenced by the social organization of science in a country and by the presumed differential cognitive development of scientific disciplines. Britain and the United States offered examples of different social organization. In Britain the social organization of science is characterized by centralized policy and funding. In the United States it is characterized by pluralistic and decentralized policy and funding. Physics, chemistry, and biology offered examples of disciplines with presumed differential cognitive development.

The reason for expecting these characteristics to influence the operation of the reward system arises from previous studies. When minor assumptions are made, those studies can be located along a "universalism" continuum. The result is that generally recognized cognitive development is positively correlated with universalism. At the same time it is possible to compare the studies of British and American scientists to see which country has more universalism. Although there are few studies, the results suggest that British science is more universalistic than American science. In some ways this idea is contrary to perceptions about Britain. Britain is commonly believed to have a high degree of snobbishness and more rigid social class distinctions. But other evidence supports the idea that Britain is more universalistic than the United States. The British educational system is rather homogeneous, and competition at the institutional level (but not necessarily at the personal level) is minimized. Consequently British scientists have few opportunities to use any advantage that might accrue from unequal competitive positions. In contrast to the British system the American educational system is heterogeneous, and there are many opportunities for scientists to use advantages resulting from unequal competitive positions.

This study shows that cognitive development influences the operation of the reward system, but unexpectedly, physics, chemistry, and biology are not ranked in the usual pattern. Biology ranked second to physics, and although this does not prove that biology has greater cognitive development than chemistry, the results seem to call for reexamination of the commonly assumed order.

The results show also that British science is more universalistic than American science but only slightly more. In fact the small differences in the amount of assessed universalism suggest that physics, chemistry, and biology are too similar to offer the best evaluation of the social-organization hypothesis. Perhaps a "representative" discipline from the physical sciences, the biological sciences, and the social sciences would be a more appropriate test of the hypothesis.

The interpretation of these results stems from the Mertonian norms of science. The normative imperatives, universalism, communality, disinterestedness, and organized skepticism, are strongly institutionalized in the British and American scientific communities studied. Scientists perform their roles and receive peer recognition, primarily on the basis of the amount of research they have contributed to the collective enterprise. These results might be possible without the norms of science, but it is difficult to imagine how or why that is possible. The scientific community could, and probably would, withhold recognition from scientists who disregarded the norm of communality. If scientists did not give up their work for others to use, and if others did not use it, scientists would not receive recognition from citations. The scientific community could, and probably would, withhold recognition from scientists who pursued personal goals, rather than institutional ones. (Indeed such scientists ultimately may leave the community in such pursuit.) It could, and probably would, withhold recognition from scientists who disregarded organized skepticism, and the data show clearly that scientists' work is referred to, regardless of affiliations or social standing. The logic leads to this conclusion: The scientific community observes the norms of science, and these data substantiate the conclusion.

PROBLEMS AND PROSPECTS FOR MERTONIAN SOCIOLOGY OF SCIENCE

To assert that Robert K. Merton is the most influential sociologist in the founding, growth, and development of contemporary sociology of science will produce more consensus than any other statement in this book. (Having been elected founding President of the Society for the Social Studies of Science is sufficient indication of his stature, but see the following: Barnes, 1972:61; Barnes and Dolby, 1970:3; Cole and Zuckerman, 1975:155–162; Mitroff, 1974:579; Mulkay, 1969:22; Storer in Merton, 1973:xi. Whatever the eventual outcome of his early model of science, first proposed about 35 years ago and more fully elaborated about 20 years ago, Merton's empirical studies and theoretical work on basic processes in science are classic exemplars of scholarly work in the sociology of science.

As the foremost figure in the specialty Merton naturally enjoys the most attention and receives the most intense criticism. This is "natural," *for* if I may paraphrase and revise a question from a famous book, *what does it profit a man to spend his life criticizing the work of someone who matters not?* Merton should not receive all the criticism, for it would be impossible for him or a group to have researched all the implications of his model of science.

Several related problems are identified in thinking about such criticism (regardless of its seeming prematurity). As someone said, after lamenting the lack of love and compassion but the prevalence of war in the world: "Christianity doesn't work," only to hear in reply: "Real Christianity hasn't been tried yet." This captures the essence of a major problem: Real Mertonian sociology of science has yet to be tried.

But what is the real Mertonian sociology of science? Clearly the ethos of science has to be a major part of it, but even complete agreement on what *Mertonian* sociology of science is would not eliminate other possible sociologies of science. Merton never claims, of course, it would, but this view seems to be imputed to him.

The best source of *some* of the Mertonian sociology of science is the 1942 essay. After describing many examples of historical consequence indicating that science has been supported and has grown under a variety of conditions, Merton (1973:269–270) writes:

> But such historical facts do not imply a random association of science and social structure. There is the further question of the ratio of scientific achievement to scientific potentialities. Science develops in various social structures, to be sure, but which provide an institutional context for the fullest measure of its development?

Merton's hypothesis—and it has remained just that—is that science develops best under conditions that are compatible to the ethos of science. But what tests are there of this straightforward empirical hypothesis?

Consider such a potential test. It takes appropriate measures of only a few variables. The independent variable is *social structure*. The dependent variable is *scientific development.* The intervening variable is *scientific potential.* Several indicators of each variable are desirable. The only major problem is to select the time periods, for surely social structure interacts with the level of knowledge base at any point in time. But this important research is yet to be done.

The general lack of sociological knowledge about the development of science in Eastern Europe is particularly troublesome. From many sources it is clear that the organization of research in Eastern Europe is much different from that in Western Europe and North America (see Dobrov, 1968; Szalai, 1968; UNESCO, 1965, 1967, 1968, 1970a, 1971a, b; and Zaleski et al., 1969). While there are similarities between some countries where the teaching and research functions of scholars are separated, in few if any countries outside Eastern Europe are science so centralized and the activities of research scientists and personnel so directed by planning groups several administrative layers above the laboratory bench or research institute. On the one hand very little is known about the effect that planning has on the ultimate applied research product: in the choice of problems and methods and the outcomes. On the other hand scientists engaged in pure research and competing in the international scientific community apparently have considerable choice in their research, but even so, the social organization of research is quite different from that in societies with less central planning.

Aside from the problem of conducting international comparative research in Eastern Europe, Western Europe, and North America, not to mention the difficulties of including Japan, China, India, and so forth, there are still other reasons that explain the difficulties for testing the social structure–scientific development hypothesis. One reason why this research has not been done is that, in spite of its apparent simplicity, it is extremely complicated. The problem of determining *scientific potential* is unsolved. How could potential be determined if scientists in country *A* have twice as many resources as those in country *B* but only half the scientific personnel? It is not impossible, but it is not easy (Ben-David's comparative historical studies come closest to this type of research). A second reason why this kind of research has not been done is that the sociology of science is a relatively new specialty, in terms of its institutionalization. There has not been sufficient time to accumulate enough research to deal with these problems. A third reason is the size of the specialty. The sociology of science, and the social studies of science, may be one of the fastest growing intellectual areas, but other social institutions have been studied for decades and by hundreds of scholars. Without sufficient time and scholar research-years, it is premature to fault any specific current perspective in the sociology of science.

In the infancy of any research specialty, scholars may differ over the questions, methods, and conclusions. That the sociology of science does this shows its self-exemplary nature. Debates, discussions, disagreements, and agreements are necessary ultimately to move a research area ahead. Often, however, some types of debate can become counterproductive. Specifically, without agreement on what it is that research is trying to explain (the dependent variable as introductory methods texts teach us), new perspectives are introduced, not as *competing* perspectives, but as *alternative* perspectives.

Granted that perspectives tend to narrow the list of research questions, and granted that research questions tend to influence methodologies, there is nothing in the process that declares other areas to be illegitimate. This view is not universally shared, of course. For example, one scholar, when discussing the efforts of sociologists of science in the Mertonian tradition, points out that a characteristic of North American scholars is to ignore the cognitive aspects of science and that this has led to North America's sociology of science's becoming the study of scientists' careers. He believes that we have deliberately tried to prevent the sociology of science from including the study of scientific ideas and that this attempt has left us to see ideas as nonproblematic. He believes we see timeless, universally valid criteria that evaluate scientific ideas, and so we do not require a sociological account. As a consequence of our limits on "rationality" we concentrate on "irrationalities"—the aberrations in scientists' social behavior, aberrations because we assume cognitive rationality. He writes that

> Any attempt at a sociological understanding of science must, in my view, involve an understanding of what it is that scientists produce. By identifying someone as a scientist, the sociologist is saying that this man produces scientific knowledge which implies some idea of what such knowledge is. If the sociologist relies on "the scientific community" to identify scientists he is implying that scientific knowledge is knowledge which is currently accepted and denying the possibility of formulating any criterion for evaluating scientific knowledge over time or space. The validity of scientific knowledge is entirely relative to the particular community. However a given classification is derived for scientists, or any occupational group, some theory of what it is that people in that group do is necessarily implied. Different theories lead to different forms of sociological work and declare different topics of research to be legitimate and illegitimate.

The view of scientific knowledge maintained by much of the sociology of science has led to an ideology of "black boxism" which restricts research to the study of currently observable inputs to, and outputs from, a system. Any study of the internal processes, which may be unobservable at the moment, is declared taboo. In the next section I will briefly outline some of the implications of, and an alternative to, a black box theory of knowledge. It is my contention that an *alternative* position will lead to a more fruitful sociology of science (Whitley, 1972:62–63).

There is an important but subtle problem in the quoted material. Whitley (p. 61) previously called attention to what he considers attempts by North Americans to define the sociology of science as what North Americans do. His conclusion simply is not warranted. But is the opposite true? How does one interpret this statement (my italics): ". . . my contention that an *alternative* position will lead to *a* more fruitful sociology of science?" Is it not an attempt to declare a particular perspective legitimate, that is, to do the same thing he *sees* North Americans doing? Only slightly different wording would make a big difference in the sentence, if it were to read, for example: ". . . my contention that a different position will lead to more fruitful *research* in the sociology of science."

A second problem appears soon after the material quoted, for Whitley shows that his definition of the sociology of science involves these questions: "How do social and cognitive factors interact to produce knowledge and what effect do different forms of scientific knowledge have on society?" (Whitley, 1972:63–64). The questions themselves are not a problem, for they are clear. The problem is Whitley's alternative sociology of science. Few, if any, scholars in North American sociology of science would either (1) deny that the questions are legitimate or (2) accept his assertion that the Mertonian sociology of science precludes such questions. Indeed they are the essence of the idea that the sociology of science is interested in, among other things—the relationship between cognitive and social structure! These semantic exercises are likely to continue as the sociology of science moves from its infancy into maturity.

THE FUTURE OF THE REWARD SYSTEM

The internal debates in the sociology of science about whether scholars are studying the cognitive development of science or merely studying scientists will ultimately be resolved as the research specialty prospers. But I turn now to the problem originally discussed in the Preface. I stated that my interest in the reward system basically stems from the question of whether or not people get what they deserve. The data in this study show that, at least for scientific recognition, these 600 British and American scientists receive recognition according to what they deserve.

The question is, then, are there trends for the future that may change this process? Are the respective societies developing any new structures or adopting any new ideologies that could jeopardize the universalistic operation of the reward system? The social structure of British society has nothing on the horizon that would suggest possible drastic changes in the operation of the reward system. British society, to a degree far greater than American society, accepts the proposition that university education and university research are elite activities. In so doing, however, the British idea of democracy shows up in the notion that everyone who can qualify (showing some potential for real success) for rigorous university education should be encouraged, and financial stipends are provided to ensure participation.

If there is no trend in British society to reduce the effective influence of the operation of the reward system, this does not mean that changes in financial support are impossible or that the distribution of funds will remain unchanged. The level of funding does not pose threats to the reward system, if the funds are distributed in a fashion to promote excellence. If funds were to be distributed on a per capita or pro rata formula, then there would be negative consequences for the reward system. That appears to be unlikely.

The United States has a potential problem on the horizon that British society does not have. The problem is extensive federal regulation that has appeared to become, increasingly, a policy not designed to deal with the needs of scientific research. Instead there is a potential that the government will use funding for research and other activities as a mechanism to promote social justice. Most Americans agree that something must be done to promote social justice and to reduce the inequality of opportunities that has compounded over the decades. The problem for the reward system is, however, whether or not the institution of science will be permitted to evaluate research proposals and research contributions with universalistic criteria. The potential is present for lower level administrators in federal employment and in universities to be concerned more with "outcomes" than with "procedures," and they may tend to interpret regulations in excess of what the executive orders and laws intended when they were formulated to guarantee civil rights.

It is difficult to avoid discussing the voluminous literature in this field, but that is not my purpose now. I am not saying, and no inference should be drawn, that current (1977) interpretations of regulations are leading to interference in the operation of the reward system. I am saying that, if current interpretations are expanded and if *political* rather than *scientific* considerations become primary objectives, the universalistic reward system is in jeopardy.

As a parting word I would repeat that the primary purpose of research on the reward system to this point has been to describe the nature of the system. It is important to know what *socially* causes the reward system to take the form it does and what causes it to operate in a universalistic or particularistic fashion. It is important also to know how the reward system acts as an independent force in the growth and development of science. If a universalistic reward system has positive functions for science, then learning more about it will enable us to explicate those functions. That will not only result in intellectual advantages for the social studies of science but also will provide potential opportunities for the enhancement of science.

I hope an ever-increasing number of us will search for some answers.

BIBLIOGRAPHY

ALLISON, *Paul D., Derek J. de Solla Price, Belver C. Griffith, Michael J. Moravcsik, and John A. Stewart*

    1976   "Lotka's Law: A Problem in Its Interpretation and Application." *Social Studies of Science* **6** (May):269–276.

ALLISON, *Paul D., and John A. Stewart*

    1974   "Productivity Differences among Scientists: Evidence for Accumulative Advantage." *American Sociological Review* **39** (August):596–606.

AMERICAN MEN OF SCIENCE

    1965–1967   11th Edition. New York: Jacques Cattell Press and R.R. Bowker.

ASTIN, *Alexander W.*

    1965   *Who Goes Where to College?* Chicago: Science Research Associates.

BABCHUK, *Nicholas, and Alan P. Bates*

    1962   "Professor or Producer: The Two Faces of Academic Man." *Social Forces* **40**:341–348.

BARBER, *Bernard*

    1962   *Science and the Social Order.* New York: Collier Books (rev. ed).

BARNES, *Barry,* Ed.

    1972   *Sociology of Science.* Harmondsworth: Penguin Books.

BARNES, *S. B., and R. G. A. Dolby*

    1970   "The Scientific Ethos: A Deviant Viewpoint." *European Journal of Sociology* **11**:3–25.

BAYER, *Alan E.*

    1970   "College and University Faculty: A Statistical Description." *ACE Research Reports* **5**:1–48.

    1973   "Teaching Faculty in Academe: 1972–73." *ACE Research Reports* **8**:1–68.

BAYER, *Alan E., and John Folger*

    1966   "Some Correlates of a Citation Measure of Productivity in Science." *Sociology of Education* **39** (Fall):381–390.

BEN-DAVID, *Joseph*

    1960   "Scientific Productivity and Academic Organization in Nineteenth Century Medicine." *American Sociological Review* **25**:828–843.

1964 "Scientific Growth: A Sociological View." *Minerva* **3**:455–476.

1971 *The Scientist's Role in Society: A Comparative Study.* Englewood Cliffs, N. J.: Prentice-Hall.

BERELSON, *Bernard*

1960 *Graduate Education in the United States.* New York: McGraw-Hill.

BIOLOGICAL ABSTRACTS

1926–1972 Philadelphia: Biological Abstracts, Inc.

BLISSETT, *Marlan*

1972 *Politics in Science.* Boston: Little, Brown and Company.

BLUME, *S. S., and Ruth Sinclair*

1973 "Chemists in British Universities: A Study of the Reward System in Science." *American Sociological Review* **38** (February):126–138.

CAPLOW, *Theodore, and Reece J. McGee*

1965 *The Academic Marketplace.* New York: Doubleday.

CARLSON, *Elof Axel*, Ed.

1967 *Modern Biology: Its Conceptual Foundation.* New York: George Brazilier.

CARTTER, *Allan M.*

1966 *An Assessment of Quality in Graduate Education.* Washington, D.C.: American Council on Education.

CHEMICAL ABSTRACTS

1907–1972 Washington, D.C.: American Chemical Society.

CHUBIN, *Daryl E., and Soumyo D. Moitra*

1975 "Content Analysis of References: Adjunct or Alternative to Citation Counting?" *Social Studies of Science* **5** (November):423–441.

CLEMENTE, *Frank*

1973 "Early Career Determinants of Research Productivity." *American Journal of Sociology* **79** (September):409–419.

COLE, *Jonathan*

(forthcoming). *Women in Science.* New York: Wiley-Interscience.

COLE, *Jonathan, and Stephen Cole*

1972 "The Ortega Hypothesis." *Science* **178** (October):368–375.

1973 *Social Stratification in Science.* Chicago: The University of Chicago Press.

1974 "Letter." *Science* **183** (11 January):32–33.

COLE, *Jonathan, and Harriet Zuckerman*

1975 "The Emergence of a Scientific Specialty: The Self-Exemplifying Case of the Sociology of Science." Pp. 139–174 in *Lewis A. Coser*, Ed., *The Idea of Social Structure.* New York: Harcourt Brace Jovanovich.

COLE, *Stephen*

1970 "Professional Standing and the Reception of Scientific Discoveries." *American Journal of Sociology* **76** (September):286–306.

COLE, *Stephen, and Jonathan Cole*

1967 "Scientific Output and Recognition: A Study in the Operation of the Reward System in Science." *American Sociological Review* **32** (June):377–390.

COLLINS, *Randall*

1977 "Review Symposium: *The Idea of Social Structure: Papers in Honor of Robert K. Merton." Contemporary Sociology* **6** (March):150–154.

COMMITTEE ON RESEARCH IN THE LIFE SCIENCES

1970 *The Life Sciences.* Washington, D.C.: National Academy of Sciences.

COMMITTEE FOR THE SURVEY OF CHEMISTRY

1965 *Chemistry: Opportunities and Needs.* Washington, D.C.: National Academy of Sciences–National Research Council.

CRANE, *Diana*

1965 "Scientists at Major and Minor Universities: A Study of Productivity and Recognition." *American Sociological Review* **30** (October):699–714.

DILLON, *Lawrence S.*

1964 *The Science of Life.* New York: The MacMillan Company.

DOBROV, *G. M.*

1968 "Scientific Potential as an Object of Investigation and Control in the Soviet Union." Pp. 189–201 in *Anthony De Reuck, Maurice Goldsmith, and Julie Knight, Eds., Decision Making In National Science Policy.* Boston: Little, Brown and Company.

FAIA, *Michael A.*

1975 "Productivity among Scientists: A Replication and Elaboration." *American Sociological Review* **40** (December):825–829.

FULTON, *Oliver, and Martin Trow*

1974 "Research Activity in American Higher Education." *Sociology of Education* **47** (Winter):29–73.

GASTON, *Jerry*

1969 "Big Science in Britain: A Sociological Study of the High Energy Physics Community." Unpublished PhD dissertation, Yale University.

1970 "The Reward System in British Science." *American Sociological Review* **35** (August):718–732.

1973 *Originality and Competition in Science.* Chicago: The University of Chicago Press.

1975 "Soziale Organisation, Kodifizierung des Wissens und das Belohnungssystem der Wissenschaft." *Kölner Zeitschrift für Soziologie und Sozialpsychologie* (Fall):287–303.

GOUDSMIT, *S. A.*

1974 "Letter to the Editor." *Science* **183** (11 January):28.

GRANT, *John,* Ed.

1971 *Who's Who in British Science 1971/72.* New York: St. Martin's Press.

HAGSTROM, *Warren O.*

1965 *The Scientific Community.* New York: Basic Books.

1967. "Competition and Teamwork in Science." Final Report to the National Science Foundation (mimeographed).

1971 "Inputs, Outputs, and the Prestige of American University Science Departments." *Sociology of Education* **44** (Fall):375–397.

1974 "Competition in Science." *American Sociological Review* **39** (February):1–18.

HALSEY, *A. H., and Martin Trow*

  1971 *The British Academics.* Cambridge, Mass.: Harvard University Press.

HARGENS, *Lowell L.*

  1971 "The Social Contexts of Scientific Research." Unpublished PhD dissertation, University of Wisconsin, Madison.

  1973 *Patterns of Scientific Research: A Comparative Analysis of Research in Three Scientific Fields.* Washington, D.C.: American Sociological Association.

HARGENS, *Lowell L., and Warren O. Hagstrom*

  1967 "Sponsored and Contest Mobility of American Academic Scientists." *Sociology of Education* **40** (Winter):24–38.

HELLMAN, *Hal*

  1971 *Biology in the World of the Future.* New York: M. Evans.

HIRSCH, *Walter*

  1968 *Scientists in American Society.* New York: Random House.

INSTITUTE FOR SCIENTIFIC INFORMATION

  1972 *Science Citation Index.* Philadelphia: Institute for Scientific Information.

KAPLAN, *Norman*

  1963 "Science and the Democratic Social Structure Revisited." Unpublished manuscript.

  1965 "The Norms of Citation Behavior: Prolegomena to the Footnote." *American Documentation* **16** (July):179–184.

KING, *M. D.*

  1971 "Reason, Tradition, and the Progressiveness of Science." *History and Theory* **10**:3–31.

KLAW, *Spencer*

  1968 *The New Brahmins.* New York: Morrow.

KUBIE, *Lawrence S.*

  1954 "Some Unsolved Problems of the Scientific Career." *American Scientist* **42**:104–112.

KUHN, *Thomas S.*

  1970 *The Structure of Scientific Revolutions.* Second edition (enlarged). Chicago: University of Chicago Press.

LAZARSFELD, *Paul F., and Wagner Thielans, Jr.*

  1958 *The Academic Mind.* Glencoe: Free Press.

LEDERMAN, *L. M.*

  1969 "A Great Collaboration." Review of Robert Jungk's *The Big Machine. Science* **164** (April):169.

LIGHTFIELD, *E. Timothy*

  1971 "Output and Recognition of Sociologists." *The American Sociologist* **6** (May):128–133.

LODAHL, *Janice B., and Gerald Gordon.*

  1972 "The Structure of Scientific Fields and the Functioning of University Graduate Departments." *American Sociological Review* **37** (February):57–72.

McGERVEY, *John D.*

    1974   "Letter to the Editor." *Science* **183** (11 January):28–31.

MANIS, *Jerome G.*

    1951   "Some Academic Influences upon Publication Productivity." *Social Forces* **29**:267–272.

MELTZER, *Leo*

    1956   "Scientific Productivity in Organizational Settings." *Journal of Social Issues* **12** ʿ(December):32–40.

MERTON, *Robert K.*

    1957   "Priorities in Scientific Discovery: A Chapter in the Sociology of Science." *American Sociological Review* **22** (December):635–659.

    1973   *The Sociology of Science: Theoretical and Empirical Investigations. Norman W. Storer,* Ed. Chicago: University of Chicago Press.

    1975   "The Matthew Effect in Science II: Problems of Cumulative Advantage." The 3rd Paley Lecture. The New York Hospital-Cornell Medical Center (September).

    1976   *Sociological Ambivalence and Other Essays.* New York: Free Press.

    1977   "The Sociology of Science: An Episodic Memoir." Pp. 3–141 in *Robert K. Merton and Jerry Gaston,* Eds. *The Sociology of Science in Europe.* Carbondale: Southern Illinois University Press.

MITROFF, *Ian I.*

    1974   "Norms and Counter-Norms in a Select Group of the Apollo Moon Scientists: A Case Study of the Ambivalence of Scientists." *American Sociological Review* **39** (August):579–595.

MORAVCSIK, *Michael J., and Poovanalingam Murugesan*

    1975   "Some Results of the Function and Quality of Citations." *Social Studies of Science* **5** (February):86–92.

MULKAY, *Michael*

    1969   "Some Aspects of Cultural Growth in the Natural Sciences." *Social Research* **36**:22–52.

    1976   "Norms and Ideology in Science." *Social Science Information* **15**:637–656.

NATIONAL SCIENCE BOARD

    1973   *Science Indicators 1972.* Washington, D.C.: U.S. Government Printing Office.

NATIONAL SCIENCE FOUNDATION

    1956   *Organization of the Federal Government for Scientific Activities.* Washington, D.C.: U.S. Government Printing Office.

Nature (editors of)

    1972   "University Growth Rate to Be Pruned." *Nature* **240** (15 December):372–373.

ORLANS, *Harold*

    1962   *The Effects of Federal Programs on Higher Education.* Washington, D.C.: Brookings Institution.

PANEL ON THEORETICAL CHEMISTRY

    1966   *Theoretical Chemistry: A Current Review.* Washington, D.C.: National Academy of Sciences–National Research Council.

PANTIN, *C. F. A.*

  1968   *The Relations between the Sciences.* Cambridge, England: Cambridge University Press.

PHYSICS SURVEY COMMITTEE

  1966   *Physics: Survey and Outlook.* Washington, D.C.: National Academy of Sciences–National Research Council.

PRICE, *Derek J. de Solla*

  1963   *Little Science, Big Science.* New York: Columbia University Press.

  1969   "Measuring the Size of Science." *Proceedings of the Israel Academy of Sciences and Humanities* **4**:98–111.

  1970   "Differences between Scientific and Technological and Non-Scientific Scholarly Communities." VII World Congress of Sociology, Varna, Bulgaria, 14–19 September.

  1976   "A General Theory of Bibliometric and Other Cumulative Advantage Processes." *Journal of the American Society for Informatiion Science* **27** (September–October):292–306.

RESKIN, *Barbara F.*

  1976a "Scientific Productivity, Sex, and Location in the Institution of Science." Unpublished paper, Indiana University.

  1976b "Sex Differences in Status Attainment in Science: The Case of the Postdoctoral Fellowship." *American Sociological Review* **41** (August):597–612.

  1976c "Scientific Productivity and the Reward Structure of Science." Mimeo.

  1977   "Scientific Productivity and the Reward Structure of Science." *American Sociological Review* **42**:491–504.

ROE, *Anne*

  1952   *The Making of a Scientist.* New York: Dodd, Mead.

ROTHMAN, *Robert A.*

  1972   "A Dissenting View on the Scientific Ethos." *British Journal of Sociology* **23** (March):102–108.

SCHAFFTER, *Dorothy*

  1969   *The National Science Foundation.* New York: Frederick A. Praeger.

SCIENCE ABSTRACTS *(Physics)*

  1898–1972   London: The Institute of Electrical Engineers.

SCIENCE CITATION INDEX

  1972   Philadelphia: Institute for Scientific Information.

SHERWELL, *Chris*

  1976   "Research on the Rack?" *Nature* **260** (25 March):274–275.

SKLAIR, *Leslie*

  1972   "The Political Sociology of Science: A Critique of Current Orthodoxies." *The Sociological Review* Monograph No. 18:43–59.

STORER, *Norman W.*

  1966   *The Social System of Science.* New York: Holt, Rinehart and Winston.

  1967   "The Hard Sciences and the Soft: Some Sociological Observations." *Bulletin, The Medical Library Association* **55** (January):75–84.

STURGIS, *Richard B., and Frank Clemente*

    1973 "The Productivity of Graduates of 50 Sociology Departments." *The American Sociologist* **8** (November):169–180.

SZALAI, *Alexander*

    1968 "National Research Planning and Research Statistics: The Case of Hungary." Pp. 202–211 in *Anthony De Reuck, Maurice Goldsmith, and Julie Knight,* Eds., *Decision Making In National Science Policy.* Boston: Little, Brown and Company.

UNESCO

    1965 *Science Policy and Organization of Scientific Research in the Czechoslovak Socialist Republic.* Paris.

    1967 *Science Policy and Organization of Research in the U.S.S.R.* Paris.

    1968 *Science Policy and the Organization of Scientific Research in the Socialist Federal Republic of Yugoslavia.* Paris.

    1970a *National Science Policies in Europe: Present Situation and Future Outlook.* Paris.

    1970b *National Science Policy and Organization of Research in Poland.* Paris.

    1971a *La politique scientific et l'organisation de la recherche scientifique en Hongrie.* Paris.

    1971b *Science Policy and the European States.* Paris.

WATSON, *James D.*

    1969 *The Double Helix.* New York: New American Library.

WHITE, *D. Hywel, Daniel Sullivan, and Edward J. Barboni*

    1976 "Growth, Changes, and Dynamics of Scientific Specialties: The Interdependence of Theory and Experiment in the Life-Cycle of a Specialty in Elementary Particle Physics." Paper presented at the International Symposium on Quantitative Methods in the History of Science, Berkeley, California, August.

WHITLEY, *Richard D.*

    1972 "Black Boxism and the Sociology of Science: A Discussion of the Major Developments in the Field." *The Sociological Review* Monograph No. 18:61–92.

WILSON, *Logan*

    1958 *The Academic Man: Sociology of a Profession.* London: Oxford University Press.

WILSON, *Mitchell*

    1949 *Live with Lightning.* Boston: Little, Brown and Company.

WOLINSKY, *Frederic, and Jerry Gaston*

    1977 "British University Teachers: An Examination of the Sponsored Mobility Model." Mimeo.

WUNDERLICH, *Richard*

    1974 "The Scientific Ethos: A Clarification." *British Journal of Sociology* **25** (September):373–377.

YAES, *Robert J.*

    1974 "Letter." *Science* **183** (11 January):31–32.

YOELS, *William C.*

    1973 "The Fate of the Ph.D. Dissertation in Sociology: An Empirical Examination." *The American Sociologist* **8** (May):87–89.

ZALESKI, *E., J. P. Kozlowski, H. Wienert, R. W. Davies, M. J. Berry, and R. Amann*

    1969 *Science Policy in the USSR.* Paris: Organization for Economic Cooperation and Development.

ZIMAN, *John*

　　1968 *Public Knowledge,* Cambridge, England: Cambridge University Press.

ZUCKERMAN, *Harriet*

　　1967 "Nobel Laureates in Science: Patterns of Productivity, Collaboration, and Authorship." *American Sociological Review* **32** (June):391–403.

ZUCKERMAN, *Harriet, and Jonathan R. Cole*

　　1975 "Women in American Science." *Minerva* **13** (Spring):82–102.

ZUCKERMAN, *Harriet, and Robert K. Merton*

　　1973a "Age, Aging, and Age Structure in Science." Pp. 497–559 in *Robert K. Merton, The Sociology of Science, Norman W. Storer,* Ed. Chicago: The University of Chicago Press.

　　1973b "Institutionalized Patterns of Evaluation in Science." Pp. 460–496 in *Robert K. Merton, The Sociology of Science, Norman W. Storer,* Ed. Chicago: The University of Chicago Press.

INDEX

Advisory Board for the Research Councils, 53
Agriculture Research Council, 53
Allison, Paul D., 65, 134, 144, 146-148
American Academy of Arts and Sciences, 20
American Council on Education, 59, 137
American Philosophical Society, 20
Astin, Alexander W., 59
Atomic Energy Commission, 50

Babchuk, Nicholas, 134-135
Barber, Bernard, 159, 180
Barnard, Christiaan, 171
Barnes, S. Barry, 166-170, 179, 187
Bates, Alan P., 134-135
Bayer, Alan E., 137, 140, 147
Ben-David, Joseph, 139, 165, 188
Berelson, Bernard, 18-19, 21-22
Biological abstracts, 57
Blissett, Marlan, 182-184
Blume, Stuart S., 19, 25-28, 30, 34, 55, 74, 81, 102, 114, 121, 127
British Academy, 26

Caplow, Theodore, 18, 21
Carlson, Elof Axel, 37
Cartter, Allan M., 19, 23, 58-59
Castro, Fidel, 173
Cavendish, Henry, 8, 140, 169
Chemical abstracts, 57
Chubin, Daryl E., 62
Citations, in american biology, chemistry, and physics, 104-107
  in British biology, chemistry, and

physicis, 104-107
loss of, 69
problems in counting, 59
scientists concerns about, 59-60
to scientists publications, 59-63
Clemente, Frank, 18, 66, 141
Codification, of knowledge, 31-35
  in biology, 37-40
  in chemistry, 40-43
  in physics, 43-44
  social measures of, 45-57
Cognitive development, 31-34, 116-119
Cole, Jonathan, 18, 23, 28-29, 55, 61, 63, 67-68, 98, 100, 121-122, 125-127, 135-136, 139-143, 145, 147, 152, 155-157, 168, 187
Cole, Stephen, 18, 23, 28-29, 55, 61, 63, 67-68, 98, 100, 113, 121-122, 125-127, 135-136, 139-143, 145, 147, 152, 155-157, 168
Collins, Randall, 180
Committee on Research in the Life Sciences, 38-40
Committee for the Survey of Chemistry, 40-42, 60
Communism (communality), 5, 161, 167, 169, 171, 174-175, 182-183, 186
Council for Scientific Policy, 26, 52-53
Crane, Diana, 18-22, 24, 28, 34, 55, 121, 124, 126-127, 135

Darwin, Charles, 12
Dennis, Wayne, 17
Department of Agriculture, 50

Department of Defense, 50
Department of Education and Science, 26, 52-53
Department of Health, Education, and Welfare, 50
Department of the Interior, 50
Department of Scientific and Industrial Research, 52
Department of State, 50
Department of the Treasury, 50
Dillon, Lawrence S., 37
Disciplines, problems in hierarchy of, 116-119
Disinterestedness, 6, 161, 171, 175, 183, 186
Dobrov, G. M., 188
Dolby, R. G. A., 166-170, 179, 187

Ethos of science, 157. *See also* Norms of science

Faia, Michael A., 147-148
Folger, John, 140
Fulton, Oliver, 138

Gaston, Jerry, 12-13, 19, 24, 28-29, 55, 67, 69, 75, 121, 124, 127, 138, 178
Gordon, Gerald, 46-47
Goudsmit, S. A., 61
Grant, John, 57
Guggenheim fellowship, 20

Hagstrom, Warren O., 5-6, 12-13, 19, 21, 22-24, 28-29, 33, 55, 60, 65, 116-117, 126-127, 136, 140-141, 146, 156
Halsey, A. H., 18, 24, 26-28, 31, 52, 59, 69, 138
Hargens, Lowell L., 19, 21-24, 28-29, 33, 55, 117-118, 126-127, 156
Harmon, Lindsey, 45
Hellman, Hal, 37
Hirsch, Walter, 171-172

Kaplan, Norman, 160-163
King, M. D., 180
Klaw, Spencer, 123, 170
Knudop effect, in science, definition of, 131
Kubie, Lawrence S., 140
Kuhn, Thomas S., 33, 169, 175

Lazarsfeld, Paul F., 18
Lederman, L. M., 14
Lightfield, E. Timothy, 134, 143-144, 152, 155
Lodahl, Janice B., 46-47

McGee, Reece J., 18, 21
McGervey, John D., 61
Manis, Jerome G., 18
Matthew effect, 145
  definition of, 122
  in science, 121-124
Medical Research Council, 53
Meltzer, Leo, 18, 135
Merton, Robert K., 2-4, 8-9, 11-12, 15, 18, 32, 38, 45-46, 68, 110, 116, 118, 121-122, 124, 140-414, 145, 159-160, 162, 166-169, 172, 175-178, 186-187
Mitroff, Ian I., 168, 175-179, 187
Moitra, Soumyo D., 62
Moravcsik, Michael J., 62
Mulkay, Michael, 123, 163-166, 170, 176, 178-181, 187
Murugesan, Poovanalingam, 62

National Academy of Sciences, 20, 50
  Committee on Science and Public Policies, 38
National Advisory Committee for Aeronautics, 50
National Institutes of Health, fellowship, 20
National Opinion Research Center, 171
National Research Council, fellowship, 20
National Science Board, 48, 60, 118
National Science Foundation, 20, 38, 50, 60
Natural Environment Research Council, 53
Nature, 52
Nobel Prize, 14, 25, 55
Norms of science, 3-4, 159
  ambivalence toward, 167, 169
  Barnes and Dolby's views, 166-170
  Blissett's views, 182-184
  counternorms, 176-178
  Kaplan's views, 160-163
  Mitroff's views, 175-178
  Mulkay's views, 163-166, 178-180
  Rothman's views, 170-172
  Sklair's views, 172-175
  see also Communism; Disinterestedness;

Organized skepticism; *and* Universalism

Organized skepticism, 5, 162, 165, 167-168, 170, 183, 186
Orlans, Harold, 18

Panel on Theoretical Chemistry, 42
Physics Survey Committee, 43-44
Podunk Effect, definition of, 122
 in science, 121-124
Price, Derek J. de Solla, 17-18, 33, 38, 45, 50, 120, 133-134, 139, 147

Reskin, Barbara F., 136-138, 141, 144, 147, 153, 155-156
Reward system, in American biology, chemistry, and physics, 96-100
 and ascriptive variables, 109-113
 in biology, 86-96
 in British biology, chemistry, and physics, 96-100
 in chemistry, 86-96
 concept of, 2
 descriptive of, 1
 deviant cases in, 125-132
 effect of, 184-190
 function of, 14
 future of, 190-192
 in Great Britain, 75-85
 operation of, 65-75
 and performance variables, 109-113
 in physics, 86-96
 problems with, 28-31
 and social organization, 185
 studies of, 18-28
 in United States, 75-85
Rockefeller Foundation, fellowship, 20
Roe, Anne, 140
Rothman, Robert A., 122-123, 170-172
Royal Society, 26-27, 30

Schaffter, Dorothy, 38
Science, centralized social organization of, 34
 content of, 15
 decentralized social organization of, 34
 goal of, 10-11
 priority in, 8-9
 as social institution, 8

 social organization of, 31-35
 social structural aspects of, 15
Science abstracts, 57
Science Citation Index, 60-63
Science Research Council, 53
Scientific awards, 58, 68
 in American biology, chemistry, and physics, 102-104
 in British biology, chemistry and physics, 100-102
Scientific disciplines, goal of, 2-3
Scientific productivity, and ability, 139-140
 and awards, 70-85
 and citations, 72-85
 and contextual variables, 141
 and cumulative advantage, 144-151
 differences among, biologists, 135-136
  chemists, 136-138
  historians, 135
  mathematicians, 135-136
  Nobel laureates, 136
  physicists, 135-136, 138
  physiologists, 135
  psychologists, 135
  sociologists, 134-135
 distribution of, 156
 explanation for, 139-147
 and individual characteristics, 141
 Lotka's Law of, 134
 and motivation, 140-141
 and professional age, 67
 and reinforcement, 142-144, 152-157
 variations in, 17-18, 133-139
Scientific recognition, nature of, 11-14
 and productivity, 20, 23-28
 variation in, 17-18
Scientists, types of, biologists, 19, 21
 chemists, 25
 physical, 21
 physicists, 23-25
 political scientists, 19
 psychologists, 19
Scientists' behavior, deviance, 7
 role of norms, 3
Selye, Hans, 12
Sherwell, Chris, 51
Sinclair, Ruth, 19, 25-28, 30, 34, 55, 74, 81, 102, 114, 121, 123, 127-128
Sklair, Leslie, 172-175
Smithsonian Institution, 50

Social organization of science, in Great
    Britain, 51-54
  in United States, 48, 50
Social Science Research Council, 53
Society for the Social Studies of Science,
    187
Stewart, John A., 65, 144, 146-148
Storer, Norman W., 2, 4, 33, 140, 159, 178,
    187
Stugis, Richard B., 18
Szalai, Alexander, 188

Tennessee Valley Authority, 50
Thielans, Wagner, Jr., 18
Trow, Martin, 18, 24, 26-28, 31, 52, 59, 69,
    138

UNESCO, 188
Universalism, 4, 159, 161, 167, 170, 172-
    174, 182, 186
  in American science, 114-115
  in British science, 114-115
Universalism statistic, 107

in American disciplines, 109
in British disciplines, 109
University Grants Committee, 52-53

Velikovsky, Immanuel, 164-166, 170

Watson, James D., 33, 171
Wehttam Effect, in science, definition of,
    131
White, D. Hywel, 178
Whitley, Richard D., 180, 189-190
Wilson, Logan, 18, 135
Wilson, Mitchell, 13
Wolinsky, Frederic, 138
Wunderlich, Richard, 180

Yaes, Robert J., 61

Zaleski, E., 188
Ziman, John, 157, 174
Zuckerman, Harriet, 32, 38, 45-46, 84,
    110, 116, 118, 124, 136, 141,
    187